Hollywood, Westerns and the 1930s

Hollywood, Westerns and the 1930s: The Lost Trail recovers the context in which Westerns were produced, exhibited and viewed in the 1930s. By examining why the American film industry produced Westerns in the 1930s and by locating these films within the history of Hollywood's production cycles and trends, Peter Stanfield reveals the limitations of previous studies. Instead of constructing a canon of isolated film 'classics', his research makes it clear that the hitherto marginalised 'B' or 'series' Western was central to the genre's history in this period.

The study explains the effect that Hollywood's shift to synchronized sound had on the Western, and discusses the studios' huge financial investment in the epic Westerns of the early years of the 1930s. It traces the subsequent decline and resurgence in Western production in the mid-1930s, and examines the deluge of A-feature Westerns produced in the 1939–1940 cycle, including *Stagecoach, Dodge City, Jesse James, Destry Rides Again, Union Pacific* and *The Oklahoma Kid*. Challenging many of the conventional critical assumptions about the Western, including the firmly held opinion that it was principally aimed at male viewers, the book highlights the significance of female audiences, the role of independent exhibitors, and of censorship in shaping film production. For the first time, this book tells the 'lost' story of the 1930s Western.

Peter Stanfield is Senior Lectuturer in the Faculty of Media Arts at Southampton Institute.

Cover image: James Cagney in *Oklahoma Kid* (courtesy of BFI Films: Stills, Posters and Designs)

Exeter Studies in Film History
General Editors: Richard Maltby and Duncan Petrie

Exeter Studies in Film History is devoted to publishing the best new scholarship on the cultural, technical and aesthetic history of cinema. The aims of the series are to reconsider established orthodoxies and to revise our understanding of cinema's past by shedding light on neglected areas in film history.

Published by University of Exeter Press in association with the Bill Douglas Centre for the History of Cinema and Popular Culture, the series includes monographs and essay collections, translations of major works written in other languages, and reprinted editions of important texts in cinema history. The series editors are Richard Maltby, Associate Professor of Screen Studies, Flinders University, Australia, and Duncan Petrie, Director of the Bill Douglas Centre for the History of Cinema and Popular Culture, University of Exeter.

> *Parrallel Tracks: The Railroad and Silent Cinema*
> Lynne Kirby (1997)
>
> *The World According to Hollywood, 1918–1939*
> Ruth Vasey (1997)
>
> *'Film Europe' and 'Film America': Cinema, Commerce and Cultural Exchange 1920–1939*
> edited by Andrew Higson and Richard Maltby (1999)
>
> *A Paul Rotha Reader*
> edited by Duncan Petrie and Robert Kruger (1999)
>
> *A Chorus of Raspberries: British Film Comedy 1929–1939*
> David Sutton (2000)
>
> *The Great Art of Light and Shadow: Archaeology of the Cinema*
> Laurent Mannoni, translated by Richard Crangle (2000)
>
> *Popular Filmgoing in 1930s Britain: A Choice of Pleasures*
> John Sedgwick (2000)
>
> *Alternative Empires: European Modernist Cinemas and Cultures of Imperialism*
> Martin Stollery (2000)

University of Exeter Press also publishes the celebrated five-volume series looking at the early years of English cinema, *The Beginnings of the Cinema in England*, by John Barnes.

HOLLYWOOD, WESTERNS AND THE 1930s

The Lost Trail

Peter Stanfield

UNIVERSITY
of
EXETER
PRESS

First published in 2001 by
University of Exeter Press
Reed Hall, Streatham Drive
Exeter, Devon EX4 4QR
UK
www.ex.ac.uk/uep/

British Library Cataloguing in Publication Data
A catalogue record for this book is available from the British Library

Paperback ISBN 0 85989 694 3
Hardback ISBN 0 85989 693 5

Typeset in 11/13pt Adobe Caslon by Kestrel Data, Exeter, Devon

Printed in Great Britain by
Cromwell Press Ltd, Trowbridge, Wiltshire

Dedicated to Esther Sonnet—my co-conspirator

Contents

List of Illustrations   viii
Acknowledgements   ix

Introduction   1

1. The First Cycle of Sound Westerns   15

2. Series Westerns, Will Rogers and the Emergence of
    the Singing Cowboy, 1931–1935   56

3. Series Westerns: Masking the Modern   78

4. Class-A Western Features, 1935–1938   117

5. Democratic Art: Westerns 1939–1941   148

6. Dixie Cowboys: Representing the Nation   193

Conclusion   225

Notes   228
Bibliography   248
Index   255

Illustrations

Stills from the following films are all courtesy of BFI Films: Stills, Posters and Designs.

1.	*The Virginian*	23
2.	*In Old Arizona*	24
3.	*The Virginian*	27
4.	*The Lash*	28
5.	*Cimarron*	34
6.	*The Big Trail*	40
7.	*Billy the Kid*	44
8.	*In Old Santa Fé*	85
9.	*Tumbling Tumbleweeds*	89
10.	*Oh, Susanna!*	102
11.	*Three Godfathers*	127
12.	*Ramona*	134
13.	*The Plainsman*	136
14.	*Let Freedom Ring*	159
15.	*Stand Up and Fight*	162
16.	*Oklahoma Kid*	164
17.	*Jesse James*	165
18.	*Arizona*	167
19.	*Destry Rides Again*	169
20.	*Dodge City*	177
21.	*Oklahoma Kid*	181
22.	*Billy the Kid*	187
23.	*Trail of the Lonesome Pine*	200
24.	*The Westerner*	213
25.	*Virginia City*	220
26.	*Santa Fé Trail*	221
27.	*Union Pacific*	226

Acknowledgements

Special acknowledgement is due to Richard Maltby and Ed Buscombe, who helped guide the book from idea to completion. I have learnt much from them.

Particular thanks go to Esther Sonnet, who read and commented on more versions of the manuscript than I care to remember. Thank you also to those friends who have read parts of this book and given the benefit of their advice—a salute, then, to Michael Hammond, Peter Kramer, Lee Grieveson, Steve Neale and Mike Todd. All are herewith granted honorary membership of the Dodge Brothers Motorcycle Club Forever Lasting.

This book first began to take shape following the publication of my 'Country Music and the 1939 Western: From Hillbillies to Cowboys' in Ian Cameron and Douglas Pye, *The Movie Book of the Western* (London: Studio Vista, 1996). I am grateful to the editors and Charles Barr for the opportunity they presented. Parts of Chapters Two and Three were previously published in 'Dixie Cowboys and Blue Yodels: The Strange History of the Singing Cowboy' in Edward Buscombe and Roberta Pearson (eds), *Back in the Saddle Again* (London: BFI, 1998).

Research for this project was supported by two travel grants awarded by the Media Arts Faculty, Southampton Institute.

Introduction

The task of the narrator is not an easy one, he said. He appears to be required to choose his tale from among the many that are possible. But of course that is not the case. The case is rather to make many of the one. Always the teller must be at pains to devise against his listener's claim—perhaps spoken, perhaps not—that he has heard the tale before. He sets forth the categories into which the listener will wish to fit the narrative as he hears it. But he understands that the narrative is itself in fact no category but is rather the category of all categories for there is nothing which falls outside its purview. All is telling. Do not doubt it.

(Cormac McCarthy, *The Crossing*[1])

'Like in a dime novel, we eliminate the old gent, you marry the girl and get the ranch'.

(dialogue, *West of the Divide*, Monogram/Lone Star, 1933)

Like McCarthy's narrator, my task is not an easy one. Among the possible narratives that have already accounted for the Western—Civilisation Over Savagery, Frontier Myth, American Exceptionalism, Social History, Heroic Pioneers, Cowboy as Existential Hero, Rugged Individualism, Restoration of Masculinity, and Ahistorical Social Mirror—I want to tell another story, one which restores the cultural vitality and historical dynamism that have been largely absent from those narratives' accounts of the Western in the 1930s. Beneath previous accounts of Westerns lies a buried story which is more closely embedded in the lived experience of American daily life in the 1930s. This book aims to recover the immediate context in which Westerns were produced, exhibited and viewed in the 1930s, and thereby fully to historicise them within their production and consumption contexts.

This is a narrative written from a concern to understand Western films primarily as products of Hollywood's studio system. It not only examines the changing fortunes in the production of Westerns during the 1930s, but also explains why the genre intermittently found and lost favour with the major studios. Hollywood invested in Westerns in 1930/31 and partially withdrew from producing them at the end of that season. The major studios made a limited return to the production of Westerns in 1936/37, before successfully reintegrating them into their production schedules during 1939/40. Through an examination of why Hollywood did or did not produce Westerns in the 1930s, and by locating these films within the history of Hollywood's production cycles and trends, the limitations of previous studies of the Western become apparent. Where critical studies based on the abstract modelling of generic archetypes have constructed a canon of isolated film 'classics', my research makes it clear that the hitherto marginalised 'B' or 'series' Western must be seen as central to the genre's history in this period. As the self-reflexive dialogue in *West of the Divide* suggests, the series Western has a unique history that stretches as far back as nineteenth-century dime novels. This book explores these 'lost trails' and contextualises the series Western within the legacies of previous popular cultural forms. For the first time, this book tells the 'lost' story of the 1930s Western.

Much of this study's discussion of Westerns will take place within a framework of the studios' production, marketing and exhibition strategies, which are introduced in Chapter One. Initially, this is located within reports drawn from the trade press where typological issues of film classification are covered. These are linked to a descriptive account of the trends and cycles produced between the transition to sound and the end of the 1930/31 season. Emphasis is given to the role of Westerns in maintaining habitual audiences in small-town, rural and neighbourhood theatres, and to how and why the major studios both ignored and played to this segment of the market. In this chapter, particular attention is paid to 'Prestige Westerns'. Following the box-office success of *In Old Arizona* (1929) and *The Virginian* (1929), I record the industry's attempts to exploit Westerns more fully.

The South of the Border/Old California cycle that followed *In Old Arizona* played successfully to a female audience, but issues around representations of masculinity eventually limited the production of this type of film to little more than a single season. The South of the Border Western was secure in its romantic intrigues, but Westerns set north of the border with Anglo-Saxon heroes proved less susceptible to the romantic impulse. This was particularly true of the season's three super-productions, *Cimarron*, *The Big Trail* and *Billy the Kid*, which are discussed according to each of the major marketing ploys used by the producing studios in their attempts to attract a large and diverse audience. The chapter concludes with an assessment of why these films failed to meet their producers' expectations of box-office success.

While most histories of the Western ignore or marginalise series Westerns, this study places them at the centre of debate.[2] Series or B Westerns were conceived and organised around a particular cowboy star and were produced for independent theatres and chains whose principal market was in rural, small-town and urban neighbourhoods; only at the close of the 1930s would some of Gene Autry's films play at first-run metropolitan houses. This did not, however, mean that Autry's and other series Westerns produced by either the major or independent studios inevitably played on the lower half of the exhibition bill, giving them a 'B' status. Autry's films for Republic and Tex Ritter's for Monogram, for example, were headline features that enabled their respective companies to practice the same block booking policy as the major studios: if a theatre chain wanted Gene Autry's latest season of films then they would also have to book the rest of Republic's output, sight unseen. Although it is now common currency to call Autry's films 'B Westerns', they would only play at the bottom of a bill on their second or subsequent release. Contemporary terminology labelled these films as simply 'Westerns', while prestige productions by the major studios using top-rank stars were labelled as anything but 'Westerns'. One of the features which differentiated series Westerns is the singing cowboy. In Chapter Two I consider how this figure embodies Western films' relationship to Western music as formulated within the recording and radio industries.

Chapter Two begins with an examination of the formation of Republic Pictures and continues with a consideration of that studio's most successful box-office star, Gene Autry. Central to the Autry phenomenon was the idea of the Southerner who transforms himself into a cowboy. Through the vocal motif of the blue yodel, the chapter considers why a musical novelty that was first popularised on the blackface minstrel stages was later reconfigured as a symbol for the singing cowboy. The figure of the cowboy and his appropriation by Southern vernacular musicians is bound into the commercialisation and exploitation of their music via the new media of radio and phonograph recordings. The popularity of radio shows aimed at a rural audience and a fad for cowboy songs amongst a more metropolitan audience was exploited by both the Poverty Row independents and the major studios. I suggest that the upsurge in the commercial use of the image of the cowboy was due to the figure's perceived ability to mediate and broker an accommodation between the past and the present, the rural and the urban, the farm and the factory, the premodern and the modern. The chapter concludes with an analysis of Will Rogers' persona, which served in part as a model for series Westerns, particularly for those produced by Republic Pictures starring Gene Autry.

Autry and Rogers shared an audience that keenly felt the effects of the Depression, yet still possessed faith in the American promise of self-improvement. Using Michael Denning's concept of the dime novel's appeal as located in the 'fairy tale transformations of familiar landscapes and characters',[3] I suggest, in Chapter Three, that both Rogers and Autry (along with other series Westerners) offer a synthesis of Old World and New World values that turn upon a similar set of transformations. Specifically, series Westerns are predominantly concerned with issues of labour and capital. The section concludes with an analysis of how modernity is represented in the figure of the young heroine, where I challenge the dominant critical wisdom on representations of gender in Westerns. The series Western formula is further investigated through a discussion of how disguise is used. It functions, I argue, as both metaphor and performance. As metaphor, it allowed for an engagement with contemporary concerns and tensions around work, gender, race and class. As performance, disguise borrowed from and reinvigorated older traditions of popular entertainment, particularly blackface minstrelsy.

By 1936, A-feature Westerns had reappeared as a distinct cycle in the studios' production schedules. Chapter Four examines this new-found interest and, through selected examples of the productions, considers how the studios marketed these films to a diverse audience, a significant section of whom was thought to be at best indifferent and at worse antagonistic to the genre. These productions can be accounted for not only by the need to meet (at least part way) the demands of independent exhibitors but also by the Western's popularity with an international audience, particularly in Great Britain. The chapter concludes by suggesting that the lessons learnt in scripting, casting and marketing this cycle of films were used to ensure the box-office success of the 1939/40 cycle.

Chapter Five begins by recording the very positive reception of *Stagecoach* by the American press. Contradicting André Bazin's thesis, these reviews are overwhelmingly nostalgic: the film was applauded not because it had taken the genre to Bazin's 'definitive stage of perfection',[4] but because by going back to basics it revitalised an American cinema which had become 'self-conscious' and overly 'sophisticated'. In 1939, Westerns were marketed as robust American history, and both within and outside Hollywood they were made to fit a wider concern for an overt celebration of American values. This was a response to both internal and external pressures: the escalating conflicts in Europe and Asia, and the domestic isolationist and interventionist movements.

Hollywood attempted to negotiate between these camps by offering Westerns as allegories. This proposition enabled the studios to claim that they were producing a more politically engaged set of films while being able to deny any interpretation of the films that proved controversial with a particular interest group. All this would count for nothing if an audience could not be found for Westerns, and the studios sought to achieve this by casting the leading stars of the day. Furthermore, they were able to differentiate their product from series Westerns by emphasising the films' adult themes, sex, gambling and the consumption of alcohol. This also enabled Hollywood to counter suggestions that the industry's trade association, the Motion Picture Producers and Distributors of America, Inc. (MPPDA), was acting to suppress innovative and provocative films through the Production Code. Chapter Five concludes with case studies of *Jesse James* (1939) and *Billy the Kid* (1941) where the issues raised throughout the chapter are examined in greater detail.

The title for Chapter Six, 'Dixie Cowboys', alludes to a dominant theme in this book: Westerns as a site where issues of national reconciliation and unity can be acted out. I argue that 1930s Westerns are intimately tied to questions of Southern identity and, hence, to questions of national unity. In many of the films discussed there is an ideological displacement that relocates concerns of Southern identity onto the terrain of the Western: the Southerner crosses the divide that separates him or her from the American commonwealth by being transformed into a Westerner. I use the 1939 cycle to offer textual challenges to dominant readings of the Western as primarily modelled on, and concerned with, the myth of the frontier. The rural South tended to be represented by Hollywood as existing outside a modern world which excluded the Southerner from participation in the life of the nation. Westerns, on the other hand, allowed for similar themes, around democratic participation and individual autonomy, to be approached in a manner that facilitated the Southerner's inclusion. The

5

chapter concludes by considering how representations of Southerners in Westerns produced between 1939 and 1941 both symbolise a lost rural Arcadia and function as a means to negotiate fissures in the Republic.

Combining textual analysis with empirical research, this study seeks to understand how generic play between 'repetition' and 'difference' operates. By viewing most of the major studios' significant Western productions made between 1929 and 1941 alongside a representative sample of series Westerns, and by drawing upon studio records, film scripts, and trade journal, newspaper and fan magazine discourses on Westerns, I offer the first substantial analysis of Hollywood and 1930s Westerns.

Critical Orthodoxies

Tag Gallagher (1986), Jean-Louis Leutrat (1984) and Steve Neale (1990) have each argued that Westerns (or any other genre) cannot be considered in terms of an evolutionary or teleological project. Leutrat disparages the tendency in the vast majority of critical writing on the Western to establish a canon as being based on false assumptions about the genre's history: the 'historian of the Western is always in danger of projecting onto the past the illusion of a stable generic system, whose self-identity is preserved by an evolutionary schema'.[5] Similarly, Gallagher suggests that: 'Every argument that evolution exists at all comes down not to evidence mustered through representative sampling but either to bald assertions or to invidious comparisons between a couple of titles—"a classic" Western versus a "self-conscious" Western—selected specifically to illustrate the assertion'.[6] Leutrat's and Gallagher's rejection of an evolutionary model of the genre replaces an emphasis on continuity (which attempts to link the most recent Westerns back to James Fenimore Cooper's fictions) with an understanding of the genre as marked by localised as well as more general industrial, cultural and social influences. Their proposed object of study becomes instead the Western *in* history, distinct from a solipsistic history of the genre in which the Western becomes a product of its own history. Leutrat contends that Westerns are better approached within the particulars of their historical context, principally through production and marketing.

In order to understand the 'Western as an object *in*, not *of* history', Leutrat argues that it should be analysed not as a static and integral system, but more complexly as one subject to instability, plurality and dispersion: the *'diffraction of an identity'*. Like Leutrat, Neale argues that 'genres are inherently temporal: hence, their inherent mutability on the one hand, and their inherent historicity on the other'.[7] The plasticity of the form implied in the conception of Westerns as a 'diffraction of an identity' means that Leutrat's perception approximates Hollywood's use of genre in terms of the marshalling of production and marketing strategies. My insistence on examining Westerns within the parameters of the American film industry is founded upon a recognition that the limits of what constitutes a genre are, as Neale argues, 'historically specific, they can only be determined *empirically*, not theoretically' (emphasis added).[8] Westerns, I argue, have to be understood as operating within and across Hollywood's production cycles and trends. This is a very different understanding of film Westerns from that which has characterised critical approaches to date. My chief aim is to reorient the terms through which Westerns are defined, principally by challenging their subsumption under modes of analysis derived from structuralism and the myth of the frontier.

The frontier myth is formed through an understanding of American history predicated on the idea of westward migration as the defining principle of American exceptionalism. This concept gained widespread consensus following the publication of Frederick Jackson Turner's seminal paper 'The Significance of the Frontier in American History' (1893). In counterpoint to histories that privileged European influences or the role of slavery, Turner proclaimed it was the 'existence of an area of free land, its continuous recession and the advance of . . . settlement westward' that defined American history.[9] In an essay on Western historiography, Charles S. Peterson notes how Turner's 'frontier thesis fell on ready ears': 'Before the end of 1893, Theodore Roosevelt and a few others praised it as a masterful summation of widely held views. In the years that followed, the public and the historical profession capitulated, suggesting Turner's ideas and spirit were firmly based in the general climate of opinion.'[10] Official expeditionary reports and published accounts of pioneers and other westwarding migrants transcended their immediate function to find a large market of enthusiastic readers: 'Sensitive to sales, expeditionaries trafficked in the tastes of the reading public and became slaves to deadlines and profits . . . their sights on the entertainment market'.[11]

These discourses (coupled with the late-nineteenth-century romantic inclinations of patrician historians) produced a history of 'heroic figures, elites, representative men, flesh and blood characters, creative imagination, drama, narrative force',[12] which were exploited by the purveyors of popular entertainments through forms such as Wild West shows, fiction, theatre and painting: 'From the early discovery accounts to the popular hero, an enormous body of history related writing had come into existence. In a very real way this was the voice of Western history in 1893 as Frederick Jackson Turner announced the closing of the frontier.'[13]

In *Creating the West: Historical Interpretations 1890–1990*, a reactionary riposte to the New Western Histories, Gerald D. Nash has set out historians' and cultural critics' responses to Turner's thesis which, despite the odd contestation, remained relatively unchallenged until the 1960s.[14] Indeed, Turner's thesis enjoyed something of a renaissance in the 1950s with the publication of Henry Nash Smith's *Virgin Land: The American West as Symbol and Myth* (1950), a book which furthered both popular and academic understanding of the frontier myth as the dominant means of imagining the American West in history and fiction.[15] As the American nation emerged as the world's dominant power in the postwar period, it registered a shift from a foreign policy hamstrung by isolationist interests towards a proactive policy understood to be operating within the framework of the Cold War. The resulting popular and intellectual celebration of American exceptionalism resonated within postwar A-feature Westerns. Writing in *Showdown: Confronting Modern America in the Western Film* (1985), for instance, John H. Lenihan notes: 'From the end of World War II through the 1950s, Westerns increasingly reflected contemporary yearnings for peaceful coexistence by emphasising the desirability of negotiating with, instead of militarily destroying, enemy forces'.[16] The allegorical 'reading' of postwar Westerns is aided by the films' self-conscious use of the frontier myth, which, as Richard Slotkin (1993) has observed, helped Americans both to understand and to justify their role in the new geopolitics.[17] While there may be some disagreement among critics of postwar Westerns over the interpretation of individual titles, there is a consensus that Westerns do 'speak' to contemporary concerns, and that this is best translated through the myth of the frontier.

This critical work cannot be made to account for the *prewar* Western. Series Westerns, which in any case lie outside the critical canon, need a distinct set of critical strategies because their principal concerns are situated not within the paradigm of the frontier myth but in the tensions created by modernisation. Seen in this way, these are tensions marked out by their impact on the individual and the community.

Critical work on the Western, and its representation of the individual and the community, has tended to be derived from structuralist models. Following Levi Strauss's work on myth, critics such as Jim Kitses (1969), John Cawelti (1971), Will Wright (1975) and Richard Slotkin (1993) consider the Western as a form fundamentally concerned with the conflict between savagery and civilisation, forces which stand in the balance, with the former eventually giving way to the latter through the intervention of the hero.[18] While this paradigm is able to recognise Westerns in a number of guises, it can also (as Slotkin's work shows) be used to critically evaluate forms as diverse as Edgar Rice Burrough's Tarzan adventures, gangster films, and 1930s Hollywood representations of the British Empire. The paradigm can tell much about the persistence of the myth, but its almost universal reach obscures more localised discussion of the production and reception of Westerns.

Slotkin's epic trilogy, *Regeneration Through Violence* (1978), *The Fatal Environment* (1985) and *Gunfighter Nation* (1993), provides the most persuasive of all the structuralist understandings of the Western, tracing the frontier's operation in the construction of national myths from the colonial period to the presidency of Ronald Reagan.[19] A narrative consistency across the three volumes is matched by Slotkin's unparalleled knowledge of primary and secondary source materials. Because Slotkin constructs his narrative through the frontier myth, the reader is left with a view of the Western that is dominated by a singular and unremitting 'perspective. While Slotkin is able to accommodate the Western in its many and varied incarnations, the effect of his thesis is to reduce the genre to a single structural proposition which is inadequate as an explanatory model for a significant range of Western story forms. In its attempt to establish a self-contained and self-sustaining mythic universe, the paradigm of civilisation and savagery fails to offer a means of accounting for the production and reception of Westerns.

The dominant position of the frontier myth as the key interpretative tool for both historians and cultural critics explains why, according to Charles S. Peterson (1994), Western American history had become largely moribund by the 1980s. The critical dominance of the frontier myth meant that larger national and global issues and themed studies on the roles of gender, race, class, industrialisation, urbanisation and environment marginalised Western history. Histories of the Old West had become mired in a romantic, patriarchal, Anglo-centric vision that, as New Western historians such as Patricia Nelson

Limerick have argued, 'precluded any understanding of the West's role in the contemporary world'.[20] Amongst much public debate, which became focused on the Smithsonian exhibition 'The West as America: Reinterpreting Images of the Frontier' (1991), New Western historians moved decisively to confront the frontier myth and to supplant it with a history that saw the region as part of larger historical forces, rather than being principally formed through local determinants. In studies such as Richard White's *It's Your Misfortune and None of My Own': A New History of the American West* (1991) the West's place in a world economy, its relationship with the federal authorities, the exploitation of land, the conflicts between labour and capital, and an emphasis on those who lost out to 'progress' as well as those who gained from it are central. Rather than ending with the closing of the frontier, White's history continues to cover the twentieth century. Indeed, references to 'the frontier' and Frederick Jackson Turner are entirely absent from his six-hundred-plus pages of text.[21]

The New Western American histories suggest the possibility of imagining a West that operates autonomously from the frontier myth, in a perspective that complements my argument that the frontier myth is wholly inapplicable to the mass of series Westerns that were produced in the 1930s. These series Westerns are far more prone to deal with acts of intrigue between labour and capital than with the historical imperatives of the winning of the West. Their heroes are not concerned with regenerating their masculinity through immersion in the wilderness. Indeed many, if not most, series Westerns are set in a geographical West in which the frontier has long since gone and the modern world eventually sits comfortably alongside the old: one of my principal objectives is to understand the meaning produced by this tension between old and new worlds.

Against the work of critics who tend towards an evolutionary model of the genre, Michael Denning (1987) has argued for profound breaks in the Western's development. In his seminal study of nineteenth-century dime novels, Denning argues that this literary form of the Western is more clearly marked by the impact of industrialisation than by the encounter of civilisation and savagery on America's frontiers:

> The dime novel outlaws . . . are perhaps less sons of Leatherstocking than sons of Molly Maguire, less stories of the Wild West than stories of Labour and Capital. The enemies of

the James brothers are Pinkertons not Indians. Read in this light, the mining towns in which Deadwood Dick lives, and his 'concern with social problems', are not anomalous but are central.[22]

Breaking from the evolutionary model of the Western, Denning demarcates distinct lines of development within the genre's history, rather than outlining a monolithic whole.

In a complimentary analysis of turn-of-the-century Westerns, Zeese Papanikolas in *Trickster in the Land of Dreams* (1995) offers an alternative and conflicting version of the West to the myth of the noble cowboy found in the work of Roosevelt, Remington and Wister. The key themes in their work were the frontier myth, social Darwinism, feminisation of the public sphere and strenuous masculinity, immigration and Anglo-Saxon supremacy, imperialistic expansion and a valorisation of the Old West. Their Western productions were designed to appeal to the moneyed classes, and represent an *embourgeoisement* of the Western, created as a defence of 'American' culture, class, race and gender hierarchies, which were, they believed, threatened by the new urban working classes.[23]

In a chapter titled 'Cowboys, Wobblies, and the Myth of the West', Papanikolas scratches away at the surface of the myth to argue that it functions as a 'tool for the distortion of historical reality, [which] was paid for by the laboring men and women whose lives and struggles it attempted to devalue or deny'. Papanikolas considers Roosevelt *et al.*'s version of the West against the counter-myth produced by the Industrial Workers of the World:

> [a] myth of the western worker that matched and opposed [the eastern establishment's] view of human possibility, that parodied it when it had to, and erected its own version of an imagined future. This counter-myth is embedded in the ideology, the propaganda—in the very style—of that most radical of labor and political movements, the I.W.W.[24]

In *Easterns, Westerns, and Private Eyes* (1994), Marcus Klein develops his understanding of the turn-of-the-century Western from similar material to Denning (though Denning's work is not acknowledged), arguing that the genre needs to be understood as produced by urban writers for urban consumers: 'The Western obviously is not a Shepherd's Tale . . . the appeal of the Western has to do with bringing a recent past to present contemplation, but more to the point, the literary discovery of the West was conducted largely | by easterners whose investment, high and low, was in the East'.[25]

Deadwood Dick helped to popularise the figure of the Western outlaw with his first appearance in 1877, and, like the equally popular figures of the James gang, he found his adversary in the detective. Klein writes:

> The Westerns were written by easterners for easterners, and the villains of the tales were eastern types, instantly recognisable as such, and were such as were thought to be the enemies of the East, from a certain point of view.
> The villains in the romance of the West were Mosensteins, not Indians or 'bad men,' or they were other foreigners, or radicals, or bankers, or Eastern politicians, or some several others who, similarly, were the natural enemies of the older and better scheme of things.[26]

According to Denning, by the mid-1880s the 'outlaw joined the genealogy of the detective, as Deadwood Dick, Jr becomes a detective, in stories often set in Eastern cities, and is fully distanced from his outlaw past'.[27] Rather than being forced to operate outside the law, he now functions as a force for social control.

The critical works of Denning, Klein and Papanikolas suggest that the formulation of Westerns as sites of confrontation between the old and the new has a particular history located in a genealogy shared by the cowboy and the detective. I am less concerned with the merging of these archetypal figures than with the idea of the cowboy as a figure produced by the social tensions engendered by industrialisation. I argue that these tensions are overdetermined by a specific ideological context, within which the West is the site of displacement for concerns around modernisation which are figured as intrinsically Southern. Prewar A-feature Westerns, while less concerned than series Westerns with modernisation, are concerned with holding together a community against both internal and external forces. These struggles are generally represented as a continuation of the conflict between the States fought out in the post-Civil War West. The frontier is the space where these tensions are resolved, but it does not, as in postwar Westerns, define the conflict. As such, 1930s Westerns can be read as complex allegorical narratives, which articulate issues of national cohesion, American identity and experiences of modernity.

This study's focus on the 1930s is not an attempt to divide Western film production into neatly self-contained decades. Rather, the period from Hollywood's transition to sound (1927–29) to the Western's 'renaissance' in 1939/40 has been systematically ignored in scholarly examination. From most accounts it would seem that between 1931 and 1939 the major studios abandoned the genre and left the market for Western films to independent producers who concentrated their efforts on series Westerns and singing cowboys, areas with little appeal for the academy. Professors of English dominate recent writings on the Western: Jane Tompkins, Lee Clark Mitchell and Robert Murray Davis.[28] Working solely from an orthodox canon of film texts, these scholars do not produce historically grounded accounts of the Western. Davis, who wishes to explore the myth and art of the Western, can identify what he is looking for in the canon but finds this only 'feebly embodied in B-movies from Republic Pictures'.[29] I would contend instead that, though they existed predominantly outside Hollywood's mainstream production trends and cycles, series Westerns were radically revitalised by the introduction of sound. While an absence of critical accounts would suggest the genre was moribund during this period, it in fact produced material that has much to say about Hollywood, historical process and American culture.

1

The First Cycle of Sound Westerns

> Is this the masculine season? The renaissance of the Western and
> the prevalence of films stressing the male note, some being
> entirely Eveless pictures, indicates a new virility in plots.
>
> (Caroline Bell, *Picture Play*, 1931[1])

This chapter records the trade press coverage of A-feature Westerns
from the first prestige productions inaugurated by the box-office
success of *In Old Arizona* (Fox, 1929) and *The Virginian* (Paramount,
1929), culminating in the relative failure of *Cimarron* (RKO, 1931),
The Big Trail (Fox, 1930) and *Billy the Kid* (MGM, 1930). Hollywood tried to solicit a diverse audience for its A-feature Western
productions, undertaken through an overt address to the female
filmgoer. With varying degrees of success, this first cycle of sound
Westerns attempted this feat by emphasising the drama of courtship
and romance.

Hollywood pinned its hope for success not on the limited notion of
genre that film studies has inherited from literature but on the broad
trends of audience preferences and on the cycles within those trends.
Writing in December 1931 for the *New York Times*, Anne O'Hare
McCormick endeavoured to explain the decision-making processes
behind Hollywood's attempts to predict its audiences:

> The business men who control Hollywood . . . grope and bluster
> in the dark, befogged and irritated as men are who are involved
> in a vital conversation carried on in a language they do not
> understand. Their attitude toward art resembles President
> Hoover's toward politics; they fumble with the slippery thing,
> resentful but intimidated. Since their only art standard is box
> office, they maintain an elaborate system for reporting, analysing

and trying to anticipate what the public likes. Again I am reminded of the great game of politics. You hear as much talk of 'trends' in Hollywood as in a Democratic headquarters during a campaign.

McCormick continues her inquiry by listing some of the means available to Hollywood for forecasting the public's 'insatiable appetite for novelty and variety':

> . . . the kind of news that holds the front page, magazine features, books that sell, the subjects oftenest discussed at noontide women's clubs, criticisms of plays and pictures, college bulletins. Theatre ushers' report comments on pictures. Door receipts are tabulated in respect to sections of the country, city and small town, rises and falls of attendance after the first showing. Hollywood has as faithful a graph as can be drawn of America in quest of entertainment, but it laments that the picture is of little value as a guide. Its only sure index of success is success.[2]

'Studios reduced risk by producing a variety of pictures every season', writes Tino Balio in his exemplary study of 1930s Hollywood: 'Only a few pictures provided something different; whenever one struck the public's fancy, a new cycle began'.[3] Using definitions provided by industry discourse, Balio supplies a hierarchical ranking of the decade's dominant trends based on 'relative production costs, duration, and box-office performance':

1 prestige pictures
2 musicals
3 the woman's film
4 comedy
5 social problem films
6 horror films.

It is noteworthy that 'Westerns' do not appear as an isolated trend: excluding horror films, class A-feature Westerns operated *across* the range of these production trends. At the end of the 1930s, Westerns made up the largest mass of films within the 'outdoor' cycle which dominated the trend in prestige pictures-'typically a big-budget special based on a pre-sold property, often as not a "classic", and tailored for top stars'.[4] Hollywood actively sought to infuse and embolden Westerns with elements from other types of films which the industry considered had occasioned an individual film's success with an audience. Westerns offered producers historical pictures full of action and spectacular scenery, but by incorporating a romance narrative or a star who had succeeded in an urban melodrama, it hoped to bolster a film's box-office appeal. Such generic hybridity is especially significant for gauging intended audiences. In general terms, the most significant segment of Hollywood's audience was female, and the story of 1930s A-feature Westerns is intimately tied up with finding ways and means of attracting women, whom the studios recognised were not the Western's foremost consumers.

During the late 1920s and early 1930s, *Exhibitors Herald-World* classified films as belonging to one of ten types:

1 comedy
2 drama
3 romance
4 musical comedy
5 farce
6 melodrama
7 Western
9 operetta
10 mystery.

This typology acted as a 'quick reference' guide for exhibitors, an aid to identifying audience preferences, and a means for plotting production trends and cycles. Since the 1910s Westerns had constituted between a quarter and a fifth of the films produced by American companies, but the production of Westerns was noticeably absent throughout 1928 and into 1929. In large part this was due to technical difficulties in recording on location, but with the production of *In Old Arizona* and *The Virginian* this was no longer an issue. In August 1929, the *Exhibitors Herald-World* published the first of a short series of reports gleaned from a questionnaire sent to all exhibitors throughout the United States. The primary purpose of the survey was to get a better picture of the distribution of sound technology and its reception. Secondly, the survey asked questions about audience preferences (as categorised above) for particular types of films. Because of the lack of Western productions the survey also asked whether the 'public wants talking Westerns'. The response was a resounding, but qualified, 'yes'.

> More talking Westerns, would be appreciated by the theatre-going public, in the opinion of a large number of exhibitors who

have sounded out their patrons' preferences, in line with the
HERALD-WORLD survey on sound in the theatre.

The belief that such a policy would be a winner at the box office
was expressed by managers of some of the largest circuit houses as
well as the smallest wired houses, and practically all the small
theatres as yet not wired stated a definite opinion that the
Western audien [*sic*] is box office material.

In Old Arizona became the bench-mark from which this opinion
was formed. The high production values and the film's emphasis on
romance were demanded from both small-town and metropolitan
exhibitors, particularly Westerns of the 'Zane Grey type and quality'.
These were stories that gave an equal space to romantic intrigue and to
action adventure. Again and again, small-town exhibitors noted how
essential the genre was in maintaining a regular audience:

> I have tried to get along without Westerns, but have had it proven
> to my satisfaction that you can't get along without Westerns in
> the small town. Since the advent of sound pictures there has been
> a lot of talk about discontinuing the production of Westerns. In
> my estimation this would be a fatal move, if the small town is to
> be given any consideration.[5]

Following these reports the journal kept a steady eye on the re-
emergence of the genre. Reports on new contracts signed by Western
stars, such as Hoot Gibson, Buck Jones and Ken Maynard, were
accompanied by news stories of planned Western series by new Poverty
Row production companies, like 'The Big Four' (a company that was
to specialise in Westerns), as well as the majors' increasing forays into
Western production. By April 1930 there was enough production
activity to justify an eighteen-page special on the genre's revival.[6]

The special supplement was headlined 'Outdoor Pictures (*Westerns*)
Enjoy a Revived Popularity. Sound Renews Interest in Robust
American life. The spirit of America! That's what the public wants in
pictures'. The emphasis is not just on revival but on progress, noting
that the new Westerns are 'logical developments of the famous so-
called "Westerns", which came in for so much kidding and yet did
so much to advance the popularity of motion pictures'. The piece
added that the 'best of our typically American pictures of outdoor life
today are as far superior to the Westerns of olden times as *The Covered
Wagon* was superior to a two-reeler made up of the cuttings from the
floor'.[7]

The schizophrenic labelling by the trade press of prestige genre productions as sometimes 'Westerns' and sometimes 'outdoor pictures' would continue throughout the decade as the producers attempted to capture both a metropolitan and a small-town market. Depending on context, *In Old Arizona* was typed as both a 'drama' and a 'Western', but a Buck Jones or Ken Maynard series production was always simply a 'Western'. Prestige Westerns would also be singled out as offering a peculiarly nativist slant, thereby transcending the suspect legitimacy of series Westerns: 'Broad-shouldered pictures of robust American life, stories with the flavor and tang of that outdoor activity so typical of American life'.[8]

The supplement reviewed various studios' intended Western output for the coming season. Its coverage was fragmentary and tentative and was partly motivated as a play to garner more advertising. Nevertheless, it revealed a distinct shift in production trends. Having picked up Buck Jones's contract after he left Fox, Columbia announced a series of eight Westerns which would help diversify its current programme of features based on 'successful stage plays, musical shows, and picturization of popular fiction'. Supplemented with *Call of the West* starring Matt Moore and Dorothy Revier, the studio promised that the series would be full of 'red-blooded action stories . . . produced on a lavish scale with spectacular sequences and several scenes in natural color showing the hues of the sagebrush and the purple mountains'.[9] Warner Bros. offered three Westerns in the guise of Rin Tin Tin adventures, while *Song of the West* and *Under the Texas Moon* were already in release. Vitaphone Varieties had recently produced a number of Western shorts, some in Technicolor. First National had five features either in work or scheduled: an adaptation of David Belasco's *Girl of the Golden West*; *Under Western Skies* from an original screenplay; *Heart of the North* adapted from a magazine story; *God's Country and the Woman* from a novel by James Oliver Curwood; and *The Bad Man* from a play by Porter Emerson Browne. In the hope of attracting a broad audience, this eclectic set of sources and story types could all be pitched as 'outdoor' dramas.

Universal 'includes in its feature program for 1930–31, three or four big outdoor pictures like *The Oregon Trail*. While eliminating entirely any suggestion of the old time horse operas, this company, aware of the increasing demand for virile stories of action, set in a natural background, has made preparations for satisfying this most commendable need.'[10] Universal also had in work or in release eight Ken Maynard and eight Hoot Gibson horse operas. In other words, it would continue to produce the kind of Westerns it always had, while emphasising in its marketing the move into prestige Western pictures. Following the 'tremendous success' of *The Virginian*, Paramount planned a series of big budget Westerns capitalising on Gary Cooper's new-found stardom. These would include *The Texan*, *Fighting Caravans*, *Rose of the Rancho* and *The Spoilers*. Richard Arlen, Cooper's co-star in *The Virginian*, was given the lead in *The Border Legion* (which also featured Mary Brian, who played Molly Wood in *The Virginian*), *Rodeo Romance*, and two others. Moreover, a number of these Paramount Westerns would have the added attraction of being adaptations of Zane Grey novels.

Fox also announced a series of Zane Grey adaptations, some of which would star George O'Brien, as well as works based on the Western novels of Max Brand, Charles Alden Seltzer, Paul Lester Ford and James Oliver Curwood. The major studios' over-reliance on adaptations of novels and short stories was due in part to the authors' pre-sold profile, but also to a believed perception that an adaptation carried connotations of 'high quality'—a mark of distinction. Pathé would produce a number of two-reel Western comedies and had signed Tom Tyler as its leading cowboy star. *The Painted Desert* (1931) would be the studio's late entry into the cycle of prestige Westerns. It was shot in monochrome but planned as an 'all color production'. MGM had the 'All-talking Singing Picture' *Montana Moon* in release starring Joan Crawford and John Mack Brown, who also starred in *Billy the Kid*, one of its key prestige pictures of the season, to be released that September.

Poverty Row and studios that specialised in short films were also covered in the report. Educational had plans for a number of Western comedy shorts, and Sono Art-World Wide Pictures had *The Dude Wrangler*, 'a new type of comedy Western, its story centred about a "pansy cowboy"', pending release. Noting how the trend in 'back-stage stories' was waning, the editor suggests that these kinds of Western comedies 'have a legitimate claim to the exhibitor's favor'.[11] The flurry of Western productions for the 1930/31 season demonstrate the speed with which Hollywood could inaugurate a production cycle following the success of two prestige pictures. Nonetheless, the box-office popularity of *The Virginian* and *In Old Arizona* should not preclude consideration that the cycle was also a response to pressures brought to bear from outside the studios.

In Old Arizona was both Fox's and Hollywood's first 'all-dialog' outdoor feature. Location sound recording was, however, by no means a novelty for the company, as a contemporary report noted:

> Those who solemnly and complacently thought that talking pictures could never be made out under the uneasy acoustics of the wide sky apparently overlooked the fact that Fox had been doing that very thing for the past two years-and successfully. William Fox has had fifty trucks with Movietone recording apparatus in various parts of the world, capturing voices and reverberations connected with important events for Movietone News.[12]

By 1929 the novelty of sound was fading, but through the use of exterior locations and judicious editing of ambient noise it was given a temporary rejuvenation. A review of *The Virginian* in the *New York Times* reports: 'The sounds, whether footfalls, horses' hoofs, rumbling wheels or voices, are really remarkably recorded and reproduced. A good deal of this film was made in the open and it would seem that stories of Western life, if pictured in a rational fashion, would be unusually successful, for they are aided immeasurably by the audibility of the screen.'[13] After two years of studio-bound dramas, which by their very nature excluded Westerns, Hollywood returned to the genre as one means of keeping the novelty of talking pictures alive. In return, as *Picture Play* magazine noted, sound brought novelty to Westerns: 'Western heroes are now human beings instead of knights of the sagebrush, thanks to speech and hoofbeats . . . *In Old Arizona*, *The Virginian* and other outdoor dramas blazed the new trail into the golden sunset where men are people and women get them into and out of trouble.'[14] In other words, sound helped Westerns to temporarily lose the impression that they were formulaic, with two-dimensional characters, short on plot and long on action.

Alongside their own pedigree as producers of *The Covered Wagon*, Paramount's publicity for *The Virginian* made much of Gary Cooper and the story's source book and the stage play derived from the novel. The film was trumpeted as 'THE NEW SHOW WORLD OF THE GREAT OUTDOORS!': 'You see and hear thousands of bellowing cattle swimming a raging river, cowboys singing as they ride range, gunfights, campfires crackling'.[15] Emphasising cinema's history and progress, publicity stunts included displays of Old West artefacts and early moving picture cameras and ephemera, linked to early Western productions which were contrasted with photographs of modern projection rooms. A campaign built around the film's historical features was aimed at schools, and students from a blind school attended a special performance. A tie-in edition of *The Virginian* was published, and advertising balloons were hung above football stadiums during the big games.[16] *The Virginian*'s reputation as novel and play made it an excellent example of the pre-sold property and this, coupled with the novelty of outdoor sound, guaranteed exhibitor and audience interest.

The Virginian has a beautifully crafted soundtrack. Ambient sound is wonderfully balanced, particularly during the scenes of cattle-herding. The braying and movement of the cattle is overlaid with the soft and harsh calls of the cowboys. Snatches of song sung by the cowboys are phased in and out unobtrusively. Dialogue is laid over the top of the ambient sound so that there are no disruptive cut-ins and breaks, and it is finely wrought and laced with neat throwaway lines: 'That boy's so smart he'd dry snow and sell it for sugar'. In the early outdoor sequences there is a tendency to shout some of the dialogue, causing Cooper to slip in and out of his character's Southern accent. But, taken as a whole, the actors manage to keep a repressed edge to their delivery of lines, maintaining a sense of imminent explosion that is kept in check until the final shoot-out between the Virginian and Trampas.

The filmmakers reworked, to good effect, the meandering plot of the source novel while keeping its latent sense of drama. The leisurely pace of the story is established in the opening few shots of the film which show the cowboys drifting a herd of cattle into the town of Medicine Bow. Here the Virginian meets up with his old saddle-pal, Steve, who has remained a loafer and a drifter while the Virginian has risen to ranch foreman. Over drinks in the saloon their differing philosophies on life are debated and then cut short as they vie for the company of the Mexican saloon girl. The scene establishes a friendly rivalry between Steve and the Virginian over women, carried on later when Molly Wood arrives in Medicine Bow to teach school. The establishment of a love triangle, not in the source novel, is essential to the dynamics of the film's plot, and is echoed in the triangle formed by the Virginian, Trampas and Steve.

The film dispenses with all of the novel's plot digressions and focuses on the romance between Molly and the Virginian and his and Trampas's rivalry for Steve's friendship. The film version takes as its theme the problems inherent in making the cowboy into a romantic lover. A central scene contrasts Molly's sentimental view of *Romeo and Juliet* with the Virginian's pragmatic approach to love-making. In a pastoral setting Molly and the Virginian discuss the various merits of Shakespeare's play. Molly tells him, 'you're no Romeo'. His response is

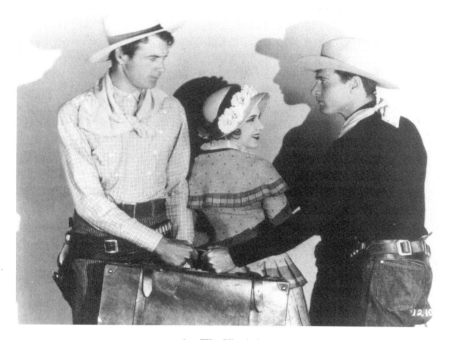

1. *The Virginian*
A romantic triangle: The Virginian (Gary Cooper), Molly (Mary Brian)
and Steve (Richard Arlen)

to take her in his arms and kiss her. He asks her to marry him, but she refuses. His coarse manners, like the West, are still 'alien' to her. The idyll is broken by the sound of cattle and the Virginian rides off to investigate. He finds Steve branding stolen cows. 'Times are changing', the Virginian tells Steve in a futile attempt to get him to give up his allegiance to Trampas. As the Virginian moves closer to winning the heart of Molly, Steve moves further into Trampas's sphere of influence. Eventually Steve is caught rustling again and this time the Virginian is not alone, and Steve must be punished. The lynching of Steve is a brilliantly staged piece of restrained direction and acting rhymed later by the Virginian's quiet walk down the streets of Medicine Bow towards his final confrontation with Trampas.

Despite Molly's status as the school teacher it is she who has to undertake the hard lessons of life. Twice she gives the Virginian an ultimatum, after the lynching and before the gunfight, and each time she backs down, having understood that she has been wrong. The film's emphasis on her education and the Virginian's attempts at

2. *In Old Arizona*
The Cisco Kid (Warner Baxter) and Sergeant Dunn (Edmund Lowe)
compete for the attention of Tonia Maria (Dorothy Burgess)

love-making, and on his friendship with Steve coupled with the under-
tow of mounting tension between the hero and Trampas, gives the
film a dramatic set of complementary conflicts that are finely balanced
and carefully paced. *Cimarron*, *The Big Trail* and *Billy the Kid* all lack
this narrative composure, in part because they are unable to produce a
credible romantic intrigue. By making the problem of courtship and
the cowboy its major theme, *The Virginian* is able to overcome the
dramatic shortcomings encountered elsewhere in early sound Westerns. The publicity for *The Virginian* promised 'hair-raising drama,
laughs and warm romance' and it delivered on all three counts.

Beyond the innovations in location sound recording, *In Old Arizona*
shared with *The Virginian* the narrative conceit of a love triangle—
'Two Men and a Senorita in a Rodeo of Love'. Poster and other
advertising campaigns visually emphasised the romantic elements. The
'Rodeo of Love' copy anchored an image of the Cisco Kid (Warner
Baxter) and Sergeant Dunn (Edmund Lowe) separated by, and
struggling over, the body of Tonia Maria (Dorothy Burgess). Posters

for *The Virginian* give as much space (if not more) to the Virginian and Molly in a lover's embrace as to the rivalry between him and Trampas.[17] Similarly, both films offered comic interludes and suspenseful drama. In *In Old Arizona*, drama is built around the alluring but treacherous figure of Tonia, who shifts her attentions between the competing men before choosing Dunn over the Kid, an act of betrayal that she is made to pay for when the Kid tricks Dunn into shooting her. The Kid then rides off singing the film's theme song: 'My Tonia'. Though the Virginian makes love with a Mexican saloon girl early in the story, flirtations with non-white women are left in the past with the arrival of Molly, and any implication of racial mixing is forgotten. In *In Old Arizona* the Cisco Kid's language of love is contrasted to the more taciturn language of the white American. When Tonia sells out the Kid it is not just a lover's betrayal but also a betrayal of race. She is a lower-class Mexican and is clearly not destined, as Molly is with the Virginian, to form a couple. Within contemporary discourse on race, miscegenation between Anglo-Americans and Mexicans is only sanctioned when the female love interest is characterised as the daughter of a 'Spanish' grandee, her European bloodline unbesmirched by the taint of the Native. The performance of romance and race was to become a key theme in the first cycle of sound Westerns. Warner Baxter won an Oscar for his performance as the Cisco Kid, an award that also recognised the box-office success of *In Old Arizona*, which at one first-run cinema broke the weekend record with a gross of $54,000.[18]

In Old Arizona was released in the last quarter of the 1928/29 season. Its box-office success, alongside *The Virginian* in the last month of 1929, meant that other studios were certain to jump on the bandwagon. But the box-office pull of these Westerns was not the only reason for the major studios' return to prestige Western production. The production of Westerns also acted as a sop to independent theatres to help quell complaints against restrictive trade practices. Paul Seale writes:

> In October 1927, the Federal Trade Commission reopened its ongoing investigation of restrictive trade practices in the film industry, an investigation fuelled in part by the complaints of independent producers and exhibitors. On 9 July 1927, Commissioner Abram F. Myers had already ordered Paramount to cease blockbooking and acquiring theaters by the time hearings reconvened in the fall. And during those fall hearings there was

increased talk of legal action or legislation against an unyielding Paramount, a threat which persisted for at least two years.[19]

With block and blind booking, where exhibitors contracted to play a 'block' of unseen films from a studio, the majors needed to pay little attention to the demands of independent exhibitors. To get the films they wanted, exhibitors had also to take a 'block' of films that might fail to meet the interests of their patrons. At a point in time when this system was under threat, the studios paid at least lip-service to the independents' demands for particular types of films; they would repeat this process in the late 1930s when antitrust litigation was reactivated.[20]

One type of film produced both to meet independent exhibitors' needs and to exploit further the popularity of *In Old Arizona* was a short cycle of films using similar characters and locations.

'Spanish—More or Less': South of the Border Westerns

Spanish—More or Less
Whether or not our gifted favorites masquerade successfully as Spaniards or Mexicans, they attempt it often enough to appear in their recent characterisations on this page.[21]

This quotation from *Picture Play* magazine was accompanied by stills of Antonio Moreno, Victor Varconi, Basil Rathbone, Gary Cooper and Don Terry dressed in the tight-fitting costumes of Spanish grandees and Mexican vaqueros. These roles allowed Hollywood's leading men to cavort in flamboyant dress, which emphasised their physique, particularly their legs and backsides. More significantly, the roles validated an image of the male lead as romantic lover *and* man of action. Romance and the language of love were an integral part of the South of the Border/Old California cycle of Westerns that followed in the wake of the success of *In Old Arizona*, based very loosely on the O. Henry stories of the Cisco Kid. The cycle itself was a reprise of an early to mid-1920s trend in Western productions. Fox capitalised on the film's success by reprising the character type played by Baxter in *Romance of the Rio Grande* (1929), *The Arizona Kid* and *The Cisco Kid* (1931). Advertising copy for *The Arizona Kid* noted it was 'Greater than *In Old Arizona* and *Romance of the Rio Grande*—two pictures that established Warner Baxter as the supreme lover in outdoor roles'.[22] First National and Warner Bros. attempted to exploit Fox's success by

3. *The Virginian*
Trampas (Walter Huston) and his villainous moustaches

offering *The Lash* (1930), a prestige production filmed in Warners'
widescreen Vitascope 65 mm process, *The Bad Man* (1930), and *Under
A Texas Moon* (1930). Tiffany added to the cycle with *Border Romance*
(1930), Beverly Productions/Columbia entered the fray with *The
Avenger* (1931) and Ken Maynard Productions contributed *Song of the*

4. *The Lash*
Don Francisco Delfino, A.K.A. Pancho, A.K.A. El Puma
(Richard Barthelmess)

Caballero (Universal, 1930). The latter produced a distinctly uncomfortable performance from Maynard, pronouncing 'Manuel' as 'Manual' while trying to assert a sexuality utterly alien to his usual straightlaced persona. In another adaptation of an O. Henry story, Paramount starred Cooper in *The Texan* (1930). All of the films draw upon the stereotype of the Latin lover and the swagger and derring-do of Douglas Fairbanks's Zorro. The setting allowed for the inclusion of a great deal of music and dance.

The Lash starred the still bankable Richard Barthelmess as Don Francisco Delfino, known more familiarly as Pancho, and more notoriously as El Puma. The story is set in 1846. California has become part of the United States, 'But while the two nations were at peace there was still hatred and friction between the two peoples—the proud and cultured Californians and the rough and forceful Americans'. Pancho's world falls apart when he delivers three thousand head of cattle to the town of Spanish Gulch. Mexicans are banished from the town and Pancho is whipped by Peter Harkness (Fred

Kohler). Pancho, in an act of reprisal, stampedes the herd through the centre of town. No one is killed but the town is a wreck: 'Every Gringo hand will be raised against you', observes Pancho's friend. 'Yes, and mine against every Gringo', Pancho replies. Pancho becomes the outlaw, El Puma, a Mexican Robin Hood—a distinct archetype in this cycle—who steals from the rich Gringos and gives to the down-trodden poor Mexicans:

> Since I've left here I've learnt many things. I've learnt that I'm a foreigner without any rights. That our people are being cheated, robbed of their lands and their homes. In the northern parts of the State I've seen them driven out like dogs and title to their land either stolen or destroyed.

Pancho's banditry is complicated by the fact that he has fallen in love with Rosita (Mary Astor). She loves him in return, but while he is an outlaw there is no future for them. To complicate matters even further, Pancho's sister Dolores (Marian Nixon) has fallen in love with the Gringo David Howard (James Rennie), who has sworn to capture and hang El Puma. When Don Mariana Delfino, Pancho's uncle, who has been running the rancho in his absence, is murdered by Harkness, Pancho must make a choice: either to follow his dying uncle's last words and accept that there is 'a new order of things here, it will do no good to fight' and disband his merry band of men, or to continue on regardless. But there is no real choice, as romance, not justice for his people, must triumph. Nevertheless there are personal quarrels to be concluded. Before avenging his uncle's death he meets with Howard and gives up the rancho to him and his sister—a marriage of the Old and New Worlds—and then heads for sanctuary in Mexico where he marries Rosita.

The emphasis on courtship and the relatively exotic settings and costumes gives the Latin hero a romantic aura that is denied, or at least suppressed, in the Anglo cowboy hero in North of the Border Westerns. The romantic aura is, however, drawn wholesale from stereotypes of Latin men, particularly as displayed by Rudolph Valentino. But as Gaylyn Studlar has noted, the meaning of Latin masculinity was reconfigured and made more acceptable by using 'actors who were thought to be from sturdy Anglo-Saxon stock',[23] such as Richard Barthelmess. Richard Maltby has suggested that this turn to Latin lovers was part of the process of renegotiating the conventions of the representation and performance of romance, masculinity and heroism in early sound cinema. The melodramatic gestural style of Valentino and John Gilbert now appeared awkward and contrived, but in the exotic space and costuming of the South of the Border Western, the exaggerated gesture of ethnic characters was still permitted.[24] Nevertheless, there still remained the question of how romance could be credibly dramatised in Westerns where the Mexicans were not the heroes, but were either fools or 'greasers', and the male lead was an Anglo cowboy who defined himself in part against the Latin lover.

The South of the Border/Old California Westerns were apt to offend the sensibilities of Latin Americans. The Mexican authorities had previously found it expedient to place an embargo on American films because of negative stereotyping, something that *The Lash* tried to overcome by restricting the role of the villain to American characters, but, as Ruth Vasey has documented, this caused 'a new kind of diplomatic backlash'. Frederick Herron, of the MPPDA's foreign department, complained:

> I was so mad after I saw [*The Lash*] that I saw red for days. If the picture had been made abroad it would never have been allowed distribution in this country . . . I feel I am a lot to blame on pictures of this type because of the continual harping I have been going through in telling people to lay off the foreign villains and make the villains American, but I didn't know they would go quite as far as this.[25]

Herron was not just reacting to the negative portrayal of Americans but also to the sexual potency of non-white characters. His distaste for *The Lash* echoes the reaction of those 'paragons of virility' who viewed the marketing of Valentino as 'a blend of sexual vitality and romantic courtship' as a racial threat, and, in Miriam Hansen's account, responded 'in a strongly nativist tone'.[26] Later versions of the Latin lover in Westerns would be contained by making them into comic figures. Indeed, many of the films in this initial cycle walked a very fine line between melodrama and comedy. This is exemplified in the advertising copy for First National's *The Bad Man*:

> 'I make ze love to you myself—personal . . . What? Because you are marry you do not wish to spik of love! Leesen Lady—eef Pancho Lopez want woman, he take her, dam queek!'
> Listen to him! The perfect love with a broken accent to mend broken hearts!—L'il old Cupid with a six-shooter—the Robin

Hood of the desert—the greatest character ever brought to the talking screen by Walter Huston.[27]

Comic dialect of this kind undercut any sexual threat, making the figure, at best, into a caricature. Comedic elements were given even greater prominence in Warner Bros.' *Under A Texas Moon*:

> Come on out for a hundred minutes of mirth! . . . See a new kind of hero in a new kind of romance. Laughing Lothario-Romeo of the ranchos—this carefree Caballero has a girl in every patio. As careless of love as he is of life, he carries his heart on his sleeve and his tongue in his cheek as he swaggers into love and out again with half a dozen seductive senoritas. *Under A Texas Moon* is a smile-a-minute-story—with full color, music, glorious outdoor scenes and a truly all-star cast. See it soon because you'll want to see it twice.[28]

With the exception of the low-budget *Return of the Cisco Kid* (20th Century-Fox, 1939) (which led to a series of six Cisco Kid adventures beginning the following year with *Cisco Kid and the Lady*), *The Mark of Zorro* (20th Century-Fox, 1940) and Paramount's tedious re-make of *The Texan*, *The Llano Kid* (1939), South of the Border/Old California Westerns would be noticeably absent from the genre's revival in 1939/40. What was retained from this cycle, however, was the romantic impulse. Dramas of courtship would later be incorporated into the 1939/40 North of the Border Westerns, but in terms of the 1930/31 cycle it was ruinously absent from the three biggest Western productions of 1930/31: *Cimarron, The Big Trail and Billy the Kid.* These films returned to Western archetypes that had proved successful during the silent period. In this respect they represented a different response to the needs of independent exhibitors and to studio antici-pation (following *In Old Arizona* and *The Virginian*) of renewed audience interest which characterised the 1930/31 cycle. In the following section, I examine how each of these films attempted to respond to diverse audience demands, and the way that this was negotiated within the film and within the preproduction and post-production phases.

Prestige Westerns

RKO's *Cimarron* was an adaptation of an Edna Ferber novel published in 1930. Ferber had achieved national fame through her short stories about the businesswoman Emma McChesney. She had followed these with a number of best-selling novels, most notably *Showboat* (1926). *Cimarron* had all the qualities that Hollywood looked for in a pre-sold property. The author had an established reputation and the source novel had sold well, acting as pre-publicity for the film. Moreover, like so many of Ferber's novels—*Showboat* for example—*Cimarron* was conceived as a saga of America that focused on the *woman's experience* of nation-building. This emphasis, plus the epic nature of the story, featuring a number of spectacular set pieces, must have suggested to the producers that a film adaptation would appeal to a diverse audience. Pre-release publicity in the trade press made much of the Ferber connection: 'Author of *Showboat* and *So Big* and many other best sellers, Edna Ferber writes to stupendous world-wide following. *Cimarron* got off with a rush and is setting an amazing pace at the book counters. Needless to say, Edna Ferber's name has a definite and far-reaching influence at the box office.'[29]

My analysis of *Cimarron* examines both the source novel and the film, suggesting why the novel was felt to have an appeal to a broad audience and how the adaptation attempted to replicate particular attractions. The story is overtly concerned with the building of the American nation and the consequent creation of an American people. The epic scope of the story is managed by mediating the momentous historical events through a localised and individualised set of responses. The film adaptation, however, has particular difficulty in reconciling the epic with the human, a problem also encountered in *The Big Trail* and *Billy the Kid*.

The Big Trail was not based on a pre-sold property but was rather a self-conscious attempt to emulate the success of the silent Western epics *The Covered Wagon* (Paramount, 1923), *The Iron Horse* (Fox, 1924) and *The Pony Express* (Paramount, 1925). Like *Cimarron*, the story attempts to give equal weight to male and female interests, but in this instance, it is not done through the formula of the saga but through melodrama. *The Big Trail* draws upon epic visualisations of American frontier history, specifically earlier filmic representations exemplified by *The Covered Wagon*. I examine how the film deploys melodramatic devices in order to individualise its historical attractions. The analysis concludes on the industry's attempts to promote the film as a 'showpiece' of American film production.

Billy the Kid pays less attention to giving an equal role to male and female interests, although the producers attempted rather futilely to find such a balance. The major dramatic attraction of *Billy the Kid* is, instead, the figure of the outlaw. The studio reader's report on the source novel, *The Saga of Billy the Kid* (1926), had been very positive, but it was principally the exploitable value of the myth of Billy the Kid (which had been given a new lease of life by the novel) and the romanticism surrounding the figure of the outlaw that finally sold the producers on this property. The exploitable value of 'Billy the Kid' was circumscribed by the need to stay within the Production Code. The MPPDA's self-regulatory body, the Studio Relations Committee (SRC), later renamed as the Production Code Administration (PCA), vetted properties for potentially censurable violations of the Code. The story of Billy the Kid was in clear violation of the Code on two counts: glorification of the criminal and the taking of murderous revenge. Beyond the containment of Billy's Code-breaking activities, the film-makers also sought, evidently against the odds, to give him a love interest. A study of various drafts of the screenplay suggests the difficulties the writers had in incorporating a credible romance. Between them these three films exemplify strategies to diversify and update the older cinematic and fictional tradition of historical Westerns for the 1930/31 cycle.

Cimarron

Cimarron tracks the fortunes of the Cravat family from the Oklahoma land rush of 1889 to the story's close forty years later. The story focuses on Sabra Cravat (Irene Dunne), who finds herself forced into the public sphere by the actions of her husband Yancey (Richard Dix), a man consumed by wanderlust and fired by visions of empire. The film squarely sets itself up as the story of America, an imagined community where all, except blacks and those who do not obey the laws of God and the government, are given the space in which their voices can be heard and their actions are seen to affect the nation's identity.

> You can't read the history of the United States . . . without learning the great story of those thousands of unnamed women . . . in mud-caked boots and calico dresses and sunbonnets, crossing the prairie and the desert and the mountains enduring hardship and privation . . . And if ever it's told straight you'll know it's the sunbonnet and not the sombrero that has settled this country.[30]

5. *Cimarron*
Yancey (Richard Dix) and Sabra (Irene Dunne) on their way to church in the
frontier town of Osage

The speech comes early in the novel, spoken by Yancey. Towards
the end of the story it is repeated by Sabra, who has become the first
woman in Congress. Yancey is a 'civilised barbarian',[31] a character that
fits comfortably into Richard Slotkin's notion of personal 'regeneration
through violence'. However, the story is less concerned with this
turn-of-the-century response to the feminisation of American culture
—a Rooseveltian call for upper-class men to experience a 'strenuous
life'—than with Sabra's regeneration through the adversity she suffers
as a result of her husband's desire to find new challenges and adventures. The novel and the film attempt to confront the contradictions
inherent in the 1920s image of the 'New Woman' which, as Miriam
Hansen notes, was partly concerned with redefining 'notions of
femininity in terms other than domesticity and motherhood'. Hansen
argues that Hollywood recognised female spectators as a 'socially and
economically significant group and films were explicitly addressed to a
female spectator, regardless of the actual composition of the audience':

34

> The orientation of the market towards a female spectator/
> consumer opened up a potential gap between traditional
> patriarchal ideology on the one hand and the recognition of
> female experience, needs, fantasies on the other, albeit for the
> purposes of immediate commercial exploitation and eventual con-
> tainment.[32]

This contradiction between female experience and patriarchal containment structures both the novel and the film versions of *Cimarron*.

Writing on the film in *The BFI Companion to the Western*, Kim
Newman complains that it is 'perhaps best considered as a woman's
picture out West rather than as a true Western'.[33] Regardless of the
film's generic authenticity, this hybridity allows Sabra, rather than
Yancey, to act as the dominant mediating figure between the frontier
as a male domain and the Old South as a female domain. As one
review of the film noted, the 'progress of character through conflict
and adversity makes fascinating characters of the *men and women* in
Cimarron' (my emphasis).[34] Yancey's ceaseless craving for adventure
produces a series of patriarchal absences in the narrative. In 1893,
against the wishes of Sabra, Yancey takes leave to partake in the
opening of the Cherokee Strip. He is not heard from for another five
years, returning eventually as a Rough Rider and veteran of the
Spanish-American war. In the intermission Sabra holds the family
together by running the family-owned newspaper. Yancey's adventur-
ing forces and justifies Sabra's position as an independent woman, a
role which the narrative attempts to contain by showing her to be
steadfastly loyal in her love and respect for her husband. Yancey stays
to see Oklahoma gain Statehood and the Indians accepted as full
citizens of the United States (after oil is struck on their lands) before
he takes unexplained leave from the story after unsuccessfully running
for Governor on a Progressive Party ticket. He is not heard from again
until the end of the film, though rumours have him fighting in France
during the Great War. His constant absences from the narrative and
from Sabra means the love story is suggested rather than dramatically
and visually realised. This was not a problem in the source novel
because Sabra's romantic attraction towards her husband is manifest in
the descriptions of her conscious meditations, but the film failed to
find visual and dramatic equivalents.

Yancey Cravat is a Texan, a frontiersman, a trained lawyer, and
proprietor and editor of the *Wichita Wig Wam*. He has lived his first
five years of married life with his wife's family the Venables in Kansas,

the longest he has remained in one place. Yancey drags a despondent Sabra off to Osage—a boomer town—to set up another newspaper. Along with him comes their son, Cimarron, and the Venables' black serving boy, Isaiah (Eugene Jackson), who shows 'loyalty that money can't buy', to 'Massa Yancey'. In one of the film's most magnificent set pieces, Yancey, with glee in his eyes, leads a fearful Sabra through the main street of this emerging city. All life is represented here: the good (honest mechanics and merchants) and the bad (bandits and prostitutes). Ethnic diversity is represented by Isaiah, Sol Levy, Mexicans and Indians, whom Sabra views as a 'dirty filthy' race, while Yancy sees them as a 'race robbed of their birth right'. This conflict between husband and wife over race provides one level of dramatic tension. It is an ambiguous tension, because Sabra has married a man rumoured to have Indian blood in him while Yancey has no qualms about profiting from the Indians' misfortune. But the more significant dramatic tension, produced later in the story, is over gender. The effect of this focus is to shift the story away from being yet another exposition of the frontier myth.

Yancey's integrationist ability, which allows him to move with ease amongst classes and races, confirms the film's project of presenting a classless America that recognises and values individual achievement. His is an integrationist, not an assimilationist project because, unlike his wife, he does not seek conformity. Although Sabra resents having to live below her station in Osage, the success of her husband's newspaper means that she does not have to remain in this position for very long. Through her superior relationship with the town's other women, marked by her ability to stay one step ahead in consuming the latest fashions and home furnishings, Sabra presents an unrelenting image of middle-class values. The confirmation of this middle-class status is seen in her shift away from her pretentious aristocratic Southern roots and by her socially superior position to Osage's other representative of the South, the prostitute Dixie Lee.

Leaving Osage and respectability to seek out new adventures, Yancey returns after an absence of five years. He arrives just in time to defend Dixie in court against charges of prostitution. One of the leading petitioners for her arrest, Sabra is utterly against her husband in his support for this harlot. As with the question of race, however, he shows her to be wrong, because Dixie is a victim rather than a criminal. It is finally Sabra who makes the connection that, had the fates not been good to her, she, too, could have found herself in Dixie's position. Dixie allows the film to raise the issue of independent women.

Orphaned at the age of fifteen, Dixie unknowingly entered into a bigamous marriage. Left pregnant and on her own, she at first tried to find employment as a school teacher, but that door was closed when her past was discovered. She next tried to find work as a servant, the most 'lowly' of legitimate occupations, but even that position was denied her. Dixie's child died and she was forced to turn to prostitution to survive. Having confirmed Sabra's superior social position, Dixie's role is also to show what can happen if women are denied the means of legitimately supporting themselves. After Yancey successfully wins Dixie's acquittal, she quietly leaves the narrative.

As the city of Osage grows, so does Sabra's fortune. In 1929 she is elected as a Member of Congress. At a celebratory dinner, surrounded by old friends and male members of Congress, she offers the following speech: 'The women of Oklahoma helped build the prairie wilderness into the State it is today. The holding of public office by a woman is a natural step'. The film's assimilationist project has been achieved at the cost of repressing, through exclusion, that which would deny its success. The figure of the African-American (Isaiah is killed defending the family), like that of the lower-class sexualised woman, is simply expelled from the narrative, while the patriarchal figure of Yancey is finally, literally and figuratively, blown apart. The last scene shows Sabra touring an Oklahoma oil field. When news of an old man who has used his body to shield oil workers from an explosive blast reaches her, she senses that it is Yancey. Rushing to the site of this heroic act, she holds the dying Yancey in her arms as he repeats his mantra: 'wife and mother'. At the close, Yancey is immortalised as a statue representing the pioneer spirit, but, as viewers of the film and readers of the novel know, the truth is that it was women like Sabra who won the west—the sunbonnet not the sombrero:

> The word feminism was unknown to the Sabra Cravats, the Mrs Wyatts, the Mrs Hefners, the Mesdames Turket and Folsom and Sipes. Prim, good women and courageous, banded together by their goodness and by their common resolve to tame the wilderness. Their power was the more tremendous because they did not know they had it. They never once said, during those fifteen years, 'We women will do this. We women will change that'. Quietly, indominantly, relentlessly, without even a furtive glance of understanding exchanged between them, but secure in their common knowledge of the sentimental American male, they went ahead with their plans.[35]

The same may be said about critical writing on women in Westerns where they are neatly assigned to preconceived ideas of character types: mother, wife, school teacher, whore. Women's roles are overlooked in the critics' concentration on the 'sentimental American male'. What is highlighted is what the women seem to be rather than what they do. In 'Visual Pleasure and Narrative Cinema', Laura Mulvey cites Budd Boetticher's now much-quoted maxim on women in Westerns:

> What counts is what the heroine provokes, or rather what she represents. She is the one, or rather the love or fear she inspires in the hero, or else the concern he feels for her, who makes him act the way he does. In herself the woman has not the slightest importance.[36]

Mulvey used this idea to support her argument that women in narrative cinema act as a brake on story development, 'freezing the flow of action in moments of erotic contemplation'. While this argument may account for the role of women in the postwar Western, it fundamentally fails to account for their centrality in the prewar Westerns, particularly in the 1939/40 cycle. *Cimarron* offers the viewer the opportunity to delight in the adventures of Yancey *and* Sabra, a dual point of identification that must have been a major reason behind the producers' decision to make such an expensive film.

Variety thought the film:

> An elegant example of super film making and a big money picture. This is a spectacular western away from all of the others. It holds action, sentiment, sympathy, thrills and comedy—and 100% clean [perhaps a reference to the Dixie Lee character who was somewhat 'cleaned up' in the adaptation, but more specifically to the film's suitability for a family audience]. Radio Pictures has a corker in *Cimarron*.[37]

The *New York Times* review marvelled at the film's spectacle and its ability to hold together the narrative's episodic structure, while remarking on some of the story's more implausible elements, such as Yancey asking Sabra whether she missed him after his five-year absence, and the coincidence of his returning just in time to act for the defence in Dixie Lee's trial. In common with most of the press reviews for the film, Yancey's role is highlighted: 'In harking back over this picture one is tempted to describe one of the sequences and then revert to Yancey Cravat, for some further deed of his that escaped the mind for the moment is remembered'.[38] On the other hand, the fan magazines, while still finding much to applaud in Dix's performance and character, made more of Sabra's role:

> The struggle of Sabra, the tenderly reared young wife, to reconcile herself to the crudities of the settlement and its flaunting people; her struggle to understand her wayward, nomadic husband who, with all his tenderness and chivalry, is unable to resist the call of far places and leaves her to edit his newspaper and rear their children until he returns, flushed with the adventure of the Spanish American War, to bask in a hero's adulation . . . It is Irene Dunne, however, who is the big surprise of the picture. In what is virtually her screen début, an actress identified with musical comedy emerges gifted with all it takes to make Sabra real. Both voice and presence are extremely sympathetic, with a refinement immediately felt and gentle, though resolute, womanliness that remind one of that strength of character underlying the soft graciousness of women of the Old South.[39]

Implicitly recognising the film's failure to find a visual means to exploit the novel's romantic impulse, *Variety* noted that: 'Miss Dunne does nicely enough in a role of a loving wife and mother, which does not permit her to be much else. What she accomplishes in a political way is suggested rather than acted.'[40] The British fan magazine *Picturegoer* trumpeted Edna May Oliver's role but barely mentioned Irene Dunne, concluding: 'The whole outlook of course, is American, but is also historical-and occasionally a little hysterical'.[41] For American reviewers the historical element was spectacular rather than hysterical: 'It's doubtful if a red-blooded western such as this, another period in American history, has held as many big diverting scenes as *Cimarron*'.[42] *Photoplay* called it 'one of the year's best pictures'.[43] *Picture Play* wrote: 'At last a real picture, one with breadth and sweep, tenderness and passion and a true reflection of American life. *Cimarron* is as native as the soil.'[44]

Despite the good reviews, an Academy Award for best picture and a listing in the top box-office draws of the season, the film failed to make back its exceptionally high production costs on first release, and only its re-release in 1935 finally brought it into profit. In part, its success may have been hindered by its length, '124 minutes will interfere with the usual turnover of a picture house program, but as shown at the Globe, not a foot was padding'.[45] Other factors also militated against it. By the end of 1931 Radio Pictures were in the midst of a financial crisis brought on by over-expansion.[46] *Cimarron* would be the last major production of any kind Radio Pictures would invest in for some time.

The Big Trail

Fox had hit an impasse with the genre earlier in the 1930/31 season with *The Big Trail*, an epic story of a pioneer wagon train in the days before the Civil War. The film's subject matter drew upon *The Covered Wagon* (1923) but its producers hoped to overshadow this silent production through the sheer weight of one spectacular scene after another. *The Covered Wagon* had been a huge hit, and *The Big Trail* was clearly designed to emulate it. Both films emphasise the democratic make-up of the pioneers and their ability to endure great suffering in order to achieve their ambition of owning a piece of land. Both films are overt dramatic enactments of Frederick Jackson Turner's thesis 'The Significance of the Frontier in American History'

6. *The Big Trail*
The film's epic scale and emphasis on the spectacular undermines emotional intimacy between the characters

(1893), which posited the idea that the American nation and character was formed out of the contact with a westward-moving frontier, where civilisation meets the wilderness:

> The blood of America is the blood of pioneers—the blood of lion-hearted men and women who carved a splendid civilisation out of an uncharted wilderness
>
> title card from *The Covered Wagon*

> Dedicated to the men and women who planted civilisation in the wilderness and courage in the blood of their children. Gathered from the North, the South and the East, they assemble on the banks of the Mississippi for the conquest of the West.
>
> rolling titles from *The Big Trail*

The Covered Wagon plays heavily on the symbol of the plough as the tool with which these hardy pioneers will turn the wilderness into productive farm land. The symbolism is dramatised in contrasting scenes in which the pioneers pay homage to the creative potential of the plough and the Indians represent it as a force which will destroy their way of life. Towards the end of the film, the symbol of the plough is reintroduced as the wagon train splits into two groups, one which will continue on to Oregon to till and cultivate the soil, while the other, abandoning its ploughs, seeks its fortune in the Californian gold fields: 'The pick and the shovel never built up a country, you've got to have a plow', declares the leader of the Oregon-bound train. *The Big Trail* forgoes this particular symbolism, but it retains much else: the natural obstacles and the internal disputes that make the pioneers' journey so hazardous. Heat and cold, rivers and mountains, starvation, Indian attacks and self-serving individuals are all eventually overcome, a point emphasised in both films with symbolic images of birth and death on the trail.

The Big Trail tells its story through the agency of the Cameron family, Ruth, Dave and their little sister (their lost fortune and parents are never explained), who leave the South in hope of a brighter future in Oregon. Bill Thorpe (Ian Keith), a gambler and a liar, attempts to seduce Ruth through presenting himself as the owner of a large plantation back home in the South. She turns him down again and again, but also returns to him again and again after tirelessly mis-interpreting the actions of the hero, Breck Colman (John Wayne). The romantic triangle, unlike *The Virginian*'s, utterly lacks credibility and suspense. Thorpe's motives are as transparent as his villainy, which is announced as soon as we meet him, but the film refuses to suggest that he will ever physically take advantage of Ruth and thereby undercuts his melodramatic potential. Thorpe enters into an alliance with the film's other villain, Red Flack (Tyrone Power, Sr), whose villainy is confirmed by giving him a greasy-looking Mexican sidekick. We soon learn that he is responsible for murdering Breck Colman's friends. Despite his obvious untrustworthiness, Flack is hired to lead the wagon train to Oregon. Breck, a frontiersman of some renown, joins the train in order to get proof that it was indeed Flack who carried out the murderous deed.

Splitting the role of the villain between Thorpe and Flack adds nothing to the romantic triangle that functioned in exactly the same manner in *The Covered Wagon*, and with equal lack of suspense and tension. The villain in *The Covered Wagon*, Sam Woodhull (Alan Hale), maintains a hold on his desire for the heroine, never stepping beyond the bounds of asking for her hand in marriage. Like Thorpe, he is the melodramatic villain by convention only and not by action. The complete lack of sexual tension in *The Big Trail* (and therefore any points of censurable controversy), allied to its epic telling of American history, made it an ideal vehicle for the MPPDA to rally around and champion as a first-rate example of Hollywood's promulgation of moral values in refutation of those who would criticise it for moral degeneracy. This point was also made in favour of *Cimarron* by *Picture Play*: 'It provides a great stimulus to those of us who are tired of teacup drama, snarling gangsters, and ladies of leisure'.[47]

In July 1930, Colonel Jason S. Joy, director of the Studio Relations Committee (SRC) in Hollywood, wrote enthusiastically to William Sheehan of Fox Film Corporation:

> the picture is tremendous in scope and in a wealth of historic detail and a stirring and vividly realistic account of a pioneer wagon train from Missouri to Oregon in the days before the civil war. It has everything, gripping story, grandeur of settings, superlative photography, acting and direction. It deserves the endorsement of every outstanding official and every educational institution, civic and patriotic organization in the country.

At the same time he also wrote to Carl Milliken at the MPPDA's New York office, explaining why the Association should get behind the promotion of the film:

There are three reasons why I think we ought to make the biggest play we have ever made for support of this picture. First, the picture justly deserves it, second, it will greatly increase the reputation of the industry as a whole, third, it will help us immeasurably with our further dealings with the Fox film company, particularly Mr Sheehan.

Joy suggested to Fox that they 'regard our public relations department for the time being as part of your staff'. He supplied a list of ideas and organisations that he thought could facilitate the film's promotion, such as patriotic, religious and women's groups, like the Daughters of the American Revolution, the International Federation of Catholic Alumnae, Boy Scouts, and so on. He suggested, too, that important people in the news might also be interested in giving the picture a boost, among them the Roosevelts, 'whose interest in the West began when the former President participated in its upbuilding, Vice President Curtis, the secretary of the interior who has Indian affairs in his charge, Owen Wister, the novelist, and many others'. He ends by suggesting that they assemble the survivors of Roosevelt's Rough Riders: 'they are of course closely associated in the public's mind with the winning of the West and have a romantic value'. Apart from his enthusiastic ballyhoo for the film, Joy noted that Sheehan and the film's director Raoul Walsh were concerned that the film would not draw at the box office, because of the Depression's effect on attendance, the film's similarity to *The Covered Wagon*, and the belief that '[w]e are in a cycle of sophistication. Our reading and theatre-going public (including picture) are supporting sophisticated subjects which make it difficult to arouse their interest in a patriotic and historical document.' Joy was noting the tastes of metropolitan audiences at first-run theatres, not those of audiences who attended rural, small-town and second-run theatres. Nevertheless Fox was willing to spend 'several thousand dollars' on its publicity campaign, and Joy believed this could be successful if it emphasised to teachers and their like the film's historical authenticity and if it held out to kids the promise of thrills and action.[48] According to Richard Maltby, the MPPDA attempted to find and promote prestige pictures that appealed to moral reformist critics during the late 1920s. *The Big Trail* is a late example of this policy, and like those other films it, too, failed to find a mass audience.[49]

7. *Billy the Kid*
From silent to sound, the old gives way to the new: silent Western star
William S. Hart handing the 'real Billy the Kid's gun' over to Johnny Mack
Brown; note the microphone above their heads

Billy the Kid

While Radio Pictures' *Cimarron* and Fox's *The Big Trail* drew upon the
historical Western epic, MGM chose to make dramatic and hoped-for
box-office capital out of the historical outlaw figure with *Billy the Kid*.

The director, King Vidor, trumpeted the Kid's exploitable historical qualities in publicity campaign interviews:

> 'When all other types of stories are out of fashion, we'll still have Westerns. They are and always will be one of the strongest foundation stones of the whole structure of entertainment . . . The Western story, however, today is in perhaps the most critical spot it has ever known. Because it was so easy to put over any sort of Western story in silent pictures . . . Western stories came to be made in a set formula, which worked alright until dialogue arrived. Speech, however, revealed these old, time-worn situations in no flattering light.[50]

Vidor's solution was to go back to the 'historical characters who made up the Old West' in order to give new life to a tired formula. By giving Westerns back their historical authenticity, Vidor suggested that it was possible to strengthen the 'weak plots' that silent Western pictures had covered up by 'plenty of action' with dialogue scenes that matched the action for interest because of their historical fidelity:

> Men like William Bonney flashed across the Western prairies in such a spectacular fashion that a great deal of data exists as to their exact conversations with various people; and their actions in certain dynamic situations. Further, to use a much abused word, there is a definite epic quality to real-life stories of this type which has not existed in some of the purely fictional Westerns.[51]

In her study of popular Western fiction, Christine Bold has noted that the most common means for a writer to move beyond formula is to set his or her story within a specific historical event.[52] The formula remains relatively intact but the historical event gives it the appearance of novelty. This is how history is used in *Billy the Kid*.

MGM had fashioned a synopsis of the film's source novel as early as October 1926. By February 1927 a 57-page treatment had been completed by staff writer Harry Behn. The film was, however, put on hold until the spring of 1929 when it was prepared as a sound film with dialogue by John Thomas Neville and adaptation by W.L. Rivers. A year later, Laurence Stallings completed the screenplay and dialogue sections from a final scenario written by Wanda Tuchock; additional dialogue was added by Charles MacArthur.

The initial reader's comments on the novel *The Saga of Billy the Kid* by Walter Nobel Burns had been highly enthusiastic:

> This is magnificent material . . . a splendidly well written book;
> and a gorgeous story is told. Surely, there is a mighty big picture
> in here, playing up the aspect of the passing of the outlaw, and the
> coming of the law. Epic stuff.

The early treatments were quick to seize on the story's 'epic' quality
and to match this, not to historical imperatives, but to myth. Billy the
Kid would be treated as a noble bandit in the mould of Robin Hood:
'The youngest and most daring outlaw in frontier history . . . the Robin
Hood of the Mesas'. Considerable attention was paid to establishing
Billy's formative years in Silver City, where an insult against his mother
leads him to become an outlaw. An early meeting between Billy and
Kit Carson is used to emphasise the Kid's mythic status and to
downplay, by association, Billy's Production Code breaking act of
revenge. A following treatment dispenses with Kit Carson and has
Billy kill the man who insulted his mother with a rock, rather than
with Carson's gun. Billy gets killed in the draft versions of the story,
though it is always a noble death. By adding an epilogue, written by
W.L. Rivers, the filmmakers offered the possibility of historically
containing Billy's glorification: 'we can dissolve with the tombstone of
Billy the Kid as the last remaining monument to the Old Southwest,
now crumbling away in a land of tractors, and railroad, and airplanes,
and Albert B. Fall's, and all the paraphernalia of a safe progressive
state'. The difficulty that the scriptwriters encountered (which would
be more profoundly repeated in the drafting of the 1941 remake) was
how to retain Billy's outlaw status and not transgress the censors'
prohibitions, in W.F. Willis's words, against 'crowning the criminal
and glorifying the gun'. On reading the script in March 1930, Willis,
who worked for MGM as a studio censor and liaison with the SRC,
reported that:

> The censors have had some very strange fancies and fads at various
> times. Yet there are a few points that may be called staple
> opinions. One of these used to be that any story that made a
> criminal a hero was inimical to the public welfare which it was
> their concern to guard so far as pictures were concerned. Another
> favorite belief was that recourse to the gun was a court of last
> resort. In private quarrel it tends to exhort the gun into a force
> where it becomes dangerous to the peace of society, and this story
> slaps those two old opinions squarely in the face!

He concluded by hoping that the director could turn these problems around at the shooting stage:

> if the picture is shown it will have a generally unfavourable effect, for it will be a strong argument that censorship is needed. However there is a ray of hope, I remember that Mr Vidor has not always followed his script. I do not mention this in the way of an unfavorable comment but rather as sincere praise. I remember when he made *The Big Parade* that by departing from the script he avoided an utterly impossible picture and made an utterly great picture instead. Perhaps he will do it again.

Vidor certainly made the picture acceptable from the censor's point of view, but he failed to make an 'utterly great picture'. The film dispenses with the suggested epilogue and instead inserts a prologue provided by the Governor of New Mexico, R.G. Dillon, that gives a pseudo-official sanction to the film's coronation of the outlaw:

> It seems to me that this picture of Billy the Kid, though it has taken liberties with the details of his life, presents a true drama of his career, and proves that this gunfighter of early New Mexico played his part in the West. Billy had a keen sense of justice which had been deeply outraged, and he set about with his gun and invincible courage to even up the scores, and in that way to restore to life on the range its personal liberty.

The film opens with the real star of the picture, the landscape, empty and magnificent. The following image shows a cattle herd dwarfed by giant mesas; a cowboy sings the film's theme tune, a quiet eerie lament to a lost and lonely cowhand. The cattle belong to the Englishman John W. Tunston and his Scottish partner Angus McSween. They decide to make the town of Lincoln their home. But what they thought was free range land is controlled by a robber baron, Donovan, who has declared himself sheriff, notary public, justice of the peace, and postmaster. Donovan makes it clear that the Britishers are not welcome. He is a badman who is shown forcefully evicting law-abiding homesteaders and then bushwhacking and murdering them.

The first stand-off is not long coming, but the balance is swung over to Tunston when Billy, whom we have not yet met, shoots one of Donovan's men. 'Killing rats comes natural to me', Billy explains to Tunston. 'You see when I was twelve years old I saw one of them shoot down my mother in cold blood, and another got my father in the back.

My father was a kind-looking gent—just like you.' This is all the explanation given for Billy's outlawry and his identification with Tunston. From here on in he plays the part of a sweet-natured killer. Six months pass in relative peace. Pat Garrett (Wallace Beery) has been hired as deputy sheriff, a man of independent mind hamstrung by Donovan's control of the legal apparatus. During this lull before the storm Tunston sends for his fiancée, Claire Randall, the very picture of English reserve: 'Say, don't you know that Englishers don't kiss until their silver anniversary', as one of the cowboys explains to Santiago, Billy's sidekick, after he observes that Tunston 'doesn't even bruise her' when she steps down from the stage that has brought her to Lincoln.

Tunston never does get that kiss; he is killed by Donovan's men on the ride to his wedding. Billy makes his vow of revenge as he holds Tunston's limp body: 'Before I die I'm gonna shoot down like a dog every man that had anything to do with this'. Billy's cause is seen as righteous by Claire and Pat Garrett, though Garrett still holds to the law. To a lesser extent Billy is also seen as innocent by General Lew Wallace, who brings martial law to the territory. He offers Billy an amnesty, but Billy has one more act of revenge to exact. Billy's thirst for revenge has been doubled by the killing of McSween, who dies in the film's great set piece—the siege and burning of his home. Along with Billy's escape from the Lincoln jail, this is a key event in the story of Billy the Kid. Billy is caught after holing up in a cave for over a week as Garrett, and what is left of the Donovan gang, starve him out. In a scene that beggars belief, Garrett, in order to take Billy alive, gets him to give himself up by frying bacon outside the cave. The smell drives Billy wild and eventually he submits to his hunger.

The last ring-leader of the Donovan gang is killed when Billy breaks jail and all that is left to tell is the ending. Here Billy meets with Claire near the Mexican border: 'Oh Billy, what are you going to do? Where are you going?' 'Keep moving West', says Billy, 'like all killers do.' 'You are not that', says Claire, 'every killing you have done has been needed. You have made this town a decent place to live in.' Unbeknown to them this meeting has been orchestrated by Pat Garrett, but rather than capture Billy, he lets him get away and gives Claire his horse so she can chase after Billy. This ending is totally lacking in historical fidelity, but its larger crime is that Claire's love for Billy has hardly, if at all, been established. As an agent of civilisation, her justification of Billy's acts of revenge are obviously supposed to carry weight, but with so little screen time given to their 'romance', we have no real sense of how this English rose has met and equalled the challenge of the wilderness. Her last words to Pat Garrett are, 'You're darn tootin''. Quite why she is so willing to adopt an American persona and dispense with waiting until her silver wedding anniversary to get kissed is a mystery the film never explains.

Along with justifying Billy's outlawry, the greatest obstacle in presenting an acceptable screenplay was the early treatments' failure to provide him with a love interest. Paulita, the half-caste daughter of Pete Maxwell in whose home the historical Billy would lose his life, eventually went the way of Kit Carson, and was replaced by a wholly Anglo character, Lucy Ann Randall (her first names are later changed to Claire). Early versions of the script had Billy shot down at the end by Pat, an event the writers tried to tie in with Billy's and Claire's growing love affair. The final scene takes place either in or just outside Claire's bedroom, where earlier she had 'surrender[ed] completely— giving him everything'. As Billy dies, he tells Pat that 'He guesses that killers like himself are just a necessary part of the beginning and that they must leave broken hearts like Claire's'. The difficulty the producers encountered was that this bedroom scene would not meet with Production Code approval. Given the character of Claire and how little time Billy and she had spent in each other's company, it was barely justified. Moreover, it gave Billy the responsibility of recognising his own mythical role in all that has happened, which clashed with his established persona of damaged innocent: he could not be both innocent and self-reflective.

In the end, the filmmakers went with the compromise that was least damaging to character continuity, and that allowed Billy's actions to be rewarded through the formation of the couple, providing a romantic capstone to a romance that was barely, if ever, there. This point is borne out in the negative reviews of the film which found little in common with the advertising copy that claimed Billy was 'A Fighter to the End—A Lover Unafraid'. Despite illustrating its review with a still of Billy and Claire, *Motion Picture* magazine wrote: 'Kay Johnson furnishes the blonde love motif which is subordinate to the gun fights that form the greater part of the action. The story is episodic, and at times slow and unreal.'[53]

End of the 1930/31 Cycle

One contemporary explanation for the box-office success of *In Old Arizona* and *The Virginian* had been the introduction of the new cinematic technologies of sound into the Western. As prestige pictures, both *The Big Trail* and *Billy the Kid* made similar investments in technological innovation with a view to increasing their exploitable value. Nonetheless, as their reviews made clear, *Billy the Kid* and *The Big Trail* lacked real novelty value. *Variety* summarized *The Big Trail* as a 'big spectacle sound picture, along familiar Western pioneer lines, without box office draught beyond one week'. Fox's Grandeur (wide screen) format in which one version of the film was shot (the other was in standard size) was summarily dismissed as 'not big enough in itself to become an additional stimulant at present to the picture house trade'.[54] Similarly, Metro's *Billy the Kid*, reviewed the previous week, was shot in Realife, an alternative widescreen format, but it, too, had little holdover appeal either in the novelty of the format or the story: 'just an ordinary Western which will have to climb uphill to reach normal business'. *The Big Trail*'s epic set pieces were much praised in the *New York Times* review, but were dismissed by *Variety* as the 'same thing over and over again'. Yet it was scenes such as these that were meant to exploit the widescreen format. Metro, according to *Variety*, was limiting the use of Realife to pictures 'calling for spectacular sequences'.[55] As with *The Big Trail*, 'the more important action sequences stand up, but the connecting links are weak' and the film has 'little or no love interest'. *Variety* concluded that 'minus Realife it looks as though the youngsters will like *Billy the Kid*, but there's little chance that the adolescents and their elders will be particularly interested'.[56]

Like the reviews, the films' producers saw Westerns as perfect vehicles for exploiting widescreen processes, but in doing so they ignored stars with real pulling power, and failed to construct a narrative with enough romantic intrigue to hold together the films' spectacular elements. 'The big puzzle to *The Big Trail*', wrote *Variety*, 'is why it was not given drawing names, and more young people. According to this film only elderly people started to hike from Mississippi to Oregon.'[57] *Motion Picture* magazine was even more damning: 'Against a background, so stupendous and unremitting and powerful as to be wearisome and a real bore, is set a thin and insufficient story of people who never come alive and matter hardly at all'.[58]

Both *Billy the Kid* and *The Big Trail* are hampered by poor dialogue. It is not John Wayne's immature screen performance (which is so often faulted) that hinders the drama, so much as the dialogue and screen direction he and the other characters have to contend with. Playing the burly villain with tombstone teeth, Tyrone Power Sr has, according to the *New York Times*, 'a voice that reminds one of Captain Hook in Peter Pan'.[59] He is also supplied with dialogue drawn wholesale from dime novels, and a phony dialect that may have worked on the printed page or in intertitles, but translates poorly when spoken. If the kind of comic villainy played by Power detracts from what little suspense the narrative has, it is compounded by dialogue that foretells characters' immediate actions: 'Ther holdin' a pow wow over thar now. I'll just step over an' see what they gotta say.' John Wayne and Marguerite Churchill, the female lead, are well matched, but there is hardly any *frisson* in the scenes between them, with director Raoul Walsh content to film them from distances that deny intimacy. Early in *The Big Trail*, Walsh fills the foreground of the frame with a group of women brushing out and washing their extremely long hair. It is a wonderful, strikingly surreal image, but Breck Colman, the ostensible object of interest, is lost to the audience as he walks across the rear of the frame.

In a contemporary interview, King Vidor explained the aesthetic and stylistic changes engendered by widescreen:

> This [Realife] will probably do away with a good many of the 'cutbacks' and close-ups to which we have been accustomed. Action on the screen can be told in a more direct flowing style. For example, in one sequence of *Billy the Kid* we have a hold-up scene in the foreground of the picture. By means of the depth of illusion produced by the new wide screen a rescue party is seen starting, in the background, several miles away. The oncoming party does not know what is happening in front, but the audience observes every moment of both with more suspense than would be possible by any system of 'cutbacks'.[60]

This may have worked with a projection system capable of showing Realife in all its glory, but only ten theatres were fitted with the necessary equipment when the film opened.[61] In whatever format the film was projected, the emphasis on the spectacular nature of scenes has the effect of continually undermining any dramatic impact and emotional intimacy. In June 1930, when production of the film was first announced, the producers had promised a picture 'as romantic as it is thrilling! With a love story of surpassing power.'[62] It clearly failed to keep this promise. As far as the 1930/31 Western was concerned, film reviewers and the industry decided that neither the novelty of sound nor widescreen could compensate for what was seen to be a dramatically played-out genre. Time and again reference is made to the epic Westerns produced in the later years of silent cinema,

The Covered Wagon, *Iron Horse* and *The Pony Express*, and how little the new Westerns have to offer over their predecessors.

Casting these Westerns was also a problem. The actors most identified with the genre, such as Harry Carey and William S. Hart, were too old to play the young romantic leads that the stories called for. Western stars such as Hoot Gibson, Tom Mix and Ken Maynard carried connotations of the formula that King Vidor had hoped to overcome. Even if age had not been a problem for the former two, their strong identities would have played havoc with the characters as originally conceived. John Mack Brown was cast as Billy because of his athleticism and strong facial and vocal features. His languid Southern accent, which had led a contemporary feature to call him the 'Alabam' Cowboy', had been used to good effect a year earlier when he played the romantic cowboy lead and love interest for Joan Crawford's flapper character in *Montana Moon*, but he was hardly a top box-office attraction.[63] This fact was underscored by casting Wallace Beery to boost *Billy the Kid*'s marquee appeal. Beery was a major star at MGM, but his appeal was geared for the masculine trade.

With the introduction of synchronised sound, Hollywood had not only invested in the talent of New York's radio and Broadway actors, but also in the city's playwriters and journalists. Equally, the recruitment of British stage actors and Broadway musical personnel, singers, composers, song and dance directors would also have an impact.[64] The industry was hiring creative personnel who had a proven track record of working with dialogue or some other area important to the production of sound features and who were also cheap, particularly the new acting talent.[65] These new recruits knew how to write and deliver credible dialogue for the urban dramas that the major studios concentrated on producing, but they had little experience of working on genre stories such as Westerns. Similarly, the new acting talent offered little in the way of a convincing physical presence that would suit Westerns.

The Virginian had a male star, Gary Cooper, in his first talking role, who physically and vocally appeared natural for the part. 'A Montana cowboy in real life and a splendid type of tall, sinewy, wholesome American manhood, Gary is the ideal talking picture star that the public today demands'[66] and 'Gary is a cowboy at heart, scorning alike the glitter of the Boulevard and the whims of public approval'[67] was how two reports helped construct an aura of authenticity around Cooper after his success in *The Virginian*. Five months after the release of the film, *Exhibitors Herald-World* confirmed Cooper's extraordinary appeal by announcing that 'Paramount's Cowboy Star' had posed for

Norman Rockwell and he was to be the first screen star to grace the cover of the *Saturday Evening Post*.[68] On the other hand, Cooper's co-star Richard Arlen, at least in his cowboy roles, was not received with universal popularity:

> What's all the hullabaloo about the waste of Richard Arlen on Western films? They're financially successful, else they wouldn't be made, and Dick's performance is always *ne plus ultra*. You don't hear *him* complaining. Time enough for dress-cast later.[69]

The sense of dissatisfaction with Arlen's portrayals of cowboys, to which this quotation from *Picture Play* magazine alludes, was not because his characters lacked authenticity but because of a feeling of ennui. Between 1929 and April 1931 when this note was published, Arlen had appeared in six low-budget Westerns (relative to *The Virginian*). The cycle, which had begun with such high expectation, was now becoming jaded and lacking in new attractions. This point was emphasised in *Gun Smoke* (Paramount, 1931), one of the final Westerns Arlen made that season, wherein Eastern gangsters are pitched against Western cowboys, creating a hybrid of that season's most discussed cycles of films. By July 1931, fan magazines had decided that both the gangster and the cowboy were over-exposed. In an article entitled 'Hunting for a Hero' *Motion Picture* magazine asked 'First, It Was Cowboys—Next, Aviators—Then Gangsters. *What Next?*' Cowboys, it suggested, are old-fashioned, surpassed by the modern hero exemplified by the aviator who was given a lead by Lindbergh. But the problem with aviators was that 'it is hard to make a man look dashing in goggles. And flying, once you are in the air, is a monotonous business.' The alternative hero of the modern world is the gangster who 'is fast becoming our typical hero type . . . But, really, haven't we had nearly enough gang heroes now? Don't we need somebody new to admire and to surround with glamour? Someone besides criminals?[70]

Before 1927, the major studios could afford to invest in a variety of productions that would suit rural and small-town markets, which often displayed a marked dislike for the 'sophisticated' dramas succeeding in metropolitan centres. But, as Paul Seale notes, by 'mid-1927, faced with falling profits for the first time in two years, the major producers cut their players' salaries, refused to grant increases, and let all unco-operative parties walk'.[71] The resultant downscaling of productions and other rationalisations meant that studios concentrated on the more profitable metropolitan market, but under the threat of antitrust litigation, they sought products that would appease all of their domestic markets. Large-scale Westerns promoted as 'outdoor dramas' or 'historical romances' appeared as one means of achieving this. As *Cimarron*, *The Big Trail* and *Billy the Kid* would prove, however, the epic Western was an expensive commodity and did not guarantee significant box-office returns. With the suspension of antitrust litigation and the fallout from over-expansion in the areas of theatre and real estate investments, exacerbated by the stock market crash and the resulting Depression, the major producers returned to the production of films whose costs could be more firmly controlled within a studio environment.

Discussing the effect of the Depression on the industry, Donald Crafton notes: 'Though the industry tried to maintain the appearance of being depression-proof, in fact the stock market crash hit Hollywood hard, if somewhat later than it hit most other businesses. Retrenchment entailed closing unprofitable theatres, stripping away nonessential distribution services, and streamlining the Hollywood product by confining it to generic categories.'[72] Moreover, as Giuliana Muscio notes, the majors' financial debts contributed to their concentration on making the types of films which had a proven box-office record of attracting audiences to the first-run theatres: Paramount, for example, expected to amortise 80 per cent of the cost of a negative film in twelve weeks.[73] The indifferent performance of these Westerns at the box office, their poor scripts, inappropriate technological innovations, the recruitment of Broadway personnel, the poor marquee appeal of their stars, their lack of novelty, reviewers' sense of ennui, cultural prejudices, and the lack of engaging and credible romantic interest to compensate for these perceived short-comings, help to explain the genre's disappearance from the major producers' production schedules. These obstacles would all be overcome when the studios showed willing (as they were to prove with the success of the 1939/40 cycle of Westerns). The sum of these negative attributes, however, coupled with the financial constraints of over-expansion and the lifting of the government's threat to outlaw blind and block booking, meant that the first cycle of prestige Westerns came to an ignominious end.

Despite the myth that the majors wholly abandoned Westerns, a number of the studios maintained series Western units, and started another cycle of the genre in 1936/37 before fully committing themselves to Westerns in 1939. The investment that the studios had already made in personnel, original screenplays, props and recyclable footage of cattle stampedes and Indian attacks was well used in the less publicity-conscious and historically invisible arena of series Westerns. It is this 'lost' and largely unresearched history of the series Western that forms the focus of the next chapter.

2

Series Westerns, Will Rogers and the Emergence of the Singing Cowboy 1931–1935

This chapter examines the fall and rise in Western production between 1931 and 1935, by considering the shifting fortunes in the careers of the leading Western stars, the domination of the series Western by independent producers, and the consolidation of independent production with the formation of Republic Pictures. The phenomenal success of the singing cowboy (particularly Gene Autry) is examined through an overview of his antecedents in the radio and phonograph industries.

The attrition of passing years had a substantial effect on the fortunes of the series Western. Of the great silent Western stars, William. S. Hart, Dustin Farnum, Art Acord and Fred Thomson had all retired or died before the advent of synchronised sound. Tom Mix's long career at Fox came to an end in 1928, and after short stints at FBO and Universal his film career came to an ignominious halt in 1935 with a serial made for the Poverty Row studio Mascot. Harry Carey, already in his forties, moved from Pathé to a short starring stint at MGM, most notably in *Trader Horn* (1931), but thereafter he made serials for Mascot, starred in Poverty Row productions by Art Class, Ajax/Commodore, and played down the bill from Randolph Scott in some of Paramount's series adaptations of Zane Grey's novels. Buck Jones's contract with Fox ended in 1929, whereupon he moved first to Beverly/Columbia and then to Universal in 1934. Tim McCoy, who was MGM's only series Western star, moved to Universal for a one-off starring appearance in a serial, and then joined Buck Jones at Columbia before leaving in 1934. He played out his career at a number of Poverty Row studios: Puritan, Victory, PRC and Monogram. Hoot Gibson left

Universal in 1930 and moved to Allied before making a slight return to major studio productions with two films in the mid-1930s for RKO. In 1929, Ken Maynard shifted from First National to Universal with short stints at Tiffany and KBS/World Wide, before returning to Universal in 1933. In 1934, he made one feature and a serial at Mascot and then joined the roster at Columbia.

In the years immediately following the transition to sound, all the contracts between the old guard of Western stars and the major studios were terminated in an act of collective house-cleaning and reorganisation that helped dampen the effects that a disabled economy was having on Hollywood. This retrenchment did not mean a complete abandonment of the series Western by the major studios, but their lack of investment and the poorly financed state of the independent sector help to explain the rapid fall in Western productions between 1931 and 1935. Fox had George O'Brien on its books until 1934, and the company continued to distribute his films until he moved to RKO in 1936. RKO's flagship Western series starred Tom Keane, Paramount had Randolph Scott, and for a series of six films Warners had John Wayne. These four actors offered a somewhat youthful contrast to the old guard, and their much smaller wage packets must have appealed to their respective studios. Nevertheless, the big studios found it difficult to match cost-cutting Poverty Row productions. According to Paul Seale, by 'Paying bottom dollar for everything, the Poverty Row producer could turn out a film for as little as $3,000 (though often closer to $10,000 or $15,000, still one tenth the budget of a low-budget major film), calculated to return its costs and a small profit in distribution'.[1] Citing *Variety*, Seale notes that prior to 1928 'the chief producers of Westerns were the major companies and larger independents: Paramount, Universal, First National, Fox, FBO, and Pathé. The smaller independents avoided Westerns because of the formidable competition'.[2] By 1932, however, most of the major studios had ceased production of Westerns, unable to afford the cost of prestige Westerns and unable to match the economies of the Poverty Row producers.

The effect on the quality of series Westerns brought about by the downscaling of production values can be seen by contrasting the series John Wayne made for Warners and the following series he made for Monogram. The Warners' films show a concern for maintaining a variety of situations to enliven the narrative formula, offering late entries in the South of the Border cycle and mining the then popular horror cycle, alongside the more familiar formulaic fare: threat to property and person, hidden identity and disguise, chase, capture and escape. The story quality is maintained by reusing plots from First National's Ken Maynard films and maintaining a higher than usual set of production values through the judicious use of stock footage (often drawn from the silent Maynard series). Moreover, with creative personnel of the quality of cinematographer Nick Musuraca (*Haunted Gold*, 1932) working on these films, a pleasing technological control over the aesthetic look and sound of the films is maintained.

In contrast, the Monogram films are mind-numbingly inter-changeable. Attempts to interject novelty, such as the idea of the cowboy who sings before he shoots the villain, or the mystery of the saloon whose patrons have all come to a violent end, read better on the page than visualised on the screen. Nevertheless, with Yakima Canutt as the villain and stunt coordinator, these films are rightly celebrated today for their novel stunts and carefully choreographed fist-fights. Towards the end of the 1934 season, independent exhibi-tors, through the pages of the *Motion Picture Herald*, began a much more vocal campaign against the poor quality series Western, which for many constituted their bread and butter programming: 'The John Wayne Westerns at one time spelled B.O. for me, but it's impossible for anyone to make several pictures a year and make good ones and this one [*Rainbow Valley* (1935)] is a very weak sister'.[3] *Trail Beyond* (1934) was lambasted by two other exhibitors as 'terribly amateurish'.[4] The situation was speedily reversed with the formation of Republic Pictures.

Republic Pictures grew out of Consolidated Laboratories, a film-processing corporation owned by Herbert J. Yates. Yates's company took most of the business offered by the expanding independent sector. When these under-financed studios felt the bite of the Depression, and fell into debt with Consolidated, Yates took several of them over. The merger of these independents provided a greater degree of financial stability, which enabled improved quality control over the planning and production of films. Although Republic did not own its own chain of theatres, it nevertheless had exchanges in the larger cities. Brian Taves notes that unlike 'most of its immediate competitors, and because of its emergence from Consolidated Labs, Republic successfully mated low-budget material with a degree of polished Hollywood seamlessness never equalled by the other smaller studios'.[5] Announcing its first season's offerings in 1935, Republic hoped both to maintain the existing audience for the product produced by the companies it amalgamated under its banner—Mascot, Liberty, Majestic,

Chesterfield, Monogram—and to expand by offering a 'superior' product. In May 1935, it announced that it was to increase annual production from twenty features and eight Westerns to twenty-six features and sixteen Westerns. The Westerns, clearly identified as a distinct product and separately accounted for, would be split equally between Gene Autry and John Wayne (*The New Frontier* was the second of the Wayne series, but the first made with the new resources available from Republic; *Westward Ho!*, the first film released, was produced before Republic's absorption of Monogram). The increase in production values over Wayne's previous Western series was indicated by Republic's announcement that it was 'not aiming to make pictures for double-bills'.[6] Although in practice Republic's films inevitably ended up in double-bills, playing either the bottom or top end, depending on patronage and class of theatre, the studio's statement signalled to exhibitors its intention to produce a consistently high-class Western product for a market that had come to feel inundated with shoddy films. *The New Frontier* was hyped as distinct from the run-of-the-mill Westerns: 'Not a Western in the strict interpretation of that term, it is an outdoor, action-packed adventure yarn which carries a charming romantic contrast to its vibrant drama'.[7]

According to the *Motion Picture Herald*, the new Republic series was endowed 'with better than ordinary production values. With John Wayne ranking as one of the foremost Western stars, his name looms as the outstanding commercial feature, but other qualities of the picture should not be ignored in its marketing.'[8] This perception was supported by letters to the magazine from exhibitors, which were in marked contrast to the reception given to the final films Wayne made for Lone Star-Monogram: 'Here is a Western that is a Western. Cowboy singing, action, theme song, everything. Give it preferred time.'[9] To confirm the self-evident improvement in production values —bigger sets, more impressive props, larger casts, better dialogue scripts, direction, cinematography, sound and editing—a number of the films were set firmly in the *past*. This was an attempt to revitalise the formula in a manner established by the major studios with their first cycle of sound Westerns: that is, to use a historically located story as a way of suggesting an authenticity for the product lacking in competing series Westerns. In the space of less than five years, Republic's yearly budget for film production had increased from $2 million to $9 million. During the Second World War, its production budget was more than doubled to $20 million.[10] Wayne's series was well received by exhibitors, but it was Gene Autry's films that would underpin the success of Republic Pictures. Given the prior period of instability characterising production by Poverty Row studios, the phenomenal effect of Autry's films on independent exhibitors and their audiences in turn profoundly altered independent production.

A history of the singing cowboy needs to look outside film and to take into account the commodification and exploitation of what was to become known as country music. To understand Autry's role within country music and Western films, it is necessary to consider not only his films and star persona but also the cultural traditions and social context out of which they were formed. Vernacular music and performance traditions were transformed by the new media industries. Due, in part, to the demands of radio programming and product promotion for a rural audience, the Southern vernacular musician found in the image of the cowboy a figure capable of transcending local and regional identities and their negative insinuations. The nationally recognised 'American' (rather than Southern) connotations of the cowboy figure facilitated a shift out of the performance circuits of a parochial audience to an audience of national consumers through commercial interests that sought to exploit his appeal. The idea of the cowboy strumming his guitar and yodelling across the high prairie may have been relatively novel to Western films, but precedents abounded within the tradition of vernacular American music that had its roots in the rural South.

Autry's success with Republic and independent exhibitors had been prefigured in his radio and recording career where he established his cowboy persona. His professional career as a recording musician had begun as an imitator of Jimmie Rodgers, producing recordings for a series of low-budget labels, in 1929. The profile gained through this activity and experience earned on small radio stations in Oklahoma eventually led to his own radio show in the early 1930s, and guest spots on the nation's leading radio barn dance. Autry's career trajectory echoes the transformation of vernacular Southern music from a localised, communally based activity into a mediated, nationally consumed product.

Blue Yodels: The Antecedents of the Singing Cowboy

One of the great misconceptions that the singing cowboy brought to Western mythology was that yodelling and being a cowpoke go hand in hand. In a history of African-Americans in the West, *The Forgotten Cowboy* (BBC Radio, 1995), in which the myth of the Anglo cowboy is contested, the programme still holds fast to another myth in claiming that yodelling was developed by cowboys out on the range to calm the cattle as they settled down for the night. The actual history of yodelling in America is not quite so prosaic.

The hero in Owen Wister's *The Virginian* (1902) did not yodel. Instead he sang blackface minstrel tunes:

> 'Yes, he'll be a missionary', said the Virginian, conclusively; and he took to singing, or rather to whining, with his head tilted at an absurd angle upward at the sky:—
>> 'Dar is a big Car'lina nigger,
>> About de size of dis chile or p'raps a little bigger,
>> By de name of Jim Crow.
>> Dat what de white folks call him'[11]

If the Virginian had yodelled at the end of the verse, it would have been in keeping with the minstrel form. Yodelling appears to have first gained a foothold in American arts when it was popularised by Tom Christian, a blackface minstrel who made his debut in Chicago in 1847. In *The Wages of Whiteness*, David R. Roediger makes the point that blackface could efface and incorporate a diversity of European ethnic character types and musical styles (when it was not holding them up for ridicule), such as Italian opera, Shakespeare, Irish songs, east European polkas, and Alpine yodelling. The difficulty in trying to disentangle the origins of the yodel is that it is caught up in this ethnic confusion.[12] Emmett Miller, a 1920s blackface vaudeville artist, appears to have been the prime mover in popularising the blue yodel, an Americanised derivation of the Alpine yodel. In 1924, *Billboard* magazine reported on a show at the New York Hippodrome and noted that Miller's 'trick singing stunt' almost stopped the show, and won him 'encore after encore'.[13] Miller's influence on Jimmie Rodgers and on other seminal figures in country music such as Hank Williams has only recently been divined, though even a cursory listen to the way he contorts and plays with the middle vowels in 'love' and 'blues' on his 1928 recording 'Lovesick Blues' suggests how significant his influence was.[14]

If Roland Barthes had ever listened to country music from this period he might have fashioned his ideas about *jouissance* on yodelling. Yodels come in many forms and carry many meanings, from the eerie otherworldly sounds in Val and Pete's 'Yodel Blues Parts 1 and 2', wherein St Peter is called up and then summarily dismissed ('I dreamt

I went to heaven, Saw St Peter there. When St Peter stood up, I sat down in his chair. St Peter said, 'I'm gonna tell you one more time, don't want a man around here with women on his mind" ') to the lonesome wail of Hank Williams looking for relief from life's torment, or the sound of pleasure and contentment in Gene Autry's later usage. At its best, as in Cliff Carlisle's 'Ash Can Blues', it gives voice to the ineffable. The singer tells of his bawdy life with a woman: 'Said, "I could haul her ashes better than any other man"—lord, lord—said, "I could sow my seed anytime in her ash can" '. In Jimmie Rodgers' first classic, 'Blue Yodel #1', the singer uses the yodel both to lighten and to darken his tale of revenge on Thelma: 'that girl who made a wreck out of me'. Jimmie gets himself a pistol—'as long as he is tall'—just to 'see poor Thelma jump and fall'. A short while later he gets himself a shotgun 'with a great long shiny barrel, I'm gonna shoot that rounder that stole away my girl'. The images of sex and violence that Rodgers conjurers up in the words and the performance get little if any recognition in the general histories of country music. It is hardly fitting subject matter for a music which has been commercially exploited as respectable since the early 1930s. The dark stain of sex and violence in 'Blue Yodel #1', which draws its power from the synthesis of black and white musical forms, is, however, never far under the surface of even the most bland and banal country performance.[15]

The effect that a well modulated yodel can have on an audience is implicit in a contemporary account of a performance by Professor Aleck Smart given at the Georgia Old-Time Fiddlers' Convention in 1915. He was described as a 'quaint character . . . who . . . plays melodeon and sings ancient ballads, which end in a yodel that climbs clear out through the roof and wanders among the stars'.[16] By the 1930s the yodel had been co-opted by younger men, who found Jimmie Rodgers' 'rounder' persona, as Mark Humphries explains, 'an appealing facade through which to vent sexual desire and aggression, stirrings which could be safely voiced in this new popular musical/ poetic form, the blue yodel. At best, the yodel was more than a comic tag: it was a non-verbal statement of youthful bravado, a catharsis, Whitman's "barbaric yawp" '.[17]

There was also of course a negative image of the poor white rural citizen of the South as illustrated by the *New York Journal* of 23 April, 1900: 'A Hill-Billie is a free and untrammelled white citizen of Alabama who lives in the hills, has no means to speak of, talks as he pleases, drinks whisky when he gets it, and fires off his revolver as the fancy takes him.'[18] This image continued to hold sway and arguably became more pronounced by the 1930s. In *The Mind of the South* (1941), W.J. Cash notes: 'the people of the towns [in the South] tended to develop a kind of supercilious contempt for all countrymen, including the yeoman himself . . . In some of the lowland areas of the South the terms "farmer" and "country jake" had got to be nearly equivalent to "white trash, and fully surrogate for "boor" and "clown" words not present in the ordinary Southern vocabulary.'[19]

Before there was 'Country' music there was 'Country and Western', a term coined by *Billboard* in 1949 to head up its chart listing that had previously been 'Folk' and before that 'Hillbilly'. The changes had been brought about as one means amongst many to rid Southern vernacular music of its pejorative and negative connotations. The history of the singing cowboy is intimately tied up in this process of making country music respectable and therefore marketable. It was the image and mythology of the cowboy that provided the most accessible means of repressing the vulgarity of Southern vernacular music, while simultaneously suggesting a classless and uncontroversial image of white supremacy. Between the late 1920s and the mid-1930s the move towards respectability allowed rural audiences to maintain a sense of regional identity. It was, however, driven on one level by the recording and radio industries, which were establishing themselves as a permanent presence in people's lives, and on another level by the rapid changes to rural lifestyles brought about by industrialisation, and compounded by the traumas of dislocation, disenfranchisement and dispossession brought on by the Depression.

By the time American vernacular music confronted the possibility of broadening its appeal, the idea of the cowboy offered itself up for appropriation, allowing the Hillbilly singer a means of reinvention whilst nevertheless maintaining an identity that spoke to the needs and desires of a white rural audience. The significance of Jimmie Rodgers is that his success underscored the potential market for exploitation within this community, though his image was far too protean and coarse to appeal to a wider audience which had to contend with the prejudices of the established middle classes, as it moved from the rural South into urban areas.[20]

This attitude was displayed in a 1926 edition of *Variety*, where a writer opined: 'Hillbillies have the intelligence of morons'.[21] Historian Richard White has noted how this stigma became particularly pronounced with the migration of 'Okies' to California during the Depression: 'Many of them had left the South to avoid being reduced to doing "niggers" work,' but this loyalty to southern values only fed a second source of scorn: a general disdain for poor white southerners, the "poor white trash" of regional stereotypes.[22] James N. Gregory, a historian of Okie migration, notes that this stereotype required:

> a special combination of background and present circumstances to trigger this response. It took, first, a close association with the heavily stigmatised occupation of farm laborer, and second, association with the equally stigmatised background of Southern sharecropper. These were elements out of which the Okie stereotype emerged . . . Class was the essential dividing line.[23]

Country stars such as Roy Acuff, who, more than anyone, began to hone the Nashville image of the conservative strait-laced country star that we have today, overcame this prejudice by dropping the ribald songs, putting on a Stetson hat and changing his band's name from The Crazy Tennesseans to the rather milder Smoky Mountain Boys (he would later disclaim any Western affectation). By the early to mid-1940s this trend was so firmly established that Hank (originally Hiram) Williams dressed in cowboy duds and called his band the Drifting Cowboys, despite the fact that his music and words paid barely a passing reference to the Old West. In making his bid for wider acceptance through TV appearances, Elvis Presley had to suffer all kinds of indignities that were brought about as a direct result of his Southern working-class background. The most notable was in the Steve Allen Show, where Elvis was ridiculed by being costumed in tie and tails and made to sing to a hound dog. It should come as no surprise, then as well as now, that his first film was a Western with a Civil War backdrop, *Love Me Tender* (1956), because by that date the process of the Southern musician ridding himself of any derogatory connotations by reinventing himself as a cowboy appeared totally unremarkable.

Dislocated rural Southerners carried with them connotations of poverty, class, overt racism, regionalism, anachronistic working practices and an absolute lack of sophistication. Southern vernacular music paradoxically confirmed this identity, yet it also displayed a remarkable ability to adapt and respond to a diversity of influences. Once Jimmie Rodgers had established himself as a recording artist, he sought out all kinds of musicians to help him realise his ideas, the most notable being Louis Armstrong. Rodgers' music is American music, not caring much for musical or ethnic purity; he sings and plays blues, jazz, old ballads, popular tunes, turning all into something unique to himself. But whatever form of music he played, whatever subject he sang about, or whatever persona he adopted, he always addressed himself directly to a rural audience.

To say that Rodgers had a profound influence on country musicians is to make only the most obvious of statements. Music critic and historian Peter Guralnick considers his influence on a whole rural generation to be 'equalled only by such figures of contemporary myth as Babe Ruth and, later Elvis Presley'.[24] Gene Autry's first forays on to disc (he made his recording debut in 1929) are slavish imitations of his hero: between 1929 and 32 he recorded twenty of Jimmie Rodgers' songs.[25] By 1931 Autry had had his first sizable hit with a maudlin tune, 'That Silver Haired Daddy of Mine'. There followed a number of sentimental songs within the mountain ballad genre, before he shifted both tone and subject matter and began billing himself as 'Oklahoma's Singing Cowboy' for regular and increasingly popular appearances on WLS radio's *National Barn Dance* out of Chicago, which was picked up by the national network in 1933. Until the mid-1940s, Chicago was thought to hold the greatest concentration of country musicians.[26]

'BARN DANCES AS SHOW BIZ', declared *Variety* in a front-page lead item in December 1934. Dan Goldberg writing from Chicago reported:

> More than 10 years of steady audiences, more than 300,000 studio visitors for 140 consecutive weeks of shows to S.R.O. [Standing Room Only] business, the biggest mail-pulling strength in the history of advertising, the greatest box-office attraction in the smaller towns throughout the country, the most loyal audience ever assembled.
>
> That's the record of the radio barn dance, now the top attraction on some dozen of the major stations in the land. It's a story without precedent in show business, in radio or in the advertising and commercial world. *A hillbilly twangs a guitar and yodels into a microphone that 'she'll be coming round the mountain' and hundreds of avid listeners rush out to buy some sponsor's work-shirt or fence post.* (emphasis added)[27]

There is a certain amount of contrived disbelief and a deal of patronising guff from the writer on the potency of the barn dance phenomenon, but his breakdown of the different barn dance formats from around the country is detailed enough to suggest recognition of more than just a passing fad. He also notes that the barn dance is absent from radio station programming in the East (that is, New York and New England) and had made little impact in the Northwest. At this point, stations ranked a particular programme or performer's popularity from the amount of mail he or she pulled and, according to *Variety*, the vast majority of listeners were from the rural regions: what mail the stations did get from city audiences was almost wholly in response to the barn dances. It is safe to surmise that these urban listeners would have been recent migrants from the rural areas. From 1920 to 1930 the total urban population in the South increased by nearly 25 per cent.[28]

The products and implied sponsors mentioned in the article are clearly pitched at the rural working class—fence posts and smoke salts—and it is also clear that the radio stations have an active policy of not peddling patent medicines, leaving this to the barely legitimate radio stations that owned powerful transmitters just over the Texas border in Mexico. These stations were principally set up to get around the oligopoly that controlled radio licences in the States and as a forum for high-tech medicine show hucksters of the day, who sold outrageous products such as cancer cures, potency revivers in the form of a goat gland transplant, and the rather less fraudulent Crazy Water Crystals, a laxative by any other name. Wrapped around these products and others such as 'glow in the dark' models of Jesus, 100 unsexed chicks and prayer cloths, were occultists, astrologers, hillbilly musicians, singing cowboys and anyone else who could pull in the mail and weasel another dollar out of the listeners.[29]

Autry's move into film revealed how intimately connected were the radio, recording and film industries by the mid-1930s. In the pages of the *Motion Picture Herald* exhibitors held an ongoing debate on whether radio was a poacher or provider of potential film audiences. The advertising manager of the Kerasotes Theatre in Springfield, Illinois, wrote a letter that expounded on the benefits of putting on a barn dance style show at his cinema that was then broadcast to outlying regions:

> This type of show is very popular in the Mid West, and we were able to run this show on our stage every Saturday night at seven for almost a year straight. This was a medium to reach rural sections and brought us a lot of new business in this particular field.[30]

In cinemas drawing rural audiences, the prime slot for Gene Autry's Westerns was Saturday night, and although this kind of direct cinema and radio promotion may not have been widespread, it nevertheless reveals how closely related film and radio audiences were for the singing cowboy.[31]

During the 1930s, WLS's *National Barn Dance* was America's number one networked show of country music. It would eventually be eclipsed by *The Grand Ole Opry*, which by 1940 had an estimated audience of 10 million.[32] The show was not networked until 1939, six years after the *National Barn Dance*. 'The music of the *Barn Dance*', notes Charles K. Wolfe, 'being designed for the Midwestern as well as Southern audience, was less "pure" and more sophisticated than that of the *Opry*.'[33] Autry's popularity on WLS was recognised when he was given his own show, *Conqueror Record Time*. It was within this 'talk and sing' format that he honed the amiable and sincere cowboy persona that would take him to Hollywood. WLS (World's Largest Store) was originally owned by Sears and Roebuck, who boosted the singer's reputation and their own sales through the promotion of mail-order 'Gene Autry' guitars, song books and other goods that he endorsed. Gene Autry was not just a singing cowboy. He was a singing merchandise store.

Autry was not the only country musician to gain commercial backing. For country groups sponsorship was almost a prerequisite to turning professional. Western Swing outfits like The Swift Jewel Cowboys were formed for the sole purpose of promoting Jewel cooking products. Aladdin Lamp Company sponsored the Aladdin Laddies, formed around Bob Wills, who changed their ridiculous name when they shifted sponsors, to the equally implausible The Light Crust Doughboys, in order to advertise Light Crust Flour. These and a myriad other bands eventually found their audience through the powerful border radio stations and more legitimate broadcasting outlets.[34]

Throughout the 1930s country music increasingly became one of the primary means by which manufacturers attracted consumers from the rural South. During the 1920s Henry Ford had pioneered sponsorship of fiddle contests at his dealerships across the South which, as Wolfe notes, were promoted as 'an antidote to the jazz music and "loose morals" that [Ford believed] were sweeping the country'.[35] In his history of Georgia Old-Time Fiddlers' Conventions, which ran between 1913 and 1935, Wayne W. Daniel notes that at its height of popularity these shows could attract an audience of over three thousand to hear fiddlers battle it out for the title of state champion and a cash prize. As 'Old-Time' suggests, the songs and tunes performed at these conventions went back at least to the nineteenth century and in many cases could be traced back to the British Isles. The convention's organisers, who saw themselves as guardians of an American tradition, made it clear that Tin Pan Alley tunes would not be tolerated, nor music that presumed to carry the haughty airs of opera. But by the mid-1930s the convention's popularity had waned, its audience lost to radio, phonograph recordings and the cinema. In the face of these new technologies of entertainment, fiddlers' conventions must have appeared hopelessly anachronistic and parochial.[36]

As the use of rural music to promote goods grew, the need to present a respectable, uncontroversial yet meaningful image became paramount. At the point at which commercial interests could search out a market within the South through the new mass medium of radio, rural communities were undergoing unprecedented changes brought about by the Depression and increased industrialisation of agriculture. Early Southern vernacular recordings display an obsession with establishing regional identity and a sense of community, called up through a specific locale, either town or State, or in terms of home and family. This is particularly evident in the songs of The Carter Family, such as 'Clinch Mountain Home'. The Carter Family, often referred to as 'the first family of country', were contemporaries of Jimmie Rodgers. On the other hand, as the Depression took hold, the image of restlessness and rootlessness is endlessly highlighted in, say, Jimmie Rodgers' or Goebel Reeves' songs of drifters and hoboes. As the 1930s wore on, this tension between home and the road increasingly became displaced onto the image of the cowboy. In the search for a popular yet respectable form of music to attract audiences to commercials, the radio stations would have chosen cowboy music in part because the cowboy seemed to combine both a sense of regional identity, of roots, with a feeling of restlessness. The plurality of this appeal was neatly expressed in the title of one of the most famous cowboy songs, 'Home on the Range'—a favourite tune of President Franklin D. Roosevelt.[37]

In the 1930s, part of the cowboy's appeal was that he was a figure who could also transcend a rural and industrial divide; tied neither to a work bench in a factory nor to the seasonal vagaries of agriculture, he appeared to have freedom of movement, yet also a way of earning a living. The cowboy hero in 1930s series Westerns is rarely a large landowner. He may aspire to own a small strip of land, but generally he spends his time helping to protect the heroine from being dispossessed of her land. Moreover, the cowboy carried none of the overt racist or class connotations of the hillbilly or his white trash cousin, nor the parochialism implied in fiddlers' conventions. The cowboy was neither a Georgia Peckerwood nor an English gentleman. He was, as Walt Whitman claims for his ideal American in *Leaves of Grass*, beyond these divides:

> The vulgar and the refined, what you call sin and what you call goodness, to think how wide a difference,
> To think the difference will still continue to others, yet we lie beyond the difference.

However, if difference in *class* is effaced it is nevertheless rearticulated in racial terms. This is aided by the repression in popular narratives of the historical presence of blacks in the West; the cowboy, through deed and action, encoded Anglo-Saxon superiority while also being incontestably of American origin. The question of race as a crucial factor in understanding American popular music cannot be overstated. When *Billboard* changed its 'Folk' chart to 'Country and Western' in 1949, it also changed the 'Race' chart to 'Rhythm and Blues'. Both moves were an attempt to give a veneer of respectability to genres that at best (regardless of sales) were seen as marginal and at worst as vulgar. But, whatever the name given to these charts and musical forms, the fact remains that a recording was marketed to either a black or a white audience. Despite the industry's construction of racially separate forms of music and audiences, these divisions meant little to the musicians who shared a common stock of influences that constantly challenges our idea of racial segregation in the South. The mutual influences on blues and country only furthered the industry's desire to keep them separate, attempting to control racial boundaries through record marketing and distribution, radio programming, and the selection of records for jukeboxes.

The figure of the cowboy helped to repress the black heritage apparent in so much of early country music. When Elvis Presley, in his Sun recordings, overtly brought together black and white styles of performance it was, and still is to some extent, seen as a transgression. Yet Rodgers and his contemporaries took eagerly and unselfconsciously whatever they could from the blues and jazz. Bob Wills and his Texas Playboys fashioned a whole sub-genre, Western Swing, on mixing black and white forms, yet there was no criticism of him, Rodgers, or the myriad other Western Swing bands for having 'corrupted' white music and the minds and bodies of their audiences by importing into their performances the 'primitive sounds of Africa'. The cowboy carried with him such a transparent sense of white racial supremacy that his use in country music transcended any critique of musical miscegenation. Such 'transparency', however, cannot be separated from a turn-of-the-century ideological construction of the cowboy and his songs as 'authentically' Anglo-Saxon American.

Interest in the cowboy's musical heritage first gained scholarly attention in the early part of the century with the publication of Nathan Howard (Jack) Thorp's Songs of the Cowboys[38] in 1908 and John Lomax's *Cowboy Songs and Other Frontier Ballads* in 1910. 'Cheyenne' (1906) was the first published Tin Pan Alley cowboy song.[39] These date-lines suggest that there was no widely recognised musical signifier for the cowboy until the early years of the twentieth century. If this is so, it raises the question about what kind of music would have been played to accompany Wild West shows and theatrical Western melodramas. Owen Wister in his 1895 essay 'The Evolution of the Cow-Puncher', noted how the cowboy had yet to inspire 'minstrels' to sing of his exploits: 'it is not so much the Rob Roy as the Walter Scott who is lacking', a lack that Wister clearly saw himself filling with *The Virginian*.[40] When he adapted *The Virginian* for the stage in 1904, Wister wrote his own cowboy song, 'Ten Thousand Cattle Roaming', whereas in the novel, the Virginian sang a minstrel tune, as do the cowboys in Andy Adams' *Log of A Cowboy* (1903).[41] Interest in cowboy songs continued to grow throughout the 1920s and early 1930s. Tex Ritter, soon to be Grand National's first all-riding, all-singing sensation, was much in demand for lecture and song recitals in Eastern colleges. But as hillbilly musicians began systematically to appropriate and commercialise the image of the cowboy, interest waned amongst the intelligentsia. Their concern for white American music shifted to 'folk' music from the Appalachians and on to figures such as Bradley Kincaid, who, according to Bill Malone, 'spoke disparagingly of "hillybilly [*sic*] and bum songs" and extolled the mountain folk from whom he obtained his songs as "a people in whose veins runs the purest strain of Anglo-Saxon blood" '.[42]

Kincaid's popularity with the intelligentsia would fade, but in his place came performers like Woody Guthrie who wedded 'folk' to 'protest':

> The urban folk movement's radical origins have always affected public perceptions of it, and the linking of 'protest' and 'folk song' has contributed to false impressions about the nature of the folk

and the music they have made. Furthermore, a regrettable distinction between 'folk' and 'hillbilly' music developed in the popular mind. 'Folk' music, which had become largely the province of intellectuals and reformers, became increasingly removed from the folk, while 'hillbilly' music, the creation of the folk, developed in its own independent fashion.[43]

Malone's formulation helps explain how 'folk music' took on the mantle of radicalism and authenticity, and 'country music' commercialism and conservatism. But this opposition misreads these two forms, as does seeing country and blues as two mutually exclusive genres. Both are equally capable of criticising or supporting the status quo.

Following in the footsteps of American literary heroes such as Huckleberry Finn, who chose to withdraw from a repressive civilisation, Jimmie Rodgers in 'Blue Yodel #8' rejects the workaday world: you won't see his initials on the back end of a mule. But in Gene Autry's 'Tumbling Tumbleweeds', or in other songs of drifting cowboys by him and others, the cowboy gives Rodgers' aimless wanderings and rejection of the work ethic a purpose. In effect, the cowboy transcends the banality of work that Rodgers so freely rejected, giving back to it a sense of purpose; in film and song Gene Autry always had an objective.

The cowboy's ascetic lifestyle as personified in the later stages of Owen Wister's *The Virginian*, in William S. Hart's reconfiguration of the *Old Testament* into the Wild West or Tom Mix's exhibitionism, took the edge off the overt sexuality of Southern vernacular music. Early country recordings can be splendidly coarse:

> I ain't no sheik man,
> Don't try to vamp no girl.
> I ain't no sheik man,
> Don't try to vamp no girl
> It's my regular grinding gets me by in this world
> (Jimmie Rodgers, 'Blue Yodel #10')

The Prairie Ramblers cut a succession of *risqué* numbers under the name of The Sweet Violet Boys. In 'I Love My Fruit', the song starts with the singer telling of his delight in eating cherries in bed, and then works through every combination of fruit and sexual metaphor before ending up with bananas: 'I am always hungry for bananas (Ah Daddy!). So much so it almost seems a sin. That when I'm all through eating, I still like to nibble on the skin.' Early publicity photographs of Autry show him not as a cowboy but as a slicked-up guitar picker in a suit, showing all the signs of a man desperately trying to escape the confines of his class. Where the suit failed him, the Stetson saved him; as a cowboy Autry transcended any notion of class. Like Rodgers, Autry's early repertoire of songs ran the gamut of the sentimental and the downright obscene. In 'Do Right Daddy Blues' (1931), recorded before he became an actor, Autry sang 'You can feel of my legs, you can feel of my thighs. But if you feel my legs you got to ride me high.' In 1935 Tex Ritter recorded the cowboy's answer to this kind of ribaldry in 'I'm A Do Right Cowboy' when he sings: 'I'm a do right cowboy, top cowhand, I live away out there where the West began. Got a horse and a saddle and a ranch of my own, and I leave all the other men's women alone.' The song concludes, 'My biggest ambition is that I want to be the daddy of a great big family'.[44]

In his record and radio appearances, Autry had systematically moved away from the plurality of persona that Rodgers and others had developed and concentrated solely on his Western identity. The cowboy allowed Autry to transcend any overt associations with a particular class, but allowed him to continue to appeal to a rural or new urban audience. His mode of address became increasingly sophisticated through production values, Tin Pan Alley crafted songs and a smoothing out of his vocal delivery. Outside of the songs' subject matter and steel guitar, by the end of the 1930s his music owed more to popular song of the time than to regionalised vernacular American music making, and eventually even the yodel would go. The blackface heritage was suppressed and the coarse and bawdy subject matter of some of his earlier recordings was absolutely censored. This move towards a more urbane set of characteristics was, however, qualified by Autry's cowboy persona. The effect was to produce a figure who, at least in appearance, managed to combine New World sophistication with Old World values. Autry achieved an accommodation between the modern world of consumption that he represented and the premodern world represented by such anachronisms as the medicine show which appear frequently in his films. In series Westerns the anxieties produced by modernity are transposed into a complex film form which ostensibly appears formulaic. For instance, the repeated plot device of property under threat by an identifiable external force is a framework within which complex transactions around identity are enacted. What complicates this scenario is not just the obvious intervention of the hero, but the play with disguise and hidden identity. To elucidate this, in the following chapter I shall explore another strand of the series Western's cultural inheritance to set with that of musical vernacular traditions: nineteenth-century working-class literary and performance narratives of labour and capital. From this perspective I shall argue that Autry's films are historically specific in the way they are organised around the tensions of the rural and new urban working classes in their confrontation with modernity. In this Autry was presaged by Will Rogers, who had more recently addressed these experiences via the new mass media.

Will Rogers: 'I look backwards to see ahead'

The model for Autry's cowboy was *not* the archetype established in Owen Wister's *The Virginian*, who anyway gives up cowboying for management responsibilities, but Will Rogers. Through radio programmes, personal appearances, newspaper columns and starring roles in some of the decade's most successful box-office hits, Rogers made a virtue of using Old World values to measure the worth of modern life.

'I look backwards to see ahead' is how Will Rogers' character in *A Connecticut Yankee* (Fox, 1931) explains his seer-like powers to King Arthur. Drawing upon Mark Twain's *A Connecticut Yankee in King Arthur's Court* (1889), the film gently mocks both the excesses of mediaevalism ('funny how they only find knights and Lords as your ancestors. I guess they skip over all the horse thieves') and the modern world ('All you got to do is persuade people they need things they've been happy without all their lives'). A setting in which tradition met the new was familiar Will Rogers territory, and his ability to transcend both the mundane and the fantastic was a major factor in his popularity. It was one of his many character traits that Gene Autry would draw upon.

Autry begins his autobiography in 1927, during a period of employment as a telegraph operator on the Frisco Line, bringing together what are for him the two most significant influences on his career—the railroad and Will Rogers.

> I was picking when I should have been tapping, but the customer didn't seem to mind . . . When I had finished whatever tune I had been playing, the visitor asked me to sing another . . . When he dropped his copy on the counter, he said, 'You know, with some hard work, young man, you might have something. You ought to think about going to New York and get yourself a job on radio.'
>
> I knew who the customer was, even before I read to the bottom of the last page and saw where he had signed it, 'Will Rogers.'

> You couldn't spend any time in Oklahoma, after all, and not
> recognise that face or that voice, which had the sound of a man
> chewing on cactus.[45]

The story is apocryphal, I believe. It did not appear in Autry's promotional biographies until after Rogers' death. However, its centrality in subsequent accounts of the singer's formative influences suggests that Autry consciously positioned himself as Rogers' heir apparent.[46]

Today the name Will Rogers conjures up little more than the tag line 'humorist and homespun philosopher'. As an icon of the late 1920s and early 1930s he has little currency. Stacked up against novelists like John Steinbeck, Hollywood stars such as James Cagney or Jean Harlow, musicians like Woody Guthrie or Robert Johnson, sports personalities like Babe Ruth, or politicians like FDR, Rogers has become almost invisible. It is not that what he stood for—a sense of tradition and rootedness—no longer resonates, but that the means through which he conveyed his view of the world worked outside of neatly defined parameters. Rogers' persona cuts across generic histories of the 1930s and remains outside of notions of sex, glamour, power, art and the romantic spirit as defined in whole or in part by now more familiar figures.

Raised in an upper-middle-class Oklahoma family, Rogers rebelled against his upbringing by following dime fantasies of a cowboy life inspired by dime novels. In 1904, at the age of 21, after globe trotting and unsuccessful short stints as a working cowboy in Texas, he joined the Mulhall Wild West Show, performing riding and roping tricks. By 1915 he was performing roping tricks for Ziegfeld's *Follies* interspersed with comic asides on contemporary issues and personalities. Vaudeville was his stage, the cowboy yokel his persona and the excesses and foibles of modern life his comic material.

By playing the cowboy, Rogers gave his commentary on contemporary life a softer, less aggressive edge, making his often highly critical views acceptable across a broad spectrum of American society. This became of paramount importance when he was given a newspaper column in 1922 by the McNaught Syndicate, which eventually led to special journalistic assignments for the *Saturday Evening Post*. He also began a tentative movie career in 1919, making short films for Samuel Goldwyn and Hal Roach and as an independent producer; one of these, *The Roping Fool* (1922), shows just how spectacular his skills with the lasso were. But it was not until the sound era, when he was cast in a succession of small-town dramas, that Rogers' film career took off. Running concurrently with the syndication of his newspaper columns and magazine articles, Rogers also found time to make regular radio shows and to keep up a dizzying number of personal appearances. In 1931 he put together a touring Red Cross charity revue for the victims of the Depression that included on the bill an ailing Jimmie Rodgers.

Like Autry, in both his public and private life (that is, in his films and in his highly successful business ventures), Rogers suggested that with his rural pre-industrial persona, he was 'in a privileged position to discern what would last and what was ephemeral . . . he provided his fellow Americans with insights into how to balance the good things of tradition with the opportunities of a boom era'.[47] Moreover, he suggested what it was to be an American.

> Will Rogers was important to Americans in the 1920s and 1930s because he addressed his humour to their basic sense of rootlessness and loss. As a cowboy version of Rip van Winkle, Rogers passed through this era of change, judging new developments by the standards of the 1890s.[48]

As Peter C. Rollins makes clear, this was not the 1890s of history but the 1890s of myth, a myth constructed around patriarchal family values set in small-town rural America where regional identity was important and the country's ethnicity was unproblematically Anglo-Saxon; where what mattered was what you did, rather than who you were.

Rogers' persona suggests a man who remains unruffled and undisturbed by modernity, comfortable with himself and the world he inhabits, yet able to detect and humorously ridicule the absurdities of the day. He is someone who gets things done, is active and combative (though he rarely breaks sweat), believes in roots and tradition and suggests a point of sanity in a world often appearing to be hurtling out of control. More to the point, he shows how closely series Westerns and rural images of the 1930s coalesce.

From the mid-1920s Rogers all but dropped the cowboy persona in his screen appearances as he played up the role of the innocent abroad and at home. *A Connecticut Yankee* opens on a scene inside Hank Martin's (Rogers) storefront radio station. A string band, The Four Farm Boys, are singing 'The Times Are Hard And So Is Your Old Man'. Martin signs off with a half-stuttered self-effacing goodnight to his audience. The scene confirms Rogers' star persona as a jovial man of the people who belongs to a small rural community, linked by use of the radio. His native charm is contrasted with the neurotic characters who inhabit a mansion on a hill that locals suspect is haunted. Outside a storm is raging. Martin is called on to deliver a radio battery to the mansion. Entering the house he finds the owner attempting to get a huge radio receiver to pick up the voices of the past. Scanning through the static he believes he has come across the voices of the Court of King Arthur. Martin, nervously announcing that he is 'going home to get Amos and Andy', is startled by a loud thunder crack. He lurches back, unbalancing a suit of armour which knocks him unconscious. He awakes in Camelot.

In his study of the antimodern impulse in turn-of-the-century American culture, T.J. Jackson Lears argues that America's fascination with mediaeval Europe was a palliative for 'the hovering soul-sickness . . . the sense that modern life has grown dry and passionless, and that one must somehow try to regenerate a lost intensity of feeling'. Americans saw in the Middle Ages states of mind and character traits that they felt were being lost in the modern age: 'pale innocence, fierce conviction, physical and emotional vitality, playfulness and spontaneity, an ability to cultivate fantastic or dreamlike states of awareness, an intense otherworldly asceticism'.[49] This search for a more authentic self was made manifest in the proliferation of histories, biographies and translations of texts, through arts and craft movements, generic fiction, in boys clubs, in the fad for genealogy, the study of folk-lore, in banquets and after-dinner speeches, in the formation of Lodges and Rotary clubs, and in chivalry in sport. As Lears reveals, this preoccupation with the past was not a withdrawal from the present but a means of accommodation: 'As part of a broad and complex movement toward class revitalization the antimodern impulse helped to sustain a resilient achievement ethos'.[50]

According to Lears, Twain's novel 'pointed to deepening conflicts in the wider culture—not just the public conflict between technological progress and republican pastorialism, but also the private conflicts between overt commitments to rationality and half-conscious yearnings for a realm of fantasy and instinctual vitality'.[51] But where Twain was unable to resolve these ambivalences, Rogers' character succeeds, although only with a shift in class address. Declaring himself a democrat, he sets about modernising Camelot. He organises factories and creates demand for his products through advertising. He establishes a newspaper, a telephone exchange, and a political machine (a mediaeval Tammany Hall). The effect is not so much a critique of modernisation as an accommodation achieved through humour.

The Court of King Arthur is likened to a Rotary club, and its pomp and ritual to that of the Ku Klux Klan(!) References to contemporary issues—farm relief, prohibition, radio evangelists, the stock market, dictators, flappers, fads and fashions—abound. In a key scene, Rogers' character is challenged to a duel, but rather than use modern weapons to overcome his adversary he appears at the joust as a cowboy. With a trick pony and his lasso he sets about the humiliation of the knight. The scene both celebrates and parodies the ideas best exemplified by Owen Wister in his essay 'The Evolution of the Cow-Puncher' (1895), which drew a line of racial descent from the Knights of the Round Table to the cowboy.[52] For Rogers, the cowboy is the preeminent symbol of the democratic American, a symbol that can transform peasants into knights and knights into peasants, a figure equally at home in the premodern and the modern. Will Rogers' greatest success was the authentication of this transcendent character:

> Will Rogers was neither a sophisticated actor donning the disguise of a simple cowboy nor a character invented by a brilliant writer. He was essentially what he seemed—a country boy who had come to the big city. He had observed the city's ways, and he had become successful. But he was a success—as he was the first to recognise—because he remained a country boy.[53]

His death in an aeroplane crash in 1935 helped to fix this persona, but he was not without his critics. In an essay on 'pseudo-folk', James Agee saw Rogers as belonging to a tradition of 'professional Americanism' characterised by its 'innocent-crafty, lucrative inverted snobbery . . . Will Rogers is wholly explained by our national weakness for congratulating ourselves upon our special forms of disgracefulness'.[54] What sold tickets at the box office, created habitual listeners to his radio programmes, readers for his newspaper columns and audiences for his personal appearances, however, was his apparent sincerity. He was a man whom his audience apparently trusted, someone who had found a home in the modern world. It was not so easy for this same audience to imagine or experience for themselves such a settled and secure place, and these are the insecure conditions Autry and other series Westerns of the 1930s address.

3

Series Westerns
Masking the Modern

This chapter examines series Westerns' attempts to accommodate both the past and the present. Contemporary political concerns found their expression in a specific film form that marked them off from mainstream Hollywood productions. However circumscribed their critiques, I argue that series Westerns of the 1930s addressed themselves to the issues of class struggle and division, and that this critically disparaged and apparently simplistic genre can in fact be approached as an important site at which audiences could contest the dominant interpretations given to the socio-economic transitions of capitalism.

'There are important differences between the cowboy and the city boy in American mythology and its underlying ideology', writes Robert Sklar:

> Both embody a traditional dilemma for the American male —independence and isolation, on the one hand, attachment and responsibility on the other. The cowboy, however, was and remains fixed in the past, a permanent character, a figure of constancy. However vivid a potential role model, he is a man whom time and change must ultimately defeat.[1]

While this is no doubt true of the cowboy as he is played in A-feature productions, it clearly is not the case with his function in either country music or in series Westerns. Gene Autry appealed to an audience still feeling the effects of the Depression but who also still had faith in America's aspirant culture. His battles against modern technology gave form to the anonymous corporations out to deprive the little man of his piece of land. His tireless, good-humoured and unbowed confrontation with the forces of corporatisation spoke directly to an audience who understood the effects of dispossession and dislocation. In my analysis, the cowboy, while still speaking to the rural ideal, offered himself up as a flexible figure able to mediate between the old world and the world of modernity. Gene Autry and series Western cowboys that followed his trail to Hollywood came to personify this dialectic.

To examine the apparent contradiction between the series Western's representation of the past and the present, I offer a critical reading of selected series Westerns produced across the span of the decade. Specifically, I illustrate that the films are focused upon issues of labour and capital, and particularly the impact of new technology. But further to this, I argue that social, cultural and economic struggles in series Westerns are played out through their formulaic use of disguise, which is best understood as a metaphor for particular class locations of its audience. As with the musical vernacular traditions in series Westerns, the use of disguise and hidden identity belongs to performance traditions already embodied in earlier forms of popular culture: nineteenth-century dime novels and blackface minstrelsy. Approached from this tradition, series Western narratives' use of disguise is both general in its employment of scenarios of mistaken and hidden identity, and specific in the sidekick's 'blackface' performance. Considering the series Western from this perspective offers the possibility of correcting received critical opinion on the genre.

In his classic essay on Westerns (1954), Robert Warshow writes: 'William S. Hart or Tom Mix, who in wooden absoluteness of their virtue represented little that an adult could take seriously; and doubtless such figures as Gene Autry or Roy Rogers are no better, though I confess I have seen none of their movies'.[2] Warshow's professed ignorance of the singing cowboy phenomenon is, at least, honest, but it is also an example of the bias against Autry in histories of the genre. Warshow knows that Autry's films are at odds with much that he celebrates in a perceived authenticity and a generic ideal, in which the singing cowboy evidently does not have a stake. This is a concept of the Western which is restated in Fenin and Everson's (1977) history: 'Although Autry's place in Western history is an important one, it is difficult to regard him as a serious Western star: he was a popular singer who had something new to offer to Westerns at a time when they were slipping back into the doldrums'.[3]

Jon Tuska (1982) takes Autry to task not only for his lack of authenticity and for being an unwarranted digression from the Western ideal, but also because he does not embody a dominant conception of masculinity:

Prior to Autry's arrival on the screen, Western heroes were customarily portrayed as being strong, capable, occasionally austere men, believable frontier types who might actually have undertaken many of the heroic exploits attributed to them by the scenarios. In Autry's case this was not so because, physically and dramatically, it could not be so. So he had to be surrounded by a different kind of aura, if no less magical. He lived, it had to seem a charmed life whereby, battling against frequently staggering odds, he invariably triumphed . . .[4]

Autry's particular image of masculinity clearly lies outside of the 'ideal' as criticised by Jane Tompkins in *West of Everything* (1992) and acclaimed by Tuska.[5] With regard to the notion of 'authenticity', the problem appears to lie as much in Autry's propensity to solve problems through singing as with his films' refusal to conform to critics' prescriptive requirement that Westerns be historically placed in the latter part of the nineteenth century. On this point even Autry appears forced into a veiled apology. Writing in the foreward to Don Miller's *Hollywood Corral* (1993) he notes that: 'The fact that most of my stories were set in the "modern" West, employing cars, trains, airplanes, radio, and even television (long before that medium took hold), did not restrict the plots from including ecological and other problems that are more prevalent today than ever'.[6] The relevance to his films of environmental issues of the 1990s is not germane. Autry's identification that there is a 'problem' with his films' modern setting is , I would argue, what actually marks out the specific terrain of series Westerns. It is nonetheless indicative of how systematically his films have been denigrated for not complying with the Western ideal. Film critics often invite the reader to laugh at the apparent absurdity of Autry's plots and at specific moments isolated from the films. Tuska's work reveals this process as well as any other:

In *Mexicali Rose*, Noah Beery, Sr, playing a Mexican bandit, captures Autry and Burnette. Tied up at the campfire, Autry discovers that Beery has a secret passion. Not women, or liquor, or gambling; it's collecting Gene Autry records. When a member of the gang accidentally kicks over Beery's portable phonograph, on which he is playing Autry's rendition of the title song, smashing the record, before Beery can shoot the offender, Gene takes up the song. Beery, thus learning Autry's identity, asks him to sing another song, which Autry does. It brings tears to Beery's eyes and he resolves to reform and commits himself to helping Autry save an orphanage from the scheming of oil speculators.

The Autry fantasy said, in point of fact, that every human problem, every dislocation, every tragedy, could be dispelled, not with hard riding, not with straight shooting, but with the magic of song.[7]

This scenario is also repeated in Phil Hardy's entry under 'music' in *The BFI Companion to the Western*.[8] Tuska and Hardy make no attempt to explain or to describe the film's narrative. Tuska's blind dismissal of Autry's films simply misses the point: song in Autry's films is not a cure-all, it dispels nothing but the blues. From the perspective of Autry's career as a recording and radio star, however, an alternative view of the film becomes possible. The principal conflict in *Mexicali Rose* (Republic, 1939) is established in the film's opening scenes. Gene Autry is a radio star sponsored by an oil company on a Texas/Mexican border station. His job is to sell stock in the company. Through the agency of a young woman we discover that the company is bogus. When this is brought to Autry's attention, his credibility as an honest salesman is threatened. His objective now is to right the wrongs that his sponsors have committed by bringing them to book. Autry and his screenwriters are addressing the consumers that listen to his radio shows and buy the products he promotes. By the late 1930s, border radio was notorious for selling spurious commodities. Through establishing an image of honesty, not just in *Mexicali Rose*, but in all of his films, Autry was confirming his (and radio's) credibility. By placing fraudulent stock at the centre of the narrative, the film is addressing wider social and economic issues thrown up by the Depression. Noah Beery's character's 'secret passion' for collecting Autry's records is clearly marked within the film as a comic interlude. The audience is asked to laugh at Beery's character, but the scene also has the purpose of promoting the fact that Autry was not only a radio performer but also a recording star.

A less prejudiced view reveals that Autry's films were not just star vehicles, but also addressed the difficulties that his audience confronted in making the socio-economic change from subsistence farming to a culture of consumption, from self-employment to industrial practices and wage dependency, from rural to urban living. In short, Autry's films represent a confrontation, magnified by the Depression, with modernity. The films defy both stereotypical gender readings and the dominant conception of Westerns as frontier narratives. His multifaceted public persona as radio, recording and performing artist indicates that his films need to be understood as a syncretic operation which draws these activities together and makes them cohere.

The perception that these films were aimed predominantly at an audience of young white males is founded neither on empirical research nor on the evidence of the films themselves, but on secondary sources where the writers are clearly enamoured with a nostalgic vision of the past. David Rothel begins his book on Gene Autry by writing: 'We who were the children of the thirties and forties, and fifties grew up with Gene Autry as our hero'.[9] His is an unapologetic nostalgia and his book, like most books that deal with the series Western, is obviously written for the fan market. But boyhood nostalgia can also be found to be driving more critical studies of post-1945 Westerns such as Kim Newman's *Wild West Movies* (1990) which emphasise the films produced during the writer's formative years.[10] Douglas Pye, in his essay on 'Criticism and the Western' in *The Movie Book of the Western* (1996), writes: 'it is difficult in retrospect to resist the view that these relatively young, white male critics and teachers were in a sense making peace with, as well as critical capital out of, a genre in which as boys in the postwar period they had a substantial emotional investment'.[11] The combined effect of this process has been to construct the Western of the 1930s (and since) as an adolescent male preserve. The historical and critical work that I present challenges such exclusively masculine constructions of the genre.

Gene Autry and Series Westerns

Autry's first featured spot was in the Ken Maynard programmer *In Old Santa Fé* (Mascot Pictures, 1934), which received almost unprecedented recognition from independent exhibitors:

> This is one of the best Westerns I've ever run. I highly recommend it to any fellow exhibitor that uses Westerns. Good story, plenty of thrills, comedy and some good music and singing by Gene Autry and his band. This is the kind of Western that pleases my patrons.
> Played 21–22 December 1934. Sammie Jackson, Jackson Theatre, Flomaton, Ala. Small town and rural patronage.[12]

This was the first recommendation for the film to appear in *Motion Picture Herald*'s 'What the Picture Did For Me' column. The column acted as a bulletin board for independent exhibitors to flag up film hits and misses, as a space to moan about unfair distribution practices ('The real facts are we play Westerns because they make us money to pay for the clucks we're forced to run, against the better judgment of the wishes of our audience'[13]), and as an opportunity to publicise successful promotional events. Sammie Jackson's review was followed swiftly by a number of equally positive recommendations: 'Why, oh why, doesn't some company produce more Westerns like this one and give us small town exhibitors something to make money on';[14] 'At last they have learned how to make Westerns. Pulled and pleased 100%. More like this . . .';[15] 'No one could ask for a better Western';[16] 'This one holds house record for this year. First musical Western I ever played';[17] 'A good Western with plenty of music and fun. Not the usual shoot 'em up and drag out type, but just a good comical modern Western. Give us more of this type';[18] 'Pleased many who are not Western fans'.[19] *In Old Santa Fé* was still getting favourable reviews and notices a year after its release.[20] The longer recommendations help explain its success:

> One of the best bets you can make on Fri–Sat. It's above the average and will please not only Western fans, but others more sophisticated. The plot is good, it has historical glamor and some really delightful Gene Autry music to lift it out of the rut of the common-place shooting and fighting which are alright as seasonings but why not make more Westerns like this and the O'Brien and Randolph Scott—Zane Grey stories? They have general appeal. Most folks (not decadent) like clean outdoor adventure, and with a little music and cowboy singing, Westerns go over well weekly in my town. And don't you ever think my Western fans don't know the difference between these two types of Westerns. The box office proves it conclusively.[21]

Autry's musical interlude and the light-hearted bits of comic business and dialogue coupled with the more formulaic episodes of fist fights, shoot-em-ups and chases appeared to be pulling in a broader than usual Western audience for the film. J.W. Noah, a regular contributor to the column and proprietor of a small chain of independent cinemas (New Liberty and Ideal Theatres, Fort Worth, Texas) with a 'general patronage', wrote:

> The success we enjoyed with this picture [*In Old Santa Fé*] again proves the value of the exhibitor's reports. Had it not been for the

glowing tributes paid to this film by fellow exhibitors we would have relegated this film to our 'B' house and then forgotten about it. However, after reading reports on it we made a radical departure from our almost set policy of playing everything except Westerns at our A house and booked it. It took some clever selling and the elimination of Maynard's name from the billing to put it over, but we stood them up and also received many compliments on the picture.[22]

As the reviews of Autry's films continued to find space in the column, it became clearer that he attracted a female audience and yet did not alienate the masculine crowd: 'Gene Autry is fast becoming one of our best box-office attractions, and our cashier has forgotten Gene Raymond in her admiration for Autry'.[23] Such inclusive audience appeal is significant in accounting for Autry's box-office success and I shall later examine the means by which this was achieved. But first, I want to identify elements specific to Autry's films and to con-textualise them within a more general resurgence of Western productions in 1935/36.

In Old Sante Fé is a blueprint for the formula Autry's Westerns would use for the rest of the 1930s, except that here Autry is given the guest spot rather than the starring role. Production values would also rise along with Autry's popularity, and his films would also make more of contemporary social concerns. The story of *In Old Santa Fé* is set on a dude ranch in the contemporary West and is centred around a horse race that a gang of 'city mugs' intends to fix. The lead villain, Chandler, alias Monte Korber (Kenneth Thompson), blackmails the owner of the dude ranch, demanding half-shares in the ranch and the owner's daughter's hand in marriage. His plans, though, are foiled when one of his men betrays him and his attempted framing of Ken (Maynard) falls apart. There is plenty of fast-paced horse riding and stunts, a fist fight, a shoot-out, and chases after runaway horses and stagecoaches—'I guess stopping runaways is my specialty today' comments Ken as he wheels Tarzan around to go after a driverless stagecoach. Disguises and hidden identities, a chaste love affair, as well as comic interludes provided by Ken's partner Cactus (George 'Gabby' Hayes), keep the story moving forward. But it is the six or seven minute musical interlude from Autry, supported by Smiley Burnette, that most of the exhibitors isolated for particular praise.

Where Autry and Burnette's performances depart from musical interludes in earlier series Westerns is that, instead of attempting to

8. *In Old Santa Fé*
Ken (Maynard) 'makes love' to the ranch owner's daughter (Evalyn Knapp)

integrate them as a spontaneous singalong around the campfire, or as an unobserved and private moment as the cowboy sings his song while riding high, wide and handsome across the lone prairie, or while he serenades his sweetheart, they are highlighted as performances. The scene begins with Autry leading the dudes in a dance which segues into 'Wyoming Waltz'. At the end of the song Smiley pokes his head in front of the camera and all but steals the show with his performance of 'Mama Don't Like Music' (aka 'Mama Don't Allow It'), trading instruments with the band and making his voice swoop up high and then drop down to his trade-mark frog impersonation. The interlude finishes with Autry singing and yodelling 'In Old Santa Fé', joined on the chorus by Smiley and the audience of dudes on the final verse. Meanwhile Ken is nervously making love to the owner's daughter, though she is doing much of the running after this 'sweet cowboy'.

The problem for Maynard was that he never was, nor could he ever be, a 'sweet cowboy'. By 1935 his long affair with the bottle was showing and he looks paunchy and out of condition. On the other hand, Autry had some years to go before he reached this physical stage, and when he sings he is so sweet he almost tastes of lavender. In his autobiography Autry reflected on his early filmmaking career:

> I returned to Hollywood in 1935, to stay, and to strike paydirt in a movie called *Tumbling Tumbleweeds*. It was the first of a genre, the first Western plotted and sold around the main character's ability to sing. The Autry image was established in that film almost 100 per cent. It was tinkered with in minor ways . . . But for the most part, the Autry of *Tumbling Tumbleweeds* was the Autry of 1947's *Robin Hood of Texas*.[24]

After the studio's takeover, Autry's initial film contract with Mascot was transferred to the newly formed Republic, headed by Herbert J. Yates, who was also the head of Autry's recording company, the American Record Corporation. With Autry's accomplishments in recording, radio and live performance, Yates must have known he was onto a sure-fire bet with Autry, yodels and Westerns. Within two years of the release of *Tumbling Tumbleweeds* Autry was Hollywood's number one Western star.

Gene Autry's success in *In Old Santa Fé* may have been the catalyst that led Warner Bros. to compete again in the market for Westerns after dropping out in the early 1930s, but, as is apparent in this advertising copy, it is just as likely that the studio was reacting to the growing popularity of cowboy music on the radio:

> 'Our hat's in the ring with Westerns that sing'.
> Dick Foran 'The Singing Cowboy'
> Yessir, men, we've got the first new idea in Westerns since Broncho Billy Anderson learned to ride! All the rarin', tearin', ridin' and shootin' of the best of the old time series—plus those <u>Cowboy Songs</u> the country's crazy over, featured in every release! That's why you'll have the edge on the other fellow if you'll grab Warner Bros. six Westerns presenting the screen's New-West star Dick Foran. *Moonlight on the Prairie*.[25]

According to *Motion Picture Herald*'s listings of new films, the Dick Foran vehicle *Moonlight on the Prairie* was ready for distribution on 2 November 1935, while Gene Autry's *Tumbling Tumbleweeds* had a 9 November 1935 release date. The question of which film came first is not really the issue. Rather, the industry had recognised that there was a growing market to exploit. Columbia and Paramount both launched new Western series during this season: 'Paramount has not forgotten Sleepy Eye, Minnesota, Smackover, Arkansas, Red Lodge, Montana and 3500 other small towns where folks like red-blooded action in their moving pictures'.[26] This was part of Paramount's advertising copy for the Zane Grey and Hopalong Cassidy series and for a reissue of *The Virginian*. Columbia gave a new boost to Charles Starrett by starring him in *Gallant Defender*: 'Presenting the first of a new series . . . thrilling romantic adventure stories . . . in Western settings . . . by Peter B. Kyne—millions of men and women—boys and girls—read his famous action yarns. His name is box office!'[27] RKO came up with the novelty of featuring Harry Carey, Hoot Gibson, Guinn 'Big Boy' Williams, Bob Steele and Tom Tyler in *Powder Smoke Range*—'The Barnum and Bailey of Western shows'.[28] In early 1936 Paramount starred Bing Crosby in *Rhythm on the Range*, which featured Bing's big hit 'I'm an Old Cowhand'.[29] MGM put Jeanette MacDonald and Nelson Eddy in a wilderness setting for *Rose Marie* aka *Indian Love Call*. And the Poverty Row independent Grand National starred Tex Ritter in *Song of the Gringo*.

Dick Foran garnered far fewer recommendations than Gene Autry from exhibitors. Initially, his films had good production values, but their plots, which were set in the historical West, not the contemporary West that Autry inhabited, followed the predictable formula of rescuing a distressed maiden. His songs were also rather overblown, lacking the intimacy, if not the *bonhomie*, of Autry's. Moreover, there was too great an emphasis on him as the star. In Autry's films a deal of screen time was given over to the comic antics of Smiley Burnette, and they always featured a performance by a musical guest star or stars who had made a name for themselves on the radio. Warner Bros.' Foran Westerns did not initially feature cameos. Only twelve were made, over the two seasons 1935/37.

According to the *Motion Picture Herald*'s poll of the top ten Western box-office stars, until the arrival of Roy Rogers, Autry's greatest competition came from Tex Ritter, but the competition did not amount to much. In its first year of polling—1936—Autry came in at number 3 and Foran at 6. In 1937 Autry had risen to the top of the poll (and would stay there until 1943, when he was deposed by Roy Rogers after Autry had enlisted in the armed forces), Foran had climbed to 4 and Ritter entered at 6. In 1938 Ritter had slipped to 9 and Foran to 10.[30] Ritter's films were hamstrung by meagre budgets, and while Autry could afford to showcase the talents of, for example, Patsy Montana, the best that Ritter could do in *Arizona Days* (Grand

National, 1937) was to give a spot to the harmonica talent of Salty Holmes (a member of Patsy Montana's backing band, the Prairie Ramblers—Grand National could not afford to hire the whole band), who plays a 'fox chase' replete with animal noises, a performance style that is derisively parodied as hokey nonsense in the major studio productions *Pigskin Parade* (1936) and *Tin Pan Alley* (1940).[31]

Autry's growing box-office success, which continued throughout the 1930s, meant that his films helped to define the formula not only for other singing Westerns but also for other series Westerns. Shifts in the formula of series Westerns were incremental, novelty was sought only when it was felt, through whatever means of measurement were available to the producers, that their principal audience was tiring of particular conventions. In covering *The Old Barn Dance* (Republic, 1938) the *Hollywood Reporter*, which regularly reviewed the new Autry pictures, noted that:

> Gene Autry here drops the old West of the cattle rustlers for the new West of tractor-using farmers and radio advertising. In keeping with the change he drops the cowboy songs (though not the costumes) in favor of hillbilly ditties and typical rural entertainment . . . just so this picture is aimed at the sticks rather than the action belt. It won't please the kids like the formula Westerns, but it may very well help to earn for Autry a new and wider audience.[32]

The broadening of Autry's audience was in evidence as early as 1937, when *Boots and Saddles* became his first picture to open on Broadway, a gambit on Republic's part to give his films a greater veneer of success and respectability. In an essay on the exhibition and reception of *The Jazz Singer*, Donald Crafton has argued that Broadway runs were often not box-office successes, but that the publicity from a New York opening would be used to hype the film elsewhere.[33] Autry's appearance in films marked the most significant injection of novelty in this period, followed by the slightly less tangible 'trio' Western which was fully inaugurated with the first Three Mesquiteers' series outing for Republic, *The Three Mesquiteers* (1936).[34] The singing cowboy revitalised the generic formula, but at base it remained relatively unchanged.

Autry's first starring role in a feature film, *Tumbling Tumbleweeds*, encapsulated all of the elements described in this chapter. It is a story of nesters verses ranchers, with Autry, the son of the biggest

9. *Tumbling Tumbleweeds*
As part of Dr Parker's medicine show, Gene Autry and his minstrels
entertain the people

landowner, mediating between the two. Rejected by his father when he
fails to support the fight against the sod-busters, Autry returns to his
home town of Gunstock after an absence of five years in the company
of a travelling medicine show. His father has been recently murdered
and Autry sets out to find the culprit. Autry's first appearance in the
film is heralded, off-screen, by him singing: 'And yodel my troubles
away . . .'. The initial emphasis on his voice delays his entrance and
plays with audience expectations, introducing him in a way with which
they would have been familiar through his radio appearances. Yet the
narrative, as in all of his 1930s films, is not just concerned with
providing novel situations for Autry's singing performances but also
with the plight of the small farmer.

The film begins by introducing itself as a historical recreation with a
dramatic montage sequence and opening credits ('In the old west there
was no law . . .'). However, the electric lamp in the ranch house,
telephones and a phonograph playing Autry's first hit, 'That Silver

Haired Daddy of Mine', finish any notion of historical authenticity and fidelity. The dominant contemporary setting and the story of farmers versus corporate interests sets up Autry as a champion of the common man, overtly tying the film into the conflicts of the Depression. The film deals with the tension between past and present not through any clever narrative device but by simply avoiding the issue altogether. As Autry wrote:

> If one had to pick an example of the slice-of-life plots that tended to pop up in my films, *Guns and Guitars* would probably serve. I did not engage, for the most part, in such mundane activities as saving the old homestead or chasing bank bandits. While my solutions were a little less complex than those offered by FDR, and my methods a bit more direct, I played a kind of New Deal Cowboy who never hesitated to tackle many of the same problems: the dust bowl, unemployment, or the harnessing of power. This may have contributed to my popularity with the 1930s audiences.[35]

Indeed, Autry's ideal contemporary audience is inserted into the film through the attraction of 'Dr Parker's Phamous Purveyors Of Phun Phrolic and Painless Panaceas' medicine show, which, apart from the good doctor and Autry, contains a three-piece band and the tap dancing minstrel Eightball (Eugene Jackson)—wide-eyed and stupid. The townspeople of Gunstock, who gather to watch the show, are dressed in 1930s work wear and are bonded together via their participation in the medicine show and through their consumption of Gene Autry records. Apart from the heavies, not one of the townsfolk is seen wearing a cowboy costume. The audience are already familiar with Autry's recorded work and are offered the inducement of a free phonograph record with every bottle of dope they buy from Dr Parker.

On the posters for *In Old Santa Fé*, Autry was billed as 'The World's Greatest Cowboy Singer'. It was an accolade he had earned through live performances, as a star of his own radio show and through phonograph recordings. How he came to transform himself from a singer of material that had its roots within the tradition of vernacular American music into the most important figure in the development of series Westerns will help explain his appeal and success with rural, small town and new metropolitan audiences.

The Modern Old West

In the 1930s, over one-quarter of all Americans still lived on the farm, but throughout the decade there was also a massive migration from rural districts into towns and cities, and, as John Opie observes in *The Law of the Land*, 'prices for farm goods dropped to less than half between 1929 and 1932; net income fell by 70 percent'. Yet 'the dedicated farm family hard at work on its own land *still* represented an American ideal' (my emphasis).[36] In his study of Southwestern migration to California, James N. Gregory notes that even though 'steady work, either farm or nonfarm, eluded the majority [of migrants] and . . . nearly half finished the decade earning less than a standard subsistence income . . . there are other issues to consider':

> Property, even just a vacant lot upon which a house would someday stand, symbolised much of what had recently eluded them. It was the land they no longer or had never been able to own. It was the home that economic conditions back east and migratory compulsions out west tried to deny them. It was the security that they along with so many other Depression era Americans craved.[37]

Series Westerns work to bridge this gap between the ideal and the reality: between a successful and failing farm, between being a property owner and being propertyless, between having a home and being homeless.

Although the cowboy functions in these dramas to negotiate between a pre-industrial and an industrial way of life, between capital and labour and between production and consumption, this does not wholly explain the cowboy's anachronistic and therefore apparently disruptive presence within the films' modern settings. Writing on the working woman's genre in dime novels, where a similar situation occurs, Michael Denning suggests:

> A story to be a story had to be set in a contemporary time and knowable landscape, but its plot had to be out of the ordinary; 'everyday happenings', according to this working woman's aesthetic, did not make a story. The story was an interruption in the present, a magical, fairy tale transformation of familiar land-scapes and characters, a death and rebirth that turned the social world upside down, making proud ladies villains, and working-girls ladies.[38]

In series Westerns capital is reformed, repossessed land and property are restored to their rightful owners, broken families are reunited, the wounds in communities are healed, the crooked are revealed and unproductive land magically produces hitherto hidden mineral or real-estate wealth. These are, indeed, fairy-tale endings to what must have been everyday fears, if not familiar events in the lives of the films' contemporary audience. The cowboy is the agent who transforms the banal, the mundane, the everyday and magically sets things right again. The cowboy performs a similar function to that ascribed by Dale Cockrell to the Jacksonian blackface minstrel. He suggests that minstrelsy 'attacked' the new institutions of industrialisation: 'clocks, bosses, subordination, grimness, and "wage slavery" '. Minstrelsey's 'seeming accommodation' of racism, which benefited white middle-class America, carried with it an 'underlying subversion' of the tropes and values of the 'powerful' which worked to affirm 'traditional modes of understanding'.[39] The cowboy, like the minstrel, mediates between the 'powerful' and the 'powerless'. The cowboy costume 'works' like the black mask, to 'conceal' *and* 'promise' a 'reordering of the world'.[40] Autry's cowboy performances suggest this paradoxical state of stability and change.

In an August 1938 review of Gene Autry's *The Man from Music Mountain*, the high-quality production values of Autry's films are underscored along with the story's novelty. The reviewer also stresses the contradiction of the film's setting, inadvertently confirming Denning's argument about the transformation of familiar landscapes and characters and Cockrell's concealed yet promised reordering of the world: 'Its excellent story, diverging far from the beaten formula path, is as modern as tomorrow's newspaper, yet it retains the vitality and atmosphere of the West'.[41] The story is centred on a group of crooks who con farmers by holding out the promise of power to be provided by a new dam. Autry makes sure the crooks and the good people get what is coming to them. Novelty in Autry's films partly consists of finding a different object or environment that is intimately associated with rural communities, and then working this into the narrative formula. The tractors in *The Old Barn Dance* and the dam in *The Man From Music Mountain* provide the novelty. In *Western Jamboree* (1938) it is provided by helium gas, in *Home on the Prairie* by an outbreak of hoof and mouth disease, in *Colorado Sunset* (1939) by a milk transport protection racket, and so on.

Since the late nineteenth century, farming in the South and the Midwest had become increasingly mechanised. Richard White notes that the 'value of implements and machinery on the northern plains rose by 240 percent between 1900 and 1920. These years saw the advent of tractors and machine-powered combines that allowed farmers to plow up and harvest more and more of the native grasslands with less and less labor, but the real boom in tractors would come in the 1920s.'[42] Although mechanisation made farming more efficient and saved on labour costs, the added investment in new technologies meant that farmers had to borrow money and turn a bigger profit in order to meet their repayments. This required them to produce greater yields, which in turn led to over-production and a glut of produce. Prices fell, leaving small farmers increasingly unable to settle their debts, a situation exacerbated during the 1930s by the Great Depression, drought and soil erosion. White argues that this expansion of commercial farming 'amounted to an invasion of a pastoral, paternalistic society by an agrarian, capitalistic society'.[43] The Autry films attempt to mediate this shift in relationships between the farmer and the wider commercial community. Autry clearly cannot change progress, but he can offer reformist advice. In this the cowboy has a crucial role to play.

This process of accommodation is the central theme in the Autry film *The Old Barn Dance* (Republic, 1938). Having bought into industrialisation through the purchase of tractors, farmers are duped by the finance company who offered them 'easy payments'—when they fall behind with their payments, the company rather too eagerly forecloses on their farms. Autry is a horse trader whose business is threatened by industrialisation represented by the tractor. His only defence against this new technology is his self-evident honesty: he won't rook the farmers. But even this most sacred of Autry's virtues is threatened when he unwittingly sponsors Mammoth tractors over the radio. When this duplicity is discovered, the drive of the narrative is switched from a direct confrontation with industrialisation to the clearing of his name, and bringing the criminal finance company's agents to book.

The power to transform the everyday is held, in part, by Autry's musical performances within his films. In *The Old Barn Dance*, work and pleasure sit side by side. He sings to increase business and it appears that he is in business so that he can sing. The title song suggests that the barn dance as performed here is a tradition outside of history, a site of entertainment that only barely separates the performers from the audience. As Autry sings, a dancing old couple confirm the song's nostalgic sentiments. Supporting Autry in his performance are the comic hayseed acts the Colorado Hillbillies and the Stafford Sisters. This variety format was an innovation of radio programming, not the unmediated communal get-together that is suggested here. Moreover, Autry is performing so he can sell his horses and, although he does not know it, the show is being broadcast. In a manner similar to Will Rogers' performance in *A Connecticut Yankee*, this self-reflexivity allows Autry to display himself as a radio star *and* man of the people, someone constructed through the media, yet unaffected and apparently unaware of it. The community and its workaday rituals are transformed into spectacle. Autry is called upon to aid the community because he is one of them, but, unlike the ranchers and farmers, his cowboy and star persona gives him the currency to transcend the mundane. What he sells is his musical labour, which is consumed (at least within the film's narrative) by other labourers, not by capitalist interests. He is asked to mediate between capital and labour, to become, in effect, a site of consumption. This is indicative of the wider shifts towards the increasing centrality of mass consumer culture to the rural population in the 1930s. Importantly, within series Westerns these shifts are gendered: it is the young heroines who register as cultural representations of socio-economic changes from productivist to consumerist capitalism. Again, Autry's persona is ambivalently positioned within the films' representation of modernity. In the following section, an examination of the construction of series Westerns' female characters will demonstrate two things: firstly, a greater degree of complexity in gender roles than has hitherto been accorded to the genre, and secondly, Autry's appeal to a female audience.

Women and Series Westerns

If the ranchers and farmers in Autry's films and in other series Westerns are clearly marked as producers who find themselves impotent in the face of an exploitative capitalism (which the film's hero will attempt to keep in check), then it is left to the leading female to act out the role of consumer. What is remarkable about series Westerns (remarkable only because the genre is hardly ever taken into account in gender studies) is the number of roles constructed around young women, who are clearly signified as independent wage earners, managers, or property owners. There is a marked absence in these films of the traditional matriarch. Instead, the central family unit is often formed around the young woman who must provide either for an ailing father and/or younger or weaker brother. The mother's absence is rarely if at all remarked upon. Nor is the role assumed by the young woman questioned. Richard Maltby has suggested that this is a Depression narrative that is also found in A-feature films, particularly those starring Deanna Durbin and Shirley Temple.[44] This patriarchal 'crisis' has become a tenet of commentaries of the Depression. In his study of the cultural front, Michael Denning (1996) writes: 'If the depression years were not a moment of feminist militancy, they were surely a time of gender strife and change: many commentators at the time noted the crisis in masculinity that accompanied the massive unemployment of the depression'.[45]

In his autobiography Autry points up the often central role given to women in his films:

> The leading ladies in Autry films were not there just for decoration or to point out which way the bad guys went. As written, they gave me a lot of anything-you-can-do-I-can-do-better sass, smoked a lot of Kools—that era's Virginia Slims—and, in general, played a thirties' version of waiting for Gloria (Steinem). That may have been due, in no small part, to the presence of such screenwriters as Betty Burbridge, Luci Ward, and Connie Lee. We didn't exactly use them because they were experts on the West. Whatever their formula, those films were about the only ones in the B Western category, up to then, that had a mass appeal to women.[46]

At a number of points, Autry argues that at least half his audience was made up of women. If this is so, then it begins to shed light on his films' concern and emphasis on the domestic sphere, on his rejection of an absolute patriarchy, on his dandyish appearance, on the replacement of sex by an emphasis on friendship, and on his 'motherly' concern and protection for his aberrant 'son'/sidekick.

In her biographical history of women scriptwriters in Hollywood, Lizzie Francke devotes a section of her book to a discussion of the work of Betty Burbridge. It is offered to the reader as a curiosity, another example of women only being able to find work in 'low-grade stuff', given little value even then or now: 'Burbridge's films may be forgotten now and no doubt for good reason'. Yet Autry clearly contradicts this reading, as do the number of women working in the genre. The filmography Francke provides identifies eighteen women who scripted Westerns between 1930 and 1941. This is not an insignificant number, even if it does pale against the number of male writers within the genre. Equally, these women had a significant profile in the production of singing Westerns. Francke takes great pleasure in pointing out Burbridge's lack of authenticity in the construction of her identity as a writer of Westerns, but this is to miss the point entirely, for an 'authentic construction' of the Western was never a concern for these films or their audience.[47]

Autry's recognition of his female audience stemmed from his radio work. In an essay on Crazy Water Crystals and hillbilly music, Pamela Grundy notes:

> Women made up a large and vocal segment of the hillbilly audience. Radio surveys of the 1930s showed that despite the stories of farmers hurrying from their fields to listen to noontime shows, the major daytime audience comprised women and children. Women wrote more than two-thirds of the letters received by stations, sponsors, and performers in the period.[48]

In *Colorado Sunset* (Republic, 1939), which has a script co-written by Betty Burbridge, radio's female audience is highlighted. The story concerns the attempt by a 'Protection Association' to coerce local farmers, but its plans are foiled when the women use the radio to garner support for Autry's bid to become sheriff. In a montage sequence we see women cajole and badger their husbands into voting for Gene. Later they get involved in a big fist fight and help bring the association to book.

The film highlights three female roles. One woman runs a restaurant and finally gets to form a couple with Frog Millhouse (Smiley Burnette)—a first, so far as I can make out, in giving Autry's sidekick a love interest, although he is far from happy in this situation. Another woman, whom Autry woos through action and in song, runs the radio station; indeed having women operate and manage radio stations is a fairly common occurrence in Autry's films. Lastly, there is a star cameo from Patsy Montana, who performs a wonderful rendition of her million-seller 'I Wanna Be A Cowboy's Sweetheart'. The women are shown to be at the centre of the action and the absolute hub of the community. They are neither the harridans that plague the town of Tonto at the beginning of *Stagecoach* (1939), nor the kind of fallen woman played by Marlene Dietrich in *Destry Rides Again* (1939), but neither are they fey and submissive housewives. The women in Autry's films cannot be made to conform to the stereotypes constructed in gender studies of the Western.

Positioned as active, independent and in control of her own destiny, the female lead's autonomy is initially compromised by her male kin. Responsibility for the younger or enfeebled male pushes her into a public arena, making her visible and therefore vulnerable. It is at this point that the hero steps in to protect her, closing down her independence and activity, which has anyway been forestalled by the villain. But closure, with the villain vanquished and the hero and heroine in chaste embrace, is also ambivalent and does not necessarily reinscribe traditional patriarchal constraints on female behaviour. Rather it leaves open the possibility of her being able to play out an independent role free from the threat of villainous entreaties.

Written by Luci Ward, who also worked on some of Autry's scripts, *Overland Stage Raiders* is centred on a brother and sister who are running a failing airline. The Three Mesquiteers buy into the company along with added investment from the local ranchers. The airline effectively denies a group of bandits the easy access they had to the shipments of gold that had previously been carried by a crooked bus company. However, the brother, Ned Hoyt, has a secret criminal past, even though he is now on the straight and narrow and is chaperoned by his sister Beth (Louise Brooks). Much of the narrative intrigue grows out of this subterfuge. Beth takes the active role in the partnership and negotiates with, and provides love interest for, Stony Brooke (John Wayne).

When we first see Beth, her face is hidden by a stack of boxes containing things she has just bought at the merchandise store: a gratuitous act of consumption as well as a device to hide her from view so that she can be more dramatically revealed. Clearly, it is not the actual act of consumption that is of primary importance, but Beth herself, or at least her body as a site of display for consumer items: her make-up, hairstyle, and, of course, her clothes. Unlike the other characters, she will go through a number of costume changes. To audiences today, the disruptive narrative effect in these series Westerns is created as much by the way the female lead dresses as by cowboys on horseback chasing after cars; both work overtly as symbols of modernity. These women are rarely seen in domestic situations, operating for the most part in the public sphere where they are able to act as mannequins for the latest fashions. The fact that they have to animate these clothes to sell them, to take them outside of the home to give them significance, means that they also have to step intrepidly into modernity, into a world of consumption. In doing so they clearly begin to take on an active role in the narrative, a role that is only ever partly wrested from them by their need to have the hero help them and by their forming a couple with him at the film's closure.

Ranch Romances, a short-story magazine aimed principally at women that ran throughout the 1930s and 1940s and into the 1950s, used a similar narrative formula but gave an even greater emphasis to the heroine.[49] In his discussion of late-nineteenth-century Western dime novels, Marcus Klein notes: 'With considerable frequency, women were the protagonists of these fictions, and were in fact the more likely to be cast into roles of general retaliation just because they were the more likely to have suffered from the degradation of the true law'.[50] Michael Denning also notes that the representation of working-class womanhood in dime novels stressed 'physical action and violence': 'just as the outlaw flourished more in the mining camps of Leadville [the setting for some of the Deadwood Dick stories] than in those of Pottsville [the setting for the Molly Maguire stories], so a physically active, non-genteel woman flourished more in the streets of Deadwood than in those of New York . . . the heroines of the cheap stories skirt the boundaries of genteel codes'.[51] Though somewhat more restricted in her area of operation, this female figure is also found in the fictions of Zane Grey. In *Riders of the Purple Sage* (1912) both Jane Withersteen and Bess Erne are given a circumscribed and qualified independence. Since her father's death, Jane runs the largest ranch in the territory, but is under attack from the Mormon elders for not submitting to their wishes and control. Bess finds freedom as the best rider on the sage, yet is constrained by her captor Oldring, who poses as her father and forces her to wear the disguise of the Masked Rider. Both women find release through the intervention of the heroes Lassiter and Venters, but this puts them back into the sphere of male influence. 'The question at the end', writes Lee Clark Mitchell in his analysis of the novel, 'is whether Jane and Bess are less bound by the men they have than by those they elude.'[52]

There is, however, a necessary distinction to be made between the ending of *Riders of the Purple Sage* and those found in the series Westerns discussed here. The future life of Bess and Jane is announced in Grey's story. Bess will marry Venters and leave Utah: 'She shall have some of the pleasures of life—see cities and people. We've gold—we'll be rich. Why, life opens sweet for both of us' exclaims Venters.[53] Jane chooses a life of seclusion with Lassiter in Surprise Valley: 'I wanted to roll it—meant to—but I can't. Venter's valley is down behind here. We could—live there. But if I roll the stone—we're shut in for always. I don't dare. I'm thinkin' of you!' claims Lassiter, but Jane replies

'Lassiter! Roll the stone!'[54] In contradistinction, the future for the couple at the end of a series Western can only be guessed. This ambiguity means that alternative readings are available to its audience. Boys and girls could read it less as the formation of the couple than as a final punctuation mark: the independent hero and heroine will be back in another film once again struggling against the odds. Men and women, though, could read the final clinch as a closure that suits either party's desires—either independent or conforming woman, either non-possessive or dominant male.

Disguise and Hidden Identity

> If historical struggles do take place in borrowed costumes and assumed accents, if social and economic divisions appear in disguise, then the source for these disguises and the manifestation of these roles lie in the conventional characters of a society, played out in its popular narratives.
>
> (Michael Denning, *Mechanic Accents*[55])

My argument so far has rested upon an understanding of series Westerns in terms of their broader engagement with the forces of modernity. I want to extend this understanding to a consideration of the *specific* narrative conceits that are available to it in its invocation of traditional performance techniques. Series Westerns' play with 'borrowed costumes and assumed accents' is both performance and metaphor. As metaphor, its characters assume disguises in order to play particular types which then stand in for particular social, cultural and economic struggles: 'disguise as a narrative equivalent of metaphor rather than a sign of an enigma to be solved'.[56] In performance, it draws upon older traditions of popular entertainment, particularly melodrama, vaudeville skits, musical exhibitions and blackface minstrelsy.

The levels of reading required to make sense of the 'metaphor of disguise' is exemplified by *Texas Wildcats* (Victory Pictures, 1939). Here, Tim McCoy plays 'Lightning' Bill Carson, a Texas Ranger who masquerades as a saloon card-dealer *and* 'The Phantom'. Through the persona of 'The Phantom' he hopes to reveal that Burrows (whose Association 'controls just about everything and everybody around here') is the killer of his old comrade Jim Parker. Carson's transformation into 'The Phantom' involves the simple expedient of a change of horses and shirts and a black hooded mask. The play between the conceits of character means that Carson is both an agent of the law *and* an outlaw. He is not an outlaw who reforms and *becomes* a lawman; he is an outlaw who is *simultaneously* a lawman. In the same film, the representative of the 'law'—the 'Association's' detective whom Burrows has brought in to capture 'The Phantom'—is also a criminal.[57] Burrows and the detective are the law, they own and control the town, but they are also the villains. Towards the end of the film, Burrows' son Mort adopts the disguise of 'The Phantom' in order to terrorise Ed and Molly Ardent, who have recently discovered a gold mine on their property. This swapping of disguises, however, is not solely a plot distraction, a means of keeping the story moving forward. Instead, the play between character positions which typifies series Westerns opens them to political readings. The unjust social relationships established at the beginning of the film are eventually reversed. In this fictional world disguise takes power from the powerful and gives it to the powerless; it turns outlaws into the lawful, the authorities into criminals, and barren, worthless land into rich gold-fields. Where there is failure there is success, where there is nothing there is something.

Suspension of disbelief on the part of the audience cannot exhaust the pleasures offered by these films. If read as an ingenuous narrative form, series Westerns' appeal in their use of disguise is infantilised, suitable only for children and hillbilly morons. Importantly, character identity never breaks down into confusion over who is who because, crucially, the disguises are always transparent to the audience. Because we know that the audience was not simply composed of guileless 'children' there needs to be a more sophisticated account of its structuring presence. Denning has argued that the use of disguise in nineteenth-century dime novels is similarly transparent, allowing the characters to transcend social, class, and even racial and gender boundaries, to operate with impunity in a variety of public and private spaces, without the characters ever losing a sense of who they are. This is clearly demonstrated where boundaries are consistently crossed in *The Man From Monterey* (Warner Bros./Four Star Western, 1933), the last of the six series Westerns John Wayne made for Warners.

John Wayne plays an officer in the American army who is overseeing the shift in power after his country's annexation of California in 1848. His role is to make sure that the old Spanish landlords are not fleeced of their rightful entitlement. The central conflict is between two old patriarchal families, one good, the other bad. The latter patriarch tries to take control of the former's property, either through the marriage of his son to the other's daughter or by the nefarious means of providing misinformation as to the American's intentions and thereby getting the good family to engage violently with the army, which would leave them open to exploitation by the back door. The Americans are not imperialists but honest brokers. As this plot is being played out, Wayne's character acquires a sidekick who in the comically and absurdly haughty tones reminiscent of the dandy Zip Coon is called Phillipe Guadalupi Concepciun del Gardo Santa Cruz. As the film builds to its swashbuckling conclusion, Wayne disguises himself as a Spanish American aristocrat and his sidekick appears in drag.

There is no narrative justification for this piece of transvestitism, but the comic implications are clear, particularly in the scenes where this grotesque image of femininity is seen to be sexually desirable by Mexican men. Here the transgression of watching a white man appropriating another's racial and gender characteristics is fully in the realm of the most vulgar of blackface traditions. John Wayne's disguise as a sword-fighting Spanish aristocrat is drawn from a different tradition, one found in the world of melodrama and dime novels:

> to reveal that the mechanic is a nobleman is not to deny that he is a mechanic; the characters all continue to insist on their character as mechanics. This is why so little time and energy is spent on explaining why the nobleman is pretending to be a mechanic in the first place: the metaphoric juxtaposition of mechanic and noble is what is important, not the story's pretence.[58]

This is the ground upon which we are asked to accept John Wayne's character's transformation. He is simultaneously American soldier and knight errant. The contradiction within this dual persona recalls that also found in the name given to the leading working-class organisation of the 1880s: the Knights of Labor, of whom Friedrich Engels remarked: 'a truly American paradox, clothing the most modern tendencies in the most mediaeval mummeries'.[59] This dialectic between past and present, labourer and nobleman, was more feasibly and invisibly synthesised through the figure of the cowboy. But, Autry's films are further complicated by the possibilities within the narrative for play between his off-screen (radio, recording and live performances) and on-screen personae.

In the Autry film *Oh, Susanna!* (Republic, 1936) disguise and hidden identity are excessively played off one another to the point of almost overbearing self-reflexivity. While travelling by train to a dude ranch to perform for some old friends who have fallen on difficult times, Gene

10. *Oh, Susanna!*
On board a west bound train, Gene Autry is about to be mugged by
Wolf Benson (Earl Hodgins)

is mugged by an escaped convict, Wolf Benson (Earl Hodgins), who
switches clothes with him and tosses him out of the window of the
moving train. Autry is found unconscious by Frog Millhouse (Smiley
Burnette) and Professor Deacon Daniels of the 'Millhouse-Daniels and
Company—Entertainers Deluxe'. Autry joins up with them and they
head off for the nearest town to report the crime. Wolf successfully
continues his masquerade as Autry—'radio star'—so he can con Gene's
friends at the dude ranch out of some money they have borrowed from
Autry. In town, Autry is mistaken for Wolf, he is locked up and a
hanging awaits him the following morning.

Before Autry's death sentence can be carried out he is given the
chance to prove his real identity by playing to an audience of Gene
Autry radio fans, but his throat has been hurt during his arrest.
Coming to Gene's aid, Frog steals a phonograph and an Autry record
that is being played on a street corner and secretly places it under
the window of Gene's cell. Gene mimes along while his fans listen
appreciatively. Freed and having swapped their city suits for western
wear ('Nobody will ever recognise us now'), Autry, Frog and the

Professor set out for the dude ranch singing 'Oh! Susanna' and performing riding stunts for the sheer hell of it.

At the ranch, the Lee family are gathered around a large ornate
phonogram listening to another Gene Autry record as they await his
arrival. Instead Wolf turns up wearing dark glasses, disguised as Gene
Autry. He asks for the return of the loan the real Autry had earlier
wired to them. Only the father suspects there is something wrong, but
before he can tell the others Wolf guns him down. Autry is now
wanted for murder; when he finds out he changes his name to Tex
Smith.

Autry, Frog and the Professor sign up as performers at the ranch and
along with the Light Crust Dough Boys entertain the city dudes who
are playing weekend cowboys and cowgirls in their fancy high-fashion
western gear. While the Dough Boys give a truly remarkable performance of instrumental breakdowns formed around 'Oh! Susanna'
and 'Tiger Rag' (one of the great performance guest spots in the Autry
canon), Autry shows off his lasso tricks. At the song's end, the Dough
Boys segue into 'He Never Came Through with the Ring' and the
Professor and Frog enter the scene singing the song and riding on a
penny-farthing tandem. The Professor is dressed as a nineteenth-
century German college boy and Frog is in drag. While this is in
progress, Autry discovers a plot by some of Wolf's cronies to rob the
dudes of their jewels. The bad guys also discover that Tex Smith is
Autry when they simultaneously play a record of the song Autry is
performing live, and the voices match! The climax to this scene of
performances and revelations comes when Frog, still in drag, takes the
role of the girl in a knife-throwing act, with the by now drunk
Professor, the thrower of the knives, suffering from blurred vision (the
Freudian implications of this scene are overwhelming, but of little
relevance in this context).

The following day, Gene catches the bad guys in the act of robbing
the safe but the sheriff arrives and mistakenly arrests him and lets the
crooks go—Autry is still wanted for murder. Escaping from the sheriff,
Gene high-tails it back to the ranch. Leaping into a car he chases after
Wolf, who has the jewels in another car. Jumping from his car into
Wolf's, Autry overpowers him just as the sheriff and cowboys from the
ranch ride up. Hidden identities are cleared up and stabilised, and
Autry gets to perform a duet with a pretty girl.

Autry's composite identity is not simply constructed through the two
personae he is made to assume: ('Wolf' and 'Tex') but also through the
different media that present 'Gene Autry': a singer in front of live

audiences, on radio, on records, and on film; he is also an actor, as well as a performer of rodeo tricks. All these are highlighted in this film, and in *Mexicali Rose* (1939) he is also a sponsored entertainer, that is to say, advertiser. On one level this is self-promotion on a grand scale: witness the number of times he is called a 'radio star' in this film (and in just about all his others) and the three occasions when his records are plugged. Furthermore, he is also seen performing in front of two distinct audiences: the working-class elderly radio audience, made up of mixed sexes and races, and here brought together and made public by his jail house performance; and the middle-class audience at the dude ranch enjoying both the novelty of the show and their own masquerade as cowboys and cowgirls. The film acts to unite these multiple performances, personae and audiences, which cohere by means of Autry's visual presence projected before the cinema audience. As Frog Millhouse exclaims in *Yodelin' Kid From Pine Ridge* (Republic, 1937), it 'only goes to show deception is an art'.

Unlike the sidekicks of the more virile Western heroes, who in part have the job of reining in the star's sexuality, Smiley Burnette's principal function is to act as the comic foil to Autry. Frog's switching of genders in this film helps to lighten the load as well as to impart a 'healthy' sexuality on to the body of Autry. The shoring of Autry's masculinity counters claims of effeminacy, such as those made in *Tumbling Tumbleweeds* where the heavies call him a 'lavender cowboy'. Autry also refrains from transgressing racial boundaries, a proscription that again is not imposed on Smiley Burnette.

In her biography of Mae West, Mary Beth Hamilton outlines the shifting history of theatrical transvestitism from its post-blackface manifestations as a respectable and much-vaunted attraction in turn-of-the-century vaudeville to its decline as a legitimate variety form and eventual outlawing by a number of municipal and state authorities in the late 1920s and early 1930s. As a form of display in minstrel shows, transvestitism had used crude and vulgar caricatures of femininity that had figured as part of a coarsely sexualised performance for a predominantly male audience. In vaudeville, at least in the kind of performance that Hamilton is discussing, the emphasis was on the performer's ability, 'as if by magic', to successfully impersonate female characteristics in a refined and wholesome way that was enjoyed by middle-class families. 'Within an astonishingly short period of time female impersonation's past connotations had vanished', writes Hamilton. 'By the late 1930s it held only one meaning: it was purely and simply an act of "degeneracy". Interpreted as a vehicle of homosexual nightlife, it was banned by . . . authorities as part of a larger crackdown on gay male culture that swept the nation during the Depression.'[60] Yet the comically grotesque transvestite continued to have cultural capital during the period when female impersonation was most in dispute. Even in the most conservative of cultural industries —Hollywood—displays of transvestitism can still be found. This fact does not so much contradict Hamilton as confirm how deeply embedded into Westerns are otherwise anachronistic theatrical forms and performances which, on the surface, appear to have absolutely nothing to do with the genre. These performance traditions are most apparent in the figure of the sidekick.

The Sidekick

The sidekick is not the Western's version of the European court jester, whose function was to offer himself as a mirror reflection of the monarch, as a 'means for absolute power to practice humility'.[61] The base function of the sidekick is to keep the hero in the realm of the common man, not to confirm his preeminence. He is truly an American original. However much the court jester offers himself as a point of comparison, the sidekick draws his tomfoolery not from the courts of mediaeval Europe, but from the clowns of blackface minstrelsy.

In *Haunted Gold* (Warners Four Star Western, 1932) the African-American actor Edgar 'Blue' Washington (who had appeared in a number of Tim McCoy's silent Westerns) plays John Mason's (John Wayne) sidekick Clarence Washington Brown, or as Mason explains, 'a sort of Man Friday'. *Haunted Gold*'s hybridisation of the Western and the horror film (the film evokes the haunted house comedy, made popular by the play *The Cat and the Canary*, which received its first cinematic adaptation in 1927, but the formula also belongs to the tradition of dime novels) allows the filmmakers to exploit fully the comic potential of Clarence's minstrel characteristics.[62] Other than the 'easy laughs' claimed by the derogatory names he is given ('Darkey', 'Smokey', 'Watermelon'), much of the 'humour' is derived from the excess of his facial expressions (rolling eyes and bared teeth), his stammering blackface dialect and his constant susceptibility to being 'spooked' by his overactive imaginings of what lurks within the shadows. One scene of Clarence busting up dusty old rooms follows another as he wildly attempts to get away from grave-yard ghosts, legs and arms a-flying. That this is derived from the tradition of blackface is evoked most overtly in a scene which has Clarence falling down a mine shaft. When the dust has cleared, there he lies covered from head to foot in white powder—a black man in a white mask, a pun that is echoed at the end of the film, when he exclaims, after tripping whilst carrying flowers for 'Massa John', who is canoodling with Janet Carter (Sheila Terry), 'is mah face red'. At which, Janet and John break into fits of uncontrolled laughter and the film fades to black.

The story deals with the contested ownership of an abandoned gold-mine. John Mason claims half-shares, while the other half is claimed by Miss Janet Carter, whose father, Bill Carter, thought to be dead, had been conned out of his claim. Just out of jail and disguised as the Phantom, Bill Carter has conspired to bring together all those with interests in the mine. The plot plays out a seemingly endless repetition of capture and escape aided by hidden doors leading to secret tunnels. The gaunt and silent house keepers, along with mysterious peeping eyes, ominous shadows and unexplained noises, provide the standard horror elements.

When John Mason first arrives at the ghost-town he is invited to stay at what was once the town's grandest house. Being black, however, Clarence is told to stay in the barn. It is within this field of segregation that the dramatic limitations of a cowboy with a black sidekick are revealed. The social and legal restrictions placed on the body of a black man, in terms of his exclusion from specific public and private spaces, alongside the limitations imposed on his ability to interact with the white heroine, means that the character Blue Washington plays would remain an anomaly in the Western. Having black men appear alongside white women was a situation that Hollywood sought to avoid. During preproduction of *Showboat* (1936) the producers had hoped to cast the white actress Tess Gardella in the role of Queenie (that was eventually given to the African-American actress Hattie McDaniel). Gardella, who specialised in blackface acts and who was better known by her stage name Aunt Jemima, had played the role in the New York productions of 1927 and 1932. But the difficulties of having her share scenes with the black actor Paul Robeson were the cause of some concern on the part of Universal, who wrote to Joe Breen at the Production Code Administration for advice: 'I think you should be extremely careful, however', noted Breen, 'not to indicate any physical contact between a white woman and a Negro man for the reason that many people will know that Aunt Jemima is a white woman and might be repulsed by the sight of her being fondled by a man who is a Negro'.[63] If the African-American appears in the Western it will not usually be as sidekick, but as a peripheral figure, like the medicine show minstrel Eightball in Autry's *Tumbling Tumbleweeds*, a role that does not create situations where keeping him out of contact with white women becomes dramatically problematic.

White sidekicks in blackface are also an anomaly but there are examples, as in *Round Up Time in Texas* (Republic, 1937), where Autry's sidekick Frog (Smiley Burnette) plays the final third of the film entirely in blackface. In one of the most wildly absurd plots to be found in series Westerns, Autry and Frog transport a herd of horses to South Africa. The justification for this geographical relocation is that Autry's brother Tex has found a diamond mine and there is a shortage of horses to work the diggings. A montage scene made up of stock footage of a ship disembarking and an intertitle 'Dunbar, South Africa' finds them riding herd down the town's main street. A stock Western town 'transformed' by the odd sign, a saloon bar decorated with a couple of African shields, two or three stuffed and mounted antelope heads, shirtless black men, and some 'English' accents supplied by bit players complete this 'African' scene. The plot differs little from those set in the West; Tex's claim is stolen from him and he is taken captive, the English daughter of Tex's partner fills the female role, and together she and Autry set out to right the injustices.

The premise on which this is built is the exploitation of the contemporary popularity of the Tarzan adventures with all their accompanying clichés and stereotypes. Again the film proceeds through a repetition of capture and escape worked through disguise (bad men pretending to be good) and hidden identity (Autry mistaken by the police for an illegal diamond buyer). On escaping from the police, Autry and Frog are caught by tribesmen. Their fate is sealed until Frog teaches some children, played by The Cabin Kids, to sing a Negro spiritual, 'Revival Day'.[64] This impresses the Chief, decked out in leopard skin toga and top hat, and he is finally won over by Frog's magic tricks. Frog is, of course, believed to be a 'white god'. Using this ruse as cover, Autry escapes from the village and rides off to find his brother. Forced to remain, Frog has switched clothes with the Chief and is told to cure the Chief's ailing son on forfeiture of his life. But Frog fools the Chief once again when he disguises himself with blacking from a handy cooking pot and then races after Autry. In the most obscene of all the racial jokes on display here, Frog, still in blackface and having been chased up a tree by a lion, attempts to shoo him off by making Tarzan noises, but instead of frightening off the lion he attracts the amorous attentions of a gorilla.[65]

What is keenly of interest here is not the blackface performance, which is familiar fare in 1930s Hollywood, but its displacement into Africa (a shift which recalls that blackface performers in the 1840s were often referred to as 'Ethiopian delineators'), which also attempts to displace, once again, a Southern narrative out of the South—the South into the West and the West into Africa. This shift is nevertheless negated by the familiarity of locations which are self-evidently still those of Autry's West, disguised in the most rudimentary fashion and with 'Africans' both visually and verbally likened to Indians. Moreover, the original Southern narrative context that is doubly repressed through the Western and Tarzan narratives returns in a scene where Autry's brother is shown in a long line of black slave labourers who are forced to work by whip-cracking white bosses. The film's final racist joke, and intended irony, is to end with The Cabin Kids and the Chief costumed in cowboy outfits.

In *Texas Wildcats* the relocation of blackface performance reveals itself in the Phantom's costume. The black hood, which is pulled tightly around the Phantom's face when worn with his Stetson, gives him the appearance of a blackface minstrel with circled white eyes and white mouth, but when he removes the hat the pointed hood gives him the appearance of a Ku Klux Klan member. In this performance, the theatrical tradition of blackface minstrelsy meets its political counterpart—white supremacism. In the Three Mesquiteers' programmer *The Night Riders* (Republic, 1939) the heroes use hooded capes as disguises to frighten and foil the villain, but, as Don Miller notes, this 'gimmick was uncomfortably close to Klandom'.[66] These films are not advocating support for the Klan, but their shared concern with using theatrical disguises and the use of extra-judicial means to right perceived wrongs creates an uneasy symbolic relationship. One means of repressing the return of Southern narratives in series Westerns is to use the Mexican as the significant racial Other, but even here the character type is predominantly informed by performance traditions drawn from minstrelsy.

The major function and characteristics of the minstrel buffoon had already been transferred onto the figure of the Mexican during the Western's formation in late-nineteenth-century dime novels, and was reinforced visually in the earliest film excursions into the genre. In films such as *The Mexican's Faith* (Essanay, 1910) it is possible to see theatrical traditions of blackface minstrelsy imported into the genre through the use of make-up to differentiate racial and ethnic types from the white characters. In this film G.M. 'Broncho Billy' Anderson plays a Mexican, but he could just as easily be playing a cross between the role of Jim Crow, the lazy dim-witted pre-industrial fool, and the brutish post Civil War variant of Zip Coon, who exchanged his swallow-tail jacket for a pair of dice and a razor. The Razor Coon was a character type developed through late-nineteenth-century Coon songs, which found its most heinous manifestation in the figure of Gus, the rapacious black renegade in *The Birth of a Nation* (1915).[67] The title and the genre of *The Mexican's Faith* tell us that Anderson's character is a Mexican, but the use of grease paint to accentuate his eyes and mouth is more familiar to blackface traditions. There is no attempt to suggest any verisimilitude in the representation of non-whites, just a signalling to the audience of the character's racial otherness, which draws on an instantly recognisable theatrical tradition: his make-up, his brutish persona and at first unrepressed sexual desires for the white heroine, which he later learns to keep under check. The Mexican, if not the Indian, becomes absolutely inter-changeable with the character types first developed on stages in the urban North from the 1830s onwards: Sambo as the lazy peon; Zip Coon with his malapropisms and hopeless attempts to dress above his station in life becomes the Mexican revolutionary general; the Razor Coon finds his partner in the knife-wielding, back-stabbing Mexican; the High Yeller prostitute turns into the mixed-blood Mexican saloon girl. It should also be recalled that Western productions in the 1910s were awash with films that used 'Greasers' in their titles, a repetitious use of a racial nomenclature that clearly has parallels with turn-of-the-century Coon songs. The shifting of blackface caricatures onto the Mexican was a move, among others, that would eventually help consolidate the displacement of Southern narratives into the West. How else can the presence of Mexicans in Missouri in such films as *The Big Trail* and *Wyoming* (1940) be explained?

Despite the renown of the Lone Ranger and his Indian sidekick, Tonto (which is Spanish for 'stupid'), the red and white couple are a rarity. Mostly the sidekick is white. Though drawing upon older traditions in his musical and comic performances, Smiley Burnette in particular produced a unique character type whose importance to the series Westerns' audience cannot be overestimated. His antics bring a much-appreciated comic relief, operating as a digressive means to shift the audience's attention away from the formulaic narrative of pursuit, capture and escape—a disruptive effect that also helps fill the void of romantic intrigue and emotional intimacy. The sidekick provides the stoic individualistic hero with humanising and democratic traits which would otherwise be wholly lacking. By gratuitously offering himself as a dependant he provides the hero with responsibility, yet he does this without restricting the hero's ability to act. However, the sidekick by no means pays deference to the hero or anyone else. He is no man's servant or master. This lack of deference to established authority figures is more broadly and generally evoked across the spectrum of 1930s series Westerns, where contemporary concerns are not necessarily articulated through the explicit conceits of disguise and performance traditions.

Stories of Labour and Capital

The mediating role given to the cowboy was not unique to Autry and arguably reaches back to the dime novel cowboy. The cowboy functions in these narratives not as an agent of progress who will in turn be superseded by the arrival of the modern world in the form of organised society—the predicate of the frontier myth. Instead, the cowboy operates in dime novels or series Westerns as a figure able to forestall and moderate progress. In *Gun Smoke*, a late entry in the Richard Arlen series that followed his role in *The Virginian*, the modern urban world is represented by gangsters, who decide to take a vacation in Bunsen, Idaho. Masquerading as businessmen with plans to invest money in the town, the gang secretly plot to 'pick it clean'. The men from the city are welcomed by the good citizens, particularly the heroine who is seduced by their sophistication: 'We're still rather primitive out here, but we're doing our best to keep up with the times'. The 'primitive' is represented by the cowboys who make their living rounding-up mustangs. Immediately following the arrival of the gangsters, Brad Farley (Richard Arlen), the head cowboy, makes a 'speech':

> Maybe they'll put up a lot of factories and use all the water in our creeks for power, and our trees for paper pulp, and our kids to run the machines for them. Maybe, if we pay 'em enough, they'll put up a lot of tall buildings, so we can't see the sun for the smoke of the chimneys. And all the cowboys left in this country will get jobs driving trucks and we'll all be just as tame, dirty and crowded as a lot of them places back east . . . I want to keep this country the way it's always been: big, clean and roomy. So the people who like it can have it to live in and those who don't like it can get out.

Because the representatives of progress are evidently criminals, Farley and his men are able to vanquish the immediate threat of change and to moderate the townspeople's desire for material improvement, a desire previously identified in its gendering as feminine. *Gun Smoke* was promoted as 'A "Western" that's different!', but as the decade wore on, the gangster-out-West would become something of a cliché, for example in *The Old Corral* (Republic, 1936) starring Gene Autry.

Even if series Westerns have historical settings, as was given to John Wayne's first series for Republic, the thematic concerns remain remarkably consistent with those evoked in series Westerns with a modern setting. In *Lawless Nineties* (1936) the setting is the imminent statehood of Wyoming and functions as a celebration of democracy. In *The Lonely Trail* (1936) the setting is Reconstruction in Texas. The film begins with dramatic stock footage of Civil War battles. The years '1861' and '1865' flash across the screen followed by a text crawl: 'Following the close of the Civil War northern politicians known as carpet baggers gained control of a part of the south. In Texas they organised mounted State police and terrorised the people by a system of legalised murder and official possession'. Inside the Adjutant General's office he is paying off a slicked-up black man who is organising the votes of the freed slaves. General Holden is intent on filling his own pockets and he intends to rob the country blind while the getting is good. Through excessive taxation and selective assassinations of prominent citizens he causes the good people of Texas to take up arms again, which gives him the excuse to declare martial law.

Though the film may at first strike a similar note to Griffith's *The Birth of a Nation*, *The Lonely Trail* is not a celebration of the antebellum South. The carpetbagger is a historical version of contemporary hucksters, cheats and crooks who covet the independent farmer's property. The South, in the form of Texas, represents the dispossessed. Nevertheless, the novelty of the setting allows for some minstrel skits, Stephen Foster tunes and other bits of business around razors, chickens, and mint juleps (which are also present, though to a lesser extent, in *Lawless Nineties*). To give balance to the pro-Southern stance, John Wayne plays a Texan whose conscience caused him to side with the Yankees. Now that he is back with his own people, he must fight to regain their trust. His actions eventually prove his loyalty and when the Governor of Texas takes a stand against the carpetbagger the final rifts in the community are closed.

Winds of the Wasteland trades on similar issues of community, but ties its suggested historical setting more directly to contemporary concerns. The days of the Pony Express are over. The telegraph has made the company redundant. Out of work, John (Wayne) and his partner Larry decide to go into the stagecoach business. They buy the franchise to run a line to Crescent City, but the film's villain Drake has sold them a bill of goods. Told the city has a population of 3,500, they discover the reality is a ghost town with a population of two. Never mind, there is a mail contract in the offing, worth $25,000 dollars to the winner of a government-sponsored race. The film cracks along at a furious pace, building towards the final showdown between the two competing stagelines, a Western chariot race.

From the opening images of workers made redundant through new technology to the rebuilding of the community of Crescent City, the film suggests that any adversity can be overcome if there is the will. The first passenger on John and Larry's stagecoach is the daughter of the city's doctor. She believes the community to be thriving and can 'hardly wait to go shopping'. Her illusions are soon shattered and she tries to persuade her dad to leave. But, like John and Larry, he has been taken for a ride by Drake. He has sunk everything he owned into the town. However, things begin to pick up. First two Chinamen arrive —having been driven out of their last home for putting too much perfume on the cowboys' laundry. Next a pioneer family turns up, and they too decide to stay and make a go of it. When John saves a gang of telegraph workers from drinking poison water they promise to reroute the line through Crescent City; all they need is fifty men at $10 a day. With news of good wages the city really begins to live again. Drake sees his power slipping away and plots to get rid of John and Larry. John outwits him but Larry gets shot, the bullet lodging near his spine—a delicate operation. The doctor has lost confidence in himself and is unable to carry out the surgery. But with John's and his daughter's prompting he eventually accepts the responsibility. Along with Larry and the city, he, too, recovers. At the close, the city has attained a population of 410 and it seems safe to assume there will soon be enough stores opening in Crescent City to fulfil the young woman's desires.

In *Frontier Horizon* (Republic, 1939) the film reuses the same stock footage of the Civil War seen in *The Lonely Trail*, then cuts to a Pony Express rider being chased by Indians. But this Three Mesquiteers programmer is not set in the past. The pictured events turn out to be re-enactments to celebrate a town's fiftieth birthday. In *Three Texas Steers* (Republic, 1939) a caterpillar-tracked vehicle pulls a Conestoga wagon, which continues the play between the past and present, the old and new, tradition and progress.

These films are not stories of frontier heroics, but localised negotiations of conflicts between labour and capital. The past in *Rainbow Valley* (Lone Star/Monogram, 1935), a run-of-the-mill entry in the John Wayne series, is represented by the figure of the cowboy and the picture of Teddy Roosevelt that hangs on the wall behind the Post Office counter. The present is represented by the heroine who earns her own keep and wears smart but not flamboyant modern dress, and through the use of an old automobile which transports the mail. The cowboy steps out of the past and into the present when he comes to the aid of the town's exploited gold miners. To forestall the entry of law and order, the villains attempt to keep the town shut in from the outside world. In the film's big action sequences the miners shoot it out with the villains' stooges. With the miners dressed in 1930s work wear the scenes appear to speak more eloquently to labour unrest than to conflict on a Western frontier, while the limited number of camera set-ups give the scenes a newsreel-like verisimilitude. Press reports, if not newsreel images, of violent clashes between strikers and strike-breakers had contemporary currency: the 1929 Carolina Piedmont textile strikes, the 1931 Harlan and Bell County, Kentucky coal miner strikes, and the wave of strikes across the South by miners, steel workers, and laundry workers, and the general strikes in San Francisco in 1934 had all been met by violent opposition.[68] The villains are defeated when John Wayne's character dynamites a pass through to a connecting road. Now linked to the rest of the Union, the townspeople and miners enter into the modern world.

Although social and economic critiques are endemic to the 1930s series Westerns, they became much more pronounced towards the close of the decade in Republic's Westerns. *Wyoming Outlaw* (1939) was John Wayne's penultimate Three Mesquiteers outing and it is probably the most overt commentary in Republic's output on the issues raised by the Depression and its effects on the rural population.

The script is by Betty Burbridge and Jack Natteford, and concerns the exploitation of unemployed farmers by a crooked local politician who sells them jobs. In its representation of the outlaw, it draws upon the figure of Robin Hood. (Warner Bros.' *The Adventures of Robin Hood* was one of the most successful box-office attractions of the 1937/38 season.) A dust storm forces the Mesquiteers to find shelter in an abandoned farm house. An old newspaper from 1918 is found among the debris, and with the help of the headline story, Stony

(Wayne) explains how ranch land had been turned into rich wheat fields, but with the end of the war in Europe prices had plummeted, causing the farmers to overproduce and eventually turning the once fertile soil into dust. When the storm subsides they notice that one of their cows has been rustled. The trail leads them to the Parker family, who, rather uniquely for 1930s series Westerns, have a still living mother, a sign of a complete family that is about to be torn apart. The father is crippled and his son Will (Don 'Red' Barry), despite the best efforts of his sister (Adele Pearce), appears to be moving towards a life of outlawry. The family had been duped by the corrupt chairman of the Public Works Programme into taking out loans to buy 1,000 acres of dust. Stony rides to the State capital to appeal to the Senator to start an investigation, but the local population are terrorised into not testifying by the 'tin horn dictator' who runs the town. In a desperate attempt to feed his family, Will Parker ends up turning to crime, but he is caught illegally killing a deer (a not particularly subtle reference to *Robin Hood* in which a similar incident occurs). After breaking out of jail, Will becomes a hunted man.

In a montage sequence led by headlines in the Wyoming *Post* we see the combined might of the mass media close in on Will as film and radio crews offer live commentary on the posse's efforts to catch him. The media's distortions and outright lies about Will add to the audience sympathy for his plight. In a neat coincidence, Will hitches a lift from a radio reporter who does not recognise him; responding to his accusations about the Wyoming Outlaw, Will tells him 'everything is a lie in this Dust Bowl'. This point is dismissed rather curtly by the radio man: 'sort of a radical, ain't yer?' He is, but through necessity rather than choice. The audience is encouraged to side wholly with Will, an idea reinforced when Will visits his parents for a last goodbye. Breaking away from their loving embrace he leaves to kill the man who has pulled his family apart. In a formulaic shoot-out both Will and the bad man are killed. An epilogue tells us that the Public Welfare Committee ends the relief racket, and the victims of exploitation and the Dust Bowl get new homes.

The film was produced at the end of the decade, when America could begin to see the Depression as belonging to the past, suggested by the film's epilogue which historicises Will Parker's actions. Will's 'radicalism' is contained by this ending, which has a beneficent State authority stamp out corruption and offer a helping hand to the distressed (an ending not dissimilar to the following year's *The Grapes of Wrath*). But this cannot quite wipe out the image of a barely potent

Three Mesquiteers whose best efforts have been unable to save Will or to bring the bad men to book by legal means. No doubt the story is also a symptom of a series that was nearing its end (at least for Wayne) and that was lost for novel material—it is apparently based on a contemporary news story about a real life 'modern Robin Hood'—but it is also a continuation and confirmation of so many of the social issues that Republic had addressed since its inauguration.[69] Republic knew its audience: men, women and children who frequented small-town, rural and neighbourhood theatres, working-class families who wanted 'a magical, fairy tale transformation of familiar landscapes and characters'. This is precisely the world that series Westerns gave them, a world where conflicts between labour and capital are resolved in favour of the working man and woman.

The individual and collective transformative possibilities that series Westerns offered to their audience can account, in part, for their growing popularity during the 1930s. As the producers of A-feature Westerns were also keenly aware, however, it also offered both domestic and international audiences a melodramatic spectacle located in America's wide open spaces. In an essay on the meaning and use of the term 'Melodrama' in the American trade press, Steve Neale has argued (albeit in a footnote):

> The type of film that comes closest of all to 'classical' melodrama, with its clear-cut heroes, villains, and heroines, its comic relief, its moments of action, spectacle, and conflict, its thrills, its performing animals, its hair-breadth escapes, its chases, its jokes, and its songs is, in fact, the singing western.[70]

These attractions, so effortlessly and economically presented by series Westerns, were enjoyed by an audience who found the 'sophisticated', 'metropolitan' concerns of Hollywood's products unappealing. Recognising that this audience was growing as the economy worked its way out of the Depression, some of the major studios attempted to exploit this market but found their system of production too expensive to compete effectively with Republic and the Poverty Row studios. In October 1938 the *Hollywood Reporter* noted:

> MAJORS DROP RITZY WESTERNS; DON'T PAY. The so-called high class Westerns that came into vogue a couple of years ago and for a time proved good box office material seem

destined to fade again because of the inability of the majors making them to get back a sufficient return on investments.

The *Hollywood Reporter* was noting the poor return on Paramount's and Columbia's series westerns. 'Ritzy' does not refer to high-production-value films like *Three Godfathers* (1936) or *The Plainsman* (1936) but to films that ranged in cost from $65,000 to $85,000 each. The report claims that under present conditions '$35,000 is the top which should be expended on a horse opera and, not being geared to make pictures at this low figure, they will leave the Western market hereafter to the smaller companies'.[71] Westerns, in industry terms, equalled low budget and low return. In trade discourses the use of the term 'Western' nearly always connoted the series Western. For audiences the Western meant Buck Jones, Hopalong Cassidy and Gene Autry. The following chapter examines the major studios' un-even attempts to re-enter Western production in 1936/37, and the lessons they learnt in that season that enabled them to exploit the genre's dramatic and spectacular attractions more successfully and to broaden substantially its audience for the 1939/40 season.

4

Class-A Western Features
1935–1938

ROOMS FOR RENT
HOLLYWOOD
$6 WEEKLY—Large Rooms,
running water. *No cowboys.*
Convenient to all studios.
Oleander Arms 1312 Marion
St. nr. Hollywood Blvd.
A Star is Born, (Selznick, 1937)

In 'Reusable Packaging: Generic Products and the Recycling Process', Rick Altman (1998) sets the foundations for a theory of genre that will take account of both *industry*-specific analysis (Neale, 1990, 1993; Leutrat, 1984, Gallagher, 1986) and those founded upon *critical* concepts, derived notably from studies of *film noir* and the *woman's picture*.[1] His proposed methodology, like mine, is based upon the understanding of genre as informed by 'transience and dissemination' rather than upon a stable system of classification. He wants to account for the creation and mutation of genres, not as a means of marking out 'origins', but as an attempt to understand the processes involved in the proprietary naming of a collection of films. In the rhetoric of both industry and critical establishments he contends that genres are marked by changes recorded in the 'liberation' of the 'adjective' from the 'noun'. For example, the genres 'romance' and 'comedy' become qualified by the adjectives 'western' and 'musical', creating a sub-set of the primary categories: 'western romance', 'musical comedy'. At some point, the adjective becomes detached from the noun and becomes the substantive category: 'The Musical', 'The Western':

> Before the western became a separate genre and a household word virtually around the world, there were such things as western chase films, western scenics, western melodramas, western romances, western adventure films, and even western comedies, western dramas, and western epics. That is, each of these already existing genres could be and was produced with settings, plots, characters, and props corresponding to current notions of the West.[2]

Hybridisation and mutation help explain the dynamic of similarity and difference that is the mark of all generic subjects. The process by which a new genre comes into existence depends on three changes taking place. Firstly, a 'standardization and automatization of the reading formation' needs to occur; that is, producers need to orchestrate the similarities between films. Secondly, this orchestration needs to be based on substantive attributes that 'stretch' beyond the genre's 'eponymous material'; that is, the adjective has to shift to a noun. For example, with *western romance* the noun 'romance' is dropped and the adjective *western* is transformed into a noun. Lastly, the public must become aware of the 'structures binding disparate films into a single category'; that is, an audience will have to bring a set of expectations to their viewing of a film that will need to be met by the producers.

Less abstractly, Altman examines how this is manifest within critical discourses and the marketing of films. Pertinently, he discovers that whereas generic vocabulary is used extensively in film reviews, 'film publicity seldom employs generic terms'. Hollywood's strategy, he argues, is 'tell them [the potential audience] nothing about the film, but make sure that everyone can imagine something that will bring them to the theatre'.[3] Rather than emphasise a film's generic 'purity', Hollywood's 'stock-in-trade is the romantic combination of genres'. Through its marketing ploys, Hollywood searches for a diverse audience offering distinct but related pleasures. This observation supports my analysis of how Hollywood promoted Westerns, rarely using the noun in publicity material but alluding to it through iconography. Altman's particular claim to originality, however, is the idea that 'genres may continue to play an exhibition or reception role as convenient labels or reading formations, but they actually work against studio economic interests'.[4] This 'unexpected observation', as he notes, is derived from the idea that individual studios need to differentiate their product and this is best done through the initiation of film cycles where the 'stress' is on exclusive resources: contract actors, proprietary characters, recognisable styles. When competing studios imitate non-exclusive elements in order to exploit the success that a rival studio has had with a number of related films, the cycle becomes a genre, but the originating studio loses its ability to differentiate its films—cycles are proprietary, genres are sharable.

The cycles of films examined here do not, however, substantiate Altman's thesis. All the major studios participated in the cycles of Westerns produced during the 1930s. With perhaps the exception of Paramount during the mid-1930s, none of the studios had a monopoly on the production of Westerns, or led the way with particular plot or stylistic attributes which the other studios then appropriated.

Following the box-office success of *In Old Arizona* (Fox) and *The Virginian* (Paramount), Fox produced *The Big Trail*, MGM produced *Billy the Kid*, and RKO produced *Cimarron*, prestige Westerns that had little in common with the two earlier films. While *In Old Arizona* spearheaded a cycle of South of the Border films in 1930/31, all the major companies and a number of independents joined this cycle, with Fox continuing to exploit Warner Baxter's characterisation initiated by *In Old Arizona*. Similarly, Paramount continued its exploitation of Gary Cooper as a cowboy (this also included a film in the South of the Border cycle) and heavily promoted Cooper's co-star Richard Arlen as a new hero of the West. In these examples 'ownership' of a cycle of films principally resides in the potential to exploit the stars contracted to individual studios, *not* with a particular type of film. Altman writes: 'Without the ability to ensure a significant measure of product differentiation, studios cannot expect a substantial economic return on their investment. When a genre reaches saturation point, studios must abandon it or handle it in a new way'.[5] *Gun Smoke* (Paramount, 1931) would appear to be an example of this process. Released at the tail-end of both the Western and gangster cycles, the producers sought to continue the exploitation of the cycles by combining characters, plots and iconography, producing a hybrid which they hoped would play to audience expectations and offer a relatively unique experience: 'A "WESTERN" *that's different!*' This tag-line from a poster advertising the film shows a portrait of the star, Richard Arlen, in cowboy costume alongside an illustration of a cowboy on horseback riding through rocky country. Below the rider is a profile portrait of the film's villain, William Boyd (*not* the actor who would later find fame as Hopalong Cassidy), who has a cigarette hanging from the corner of his mouth, and is wearing a shirt and tie and fedora hat. Next to him is an illustration of a city block while in the foreground are five male figures wearing suits and 'newsboy' hats, firing automatic pistols. This collision of city and outdoor Western iconography was unique for its time, and exemplifies the process of cyclical innovation and stasis that Altman articulates. *Gun Smoke* was not, however, an A-feature production and it is notable that the film was promoted as a 'WESTERN'.

Clearly, then, 'genre' (as conceived by Altman) did not work against studios' interests when a film was intended for independent rural, small-town and neighbourhood theatres, and not pitched to a first-run metropolitan audience. Generic labelling is highly visible within the material used to promote series Westerns. Buck Jones's early 1930s films were sold as 'Whirlwind Westerns', and John Wayne's Vitagraph/Warner Bros. films were '4 Star Western' productions. The genre is a given, needing little in the way of re-promotion.

The audience for series Westerns is *not* solicited in a comparable manner to the audience for the A-feature, whose attendance cannot be guaranteed. As my analysis of independent exhibitors' programming preferences in Chapter One points out, there was an explicit demand for Westerns. Further, it was clearly not a fad akin to the cycle of gangster films or backstage musicals. There was no notable 'saturation' point. Indeed after the success of Gene Autry and the improved quality of the films produced by Republic Pictures, demand for series Westerns increased throughout the decade.

The innovations of singing and trio Westerns excepted, the star provides the necessary differentiation between the various studios' series Westerns, providing the primary point of distinction (though with a guarantee that his performance will be consistent from film to film). In this context, what is unique about series Westerns is that the cowboy star rarely performs outside the genre. The cowboy star and the Western genre are caught in a symbiotic relationship that has few parallels. One can think of horror stars such as Bela Lugosi, or sports stars turned actors such as ice skater Sonja Henie, but their appeal was short-lived. Though often given very restricted roles, A-feature stars were not confined to a particular genre. Indeed, as with matinee idols Tyrone Power and Robert Taylor, casting them in Westerns could broaden their appeal and, in turn, they helped widen the appeal of the genre by giving credence to romantic Western plots.

Altman's model suggests the processes involved in the formation and dissipation of genres as produced by the major studios, but it is an overly predefined paradigm that is unable to contain and explain

Hollywood's rather haphazard production schedules and modes of exploitation. It needs to be qualified by historically grounded analysis that seeks not just to understand genre as the end product of Hollywood's cycles but also to understand this process within the concept of the 'trends' that Tino Balio (1993) cites as one of Hollywood's principal means of predicting and catering to audience preferences. For Altman, it may be that Balio's 'trends' are trade terms synonymous with his concept of genres. But if this is the case, then generic categories during the 1930s are remarkably broad and limited in number. The consideration of genres as trends, according to this formulation, means that the Western needs to be regarded as a sub-set, its status as an adjective assured, while its status as a noun is effaced. While Westerns did function as a sub-set, for example, to prestige pictures, comedies, and musicals, they were also a substantive category in their own right and not just in the field of B-features.

Apart from series Western production and marketing, the 'confusion' over whether a film is a 'Western' or a sub-set of some other substantive category resulted from Hollywood's seeking to make its films inclusive and not exclusive. Balio argues that 'Hollywood tailored pictures for specific audiences and simultaneously promoted them to reach as many people as possible'.[6] This point was recognised by Anne O'Hare McCormick:

> In Hollywood you are told that pictures are not keyed to any particular section of the country, to any age group or to any special audience. The films that are popular in the East are said to be equally popular in the West, in city and small town alike. Yet where one might expect a desire for bright lights and city life, in the smaller places of the West, I was surprised to see 'Westerns' still in demand, either because people really like the thing they know best, the familiar background, or because the tame West of today hankers after the adventurousness of the Wild West of yesterday.[7]

McCormick's account of Hollywood's production trends and cycles comes at the end of an attempt to find a rational explanation for why it chooses to produce certain kinds of films. Her series of lengthy articles for the *New York Times* covers a period when Westerns had been seen to fail at the box office. Contemporary trade accounts tended to suggest that this was because the public was now interested in 'sophisticated' dramas (stories of moneyed characters set in an urban milieu were selling). Parallel to the trades' promotion of the new trend, however, was an awareness of the popularity of pictures of rural 'hokum'. Will Rogers, whose films best exemplify this latter trend, became one of the top box-office draws of the period and the highest paid actor in Hollywood.

Although Rogers' star persona drew heavily upon the image of the cowboy, his sound films make only passing reference to the West. Nevertheless, many of the concerns of his films are later echoed in singing and series Westerns of the mid-to-late 1930s. Rogers' work represents a significant influence on Westerns that followed his death in 1935, and his popularity suggests that there was still a considerable market for non-metropolitan, non-sophisticated dramas during the early 1930s, a point often made by the exhibitors' journal *Motion Picture Herald*.

It has been argued that a further pressure brought to bear on Westerns was produced by cultural shifts exemplified by the figure of the gangster. In his study of Cagney, Bogart and Garfield, Robert Sklar (1992) writes that in 1929 the gangster became a favoured subject in Hollywood, surpassing the cowboy:

> This may be one of the overlooked watersheds of American cultural history. In commercial popular culture, this ranks with— and perhaps completes—the historian Frederick Jackson Turner's declaration at the end of the previous century that the time of the frontier had passed.[8]

There is little doubt that the 'time of the frontier had passed', but Sklar's claims for the gangster's cultural eclipse of the cowboy is based wholly on the *major* studios' production cycles, where Westerns were clearly out of fashion. His argument is not sustained by evidence provided by the continued consumption of Western narratives and forms in other less visible cultural spheres. The major studios' withdrawal from A-feature Western production in 1932 was due to a variety of interlocking factors, rather than any single determinant.

Firstly, despite the fact that there was evidently a large demand for Westerns from independent exhibitors, the major studios' primary audience (those who attended first-run metropolitan theatres) accepted the genre only if the films had the mark of prestige productions. The failure of the three biggest Western films produced for the 1930/31 season to recoup their costs quickly meant that the major studios were unwilling to invest time and money in expensive outdoor productions.

This lack of investment in the genre was exacerbated by the onset and tangible effect of the Depression on the film industry. As Tino Balio notes, 'sound staved off the Depression for well over a year. But when the novelty of sound wore off in 1931, box office receipts plummeted and Hollywood felt the effects of a disabled economy'.[9] By 1931 Warner Bros. had a deficit of $7 million; Fox $3 million; RKO $5.6 million. In 1932 Paramount had a deficit of $21 million and in the following year it went into bankruptcy; Universal had gone into receivership; Columbia and United Artists were 'wounded, but not down'. Only Loews had remained in the black.[10] The immediate effect on production was to limit the scope of prestigious productions, particularly costly location filming. This retreat into the controlled environment of the studio curtailed the production of Westerns, which were often promoted on their spectacularisation of American land-scapes.

Secondly, if, as Balio suggests, Hollywood's principal target audience was conceived as female, then, according to Hollywood's common-sensical assumption about what kinds of stories attracted women to the movies, dramas of romantic courtship would have to be at the centre of the Western's narrative concerns. The enduring centrality of romance in Hollywood's films was a point emphasised in McCormick's series of articles:

> Now, in their extremity, they are harking back to the old, old story. Surprised though you may be to hear that its story was anything but this, static amid all the variations of time, place and treatment, Hollywood announces, as if it were news, that its present trend is toward the romantic, and when Hollywood says romantic it means a love story.[11]

The 1930/31 Westerns notably failed to provide credible love stories.

Finally, the enthusiastic welcome for the return of prestige Westerns in 1929/30, evident within the trade press, had been driven in part by the recognition that independent exhibitors' demands for a more suitable film product for their patrons were being answered. The threat of government antitrust litigation had raised its head towards the end of the 1920s. The major studios had tried to quell the independents' disquiet about blind and block booking through delivering requested generic films. But, when the effects of the Depression hit Hollywood and the government withdrew its antitrust action, the major studios returned to making films that pleased their first-run patrons and left Western productions to Poverty Row.

The years from 1932 to 1934 represent a low point in the production of Westerns by the Hollywood studio system and its independent satellites. From a high of 199 Western features produced in 1926, production dipped slightly in 1927 and 1928 with 140-odd films produced in each of those years. In 1929, for the first time since 1923, production fell below the 100 mark. In 1930, 79 Westerns were made, while there was a slight rise to 85 in 1931 and to 108 in 1932. The following two years, however, represent the nadir of Western film production until 1954. In 1933 only 65 Westerns were made, with 76 in the following year. The upswing in 1935, when 145 Westerns were produced, was therefore particularly dramatic.[12]

During the 1936/37 season the major studios returned to the production of A-feature Westerns. The trend did not produce epic Westerns in the mould of the 1930/31 season's output, nor was the genre as pervasive as it was to become in the 1939/40 season, but all the major studios contributed to the cycle. In part this was simply Hollywood's attempt to inject a little novelty into a new season's productions. Action-adventure films had made a good showing in *Variety*'s top grossing films of 1935, with *Mutiny on the Bounty* (MGM), *Lives of a Bengal Lancer* (Paramount) and *China Seas* (MGM) sitting alongside the Astaire/Rogers musical *Top Hat* (RKO), the Shirley Temple vehicle *Curly Top* (20th Century-Fox), and an adaptation of Dickens' *David Copperfield* (United Artists). In 1935 RKO produced *Annie Oakley*, starring Barbara Stanwyck, and, with *The Arizonian*, continued its re-promotion of Richard Dix as a man of the West, initiated in *Cimarron* and then continued in *West of the Pecos* (1934). MGM continued to develop Clark Gable's repertoire as a man of action by loaning him to Fox for an adaptation of the Jack London novel *Call of the Wild*. Fox made use of Warner Baxter as a Mexican Lothario again in *Under the Pampas Moon*. Paramount pursued its Randolph Scott and William Boyd series, and put Charles Laughton in a Western setting in *Ruggles of Red Gap*. After Buck Jones left Columbia in 1934, his career was supported by Universal. Warner Bros. and Columbia produced Western series with Dick Foran and Charles Starrett respectively.

Columbia, Universal, Warner Bros. and Paramount simultaneously maintained an involvement with series Westerns into 1936. According to Tino Balio, Paramount was 'almost single-handedly' responsible for keeping alive the class-A Western with *Texas Rangers* (1936) and *The*

Plainsman (1936). The studio stayed loyal to this brand of historical Western with *Wells Fargo* (1937) and *The Texans* (1938).[13] RKO sought to emulate the minor success it had had with *Powdersmoke Range* by starring Harry Carey and Hoot Gibson in *The Last Outlaw* (1936). It also picked up George O'Brien's contract and cast him as the lead in *Daniel Boone* (1936). Fox produced another adaptation of Helen Hunt Jackson's novel *Ramona* (1936), and Universal put *Covered Wagon*'s director James Cruze at the helm for *Sutter's Gold* (1936) after Howard Hawks had failed to come to grips with the spiralling cost of the production incurred by the Soviet director Sergei Eisenstein. Surprisingly, considering their reputation for prestige productions of musicals and costume dramas, MGM claimed the largest stake in A-feature Westerns after Paramount during this season: *Robin Hood of El Dorado* (1936), with Warner Baxter playing the Mexican bandit Joaquin Murrieta; *Rose Marie* (1936), which made *Variety*'s top grossing film list; *Three Godfathers* (1936), based on Peter B. Kyne's much-filmed novel, starring Chester Morris, Lewis Stone and Walter Brennan fresh from his success in *Barbary Coast* (1935); and *The Bad Man of Brimstone* (1937), starring the ever-popular Wallace Beery.

This stirring of renewed interest in Westerns was fed by the increasing popularity of Gene Autry and the parallel fad for popular songs with Western themes, which claimed a much larger audience than the rural and new urban population who were Autry's principal consumers. The adoption of cowboy songs by Bing Crosby, Jeanette MacDonald, Rudy Vallee, Nelson Eddy and other mainstream popular singers testified to the genre's appeal. The problem for the major studios was how to exploit the vogue without replicating the formula of series Westerns which, as the lack of crossover success of the Dick Foran/Warner Bros. series had shown, had limited appeal. Parody was one possible avenue. For example, *The Cowboy From Brooklyn* (1938) starred Dick Powell as an urban balladeer who assumes the identity of a singing cowboy in order to succeed in showbusiness. Individual scenes built into the backstage musical provided another possibility, but these tended to ridicule the figure of the hillbilly/ cowboy. In the following sections I examine how Hollywood attempted to exploit Westerns in ways that did not rely on parodying or replicating series Westerns. With the right promotional pitch around elements deemed to have female appeal, it was possible to erode potential audience antagonism toward Westerns and, at the same time, to attract an audience that was already predisposed to thrills and action.

The *Motion Picture Herald* review of *Three Godfathers* was intended like all its reviews to provide the exhibitor with a marketing angle. It serves as a good example of the industry's continued ambivalence about any given film's generic specificity, which is revealed, in part, through the shifting use of generic nomenclature. Is *Three Godfathers* a Western or is it something else?

> Although set in a Western locale and the three principal players are Western badmen, this is no prosaic Western picture . . . The picture has an impressive quality not ordinarily associated with outdoor Western entertainment. While it provides thrills and action, desperation, fear and heroism, it does so more in a manner to play upon the *sentimental* rather than *excitable* emotions. Brought to the attention of patrons as something entirely new and different, it is legitimate to anticipate that it will prove a popular attraction with *just as much, if not more, interest for women than men.* (emphasis added)[14]

By this point in the decade the use of the noun 'Western' within trade press discourse carried with it explicit connotations of a type of film aimed almost exclusively at male, rural, small-town and neighbourhood patronage. 'Western' implied a low budget, relative to A-features, with a recognisable Western star as its main selling point. The emphasis was, as the *Motion Picture Herald* review notes, on 'thrills, action, desperation, fear and heroism', on the 'excitable emotions', and not on the 'sentimental'. To the extent, however, that Autry's success was due to the marriage of the 'sentimental' with the spectacular, it suggested to the major studios a possible route back into the production of A-feature Westerns.

A-feature Westerns had nonetheless been and continued to be marketed not as cowboy pictures, prosaic Westerns or just Westerns, but rather as historical melodramas set in the West, romantic adventures, or sentimental dramas of the West. More precisely, *Three Godfathers* offered to 'play upon the *sentimental* rather than *excitable* emotions' felt to be missing from, for example, Buck Jones or Ken Maynard films. In this, the major studios were mining the same territory as Autry in differentiating their films through an overt address to male *and* female audiences. Significantly, though, the majors aimed to capture a similarly diverse, but more metropolitan audience than that being established for Gene Autry's films.

In this chapter I shall examine how the major studios used a variety

11. *Three Godfathers*
Three bad men (Chester Morris, Walter Brennan, Lewis Stone)
and a baby (unidentified)

of strategies to exploit the audience potential for 'sentimental' dramas set in the West. In particular I shall consider MGM's *Three Godfathers*, RKO's *Annie Oakley* and *The Arizonian*, Fox's *Ramona*, and Paramount's *The Plainsman* and *Texas Rangers* to demonstrate how the 1935/37 cycle was typified by successes and failures in the major studios' efforts to build a broader audience for Westerns.

Three Godfathers is a minor American classic in its balance of the sentimental with the hard-bitten. The three lead actors give as good a performance, if not their best, as any in their careers. They are helped by a script that is sympathetic to their characters when it could easily have patronised them and left them two-dimensional, rather than presenting them as complex individuals defined by the competing pulls of comradeship and selfishness. There are no grand star turns and the small ensemble, directed by Richard Boleslawski, produces a remarkable *frisson* which is heightened by setting this redemption parable in wholly appropriate landscapes of high buttes and miles of untracked inhospitable desert flat lands. The cowboy's insignificance within the natural arena of the West, caught by Joseph Ruttenberg's photography, has hardly, if ever, been bettered.

Christmas fills the Arizona air as four desperados overlook the peaceful town of New Jerusalem—'Full of the most clean living, sanctimonious buzzards on earth' says Bob (Chester Morris: 'a young man who made good by being bad'[15]), who is returning to his home town after a two-year absence in order to rob the bank. Along with him are Pedro, a guitar-playing Mexican who is not fated to live long, Gus (Walter Brennan), a ragged, toothless, illiterate man, by self-acclaim 'the oldest desperado in the South West', and Doc (Lewis Stone), the carrier of a PhD and consumption.

The four arrive in the town separately. Doc and Gus make their respective ways to the bar, a spit and sawdust saloon with one resident chippy, Blackie (Dorothy Tree), and a bartender who slicks his hair down with bear grease. The sheriff invites the newcomers to the Christmas social where the good and the lowly of the town, the latter represented by Blackie, begin the season's celebrations. Dinner, followed by a lecture on tooth decay, is topped by a dance, the Virginia reel, which is brought to a sudden halt by the arrival of Bob, the town's prodigal son. Moving through the suspicious citizens, Bob makes contact with Blackie and then with his old sweetheart, Molly (Irene Hervey), a picture of Western maidenhood. She is soon to be married to the boring but honest and dependable Frank, who works in the bank.

These scenes, in the bar, at the social and at the bank on the following day, establish the three main characters and the town they intend to violate, which is not quite the haven for the sanctimonious that Bob believes it to be. The town accepts that the saloon and Blackie serve a function, though they are not condoned. If the towns-people have a failing, it is that they trust too easily and condemn too slowly. Blackie and the saloon keep the townsfolk in a world occupied by fallible human beings rather than Presbyterian role models. The social niceties of the townsfolk offer a marvellous opportunity for Gus unconsciously to play on his coarse manners. At the social dinner Gus's attempts to pull the legs off a chicken are thwarted by the need to pass plates to the other diners. When it is Gus's turn with the asparagus spears he neatly cuts the tips off and puts them all on his own plate. Passing on the dish, he sucks in each tip with a self-satisfied smack of the lips. Dinner is barely finished and Gus is off and dancing with the smallest woman in town. This is not played in the Grand Guignol style of, say, Wallace Beery, but quietly and with subtle effect. Gus is also a contrast to Doc's educated respectful manner. As played by Lewis Stone, in looks, deportment and costume Doc is William S. Hart, a steely Puritan exterior hiding the most sentimental of men. Bob is the darkness that lies within them all. The youngest and most virile, he scours and lurks around the social and the saloon like a cowboy Johnny in search of his Frankie. Bob will 'kill anything from a baby to an old woman', the town's sheriff tells a suitably impressed Doc, who professes to have always wanted to meet a real Western killer. When Bob fails to seduce Molly at the social (she almost succumbs) he returns to the saloon and to Blackie, who has changed from the spinsterish clothes she wore at the social back into her dance-hall girl glad rags. To the melody of 'Frankie and Johnny', Bob and Blackie dance into the fadeout as he tells her, 'I danced at the social, but it didn't get me anywhere'. As demanded by the Production Code Administration, the fadeout eliminates the tag line: 'wonder how I'll do with you'.[16]

This is melodrama played subtly, striking its contrasts lightly and building its characterisation slowly, with the levity of comedy. The robbing of the bank is the climax to the scenes in New Jerusalem. Preparing to give the town's kids a treat, Frank, Molly's fiancé, is costumed as Santa Claus, and as the townsfolk meet to continue Christmas preparations, Bob, Gus and Doc take the bank's money with ease. But when Frank slips back into the bank's office, away from the robbers, Bob wantonly shoots him sneering, 'there ain't no Santa Claus'. High-tailing it out of the town, Pedro, who has been keeping watch outside the bank, is shot from his horse and Doc gets hit in the shoulder.

The posse is left behind and the three take stock of their situation by a poisoned water hole. Doc's wound is a problem, but it should not hinder them unduly and they have enough water to get them to the next watering place. Heading into the desert they come across the body of a man who has shot himself. They have a short debate over whether they should bury him and leave him to the maggots or leave him to feed the buzzards and vultures. As dusk comes, they reach water and an abandoned covered wagon. Inside are a dying mother, wife of the man they found on the trail, and a baby boy. Her horses have run off and, in the hope of getting more than the dribble of water he found in the natural well, her husband has dynamited it, closing it up for good. They make camp, bury the mother, and Gus and Doc tend to the baby (the PCA asked that the changing of the diaper not be shown and that Gus's line 'getting kinda swampy 'round here' be deleted). Bob will have nothing to do with the kid, and suggests they put it out of its misery. Doc reads from one of the books he carries, his constant companions; his choice is the philosopher Schopenhauer. 'What's the story?', asks Gus. 'There isn't any story', replies Doc. 'Jokes, huh?', returns Gus. 'Yes', responds a weary Doc, 'just jokes.' Doc reads aloud: 'Man is everything, woman is nothing'. Doc then tries to make an ironic parallel between the three of them and the baby and the three wise men and Christ. But the story is utterly lost on Gus and Bob does not care to listen.

Morning, and their horses have wandered off; Bob finds them dead by another poisoned water hole along with those that had pulled the wagon. Water is low and the baby has only three cans of milk, which Bob demands should be split amongst the three of them. Doc uses the money from the bank job to buy Bob's can of milk for the baby. The three men and the baby, carried by Doc who is much weakened from his wound, head back towards New Jerusalem, the only source of water within walking distance. The long walk towards redemption begins.

Bob tells a visibly wilting Doc to throw away his books, calling them 'dead weight'. 'Yes', says Doc of his John Milton, 'you were always a little heavy.' At the next stop in their journey, Doc writes a will for Gus and burns a bundle of letters tied with a ribbon (love letters from a life long past?). Gus then takes over the burden of carrying the baby and Doc stays behind: 'Funny', he says, 'where you start has nothing to do with where you finish.' He reads aloud from *Macbeth*:

> To-morrow, and to-morrow, and to-morrow,
> Creeps in this petty pace from day to day,
> To the last syllable of recorded time:
> And all our yesterdays, have lighted fools
> The way to dusty death. Out, out, brief candle,
> Life's but a walking shadow, a poor player
> That struts and frets his hour upon the stage,
> And then is heard no more. It is a tale
> Told by an idiot, full of sound and fury
> Signifying nothing

The last two words carry over to a shot, from behind, of Gus and Bob walking on, turning to pause only momentarily as a gunshot and its echo are heard. Gus's time, by the end of the day, is also played out, and, after saying a pathetic little prayer he learned as a child, he leaves the will Doc had written for him (Gus is illiterate) between his bags of loot and wanders off into the desert to die. Bob wakes to find Gus's will, which turns out to be a letter from Doc to Bob: 'If you get this letter it means that Gus is dead too. If you never did anything human before give the kid an even break—James Underwood "Doc." ' Bob throws the note away and tells the baby to go to sleep. 'If you've got any sense', he tells the baby, 'you'll never wake up.' Leaving the kid behind, Bob begins the final leg of his journey alone, but the cries of the child call him back. 'Shut up' he shouts at the baby and snaps out a shot from his pistol, but the bullet is aimed at a rattlesnake and not the child. Bob's actions begin to tell against his spoken selfish words: 'if you spill any of this', he tells the baby as he gives him the last of the water, 'I'll punch you on the nose'.

Five miles from New Jerusalem, Bob is just about played out. He has abandoned all that he once cared for, his guns and gold, and now there is just him and the baby. By the poisoned well the three badmen had stopped at on their way into the desert, Bob recalls that Doc reckoned the water would take an hour to kill a man. 'Here's to you, kid', he drinks the poisoned water; temporarily revived he continues on to New Jerusalem. Bob makes it to the church, staggering past the picket fence, into the church, down the aisle, past the hymn-singing congregation. At the front he stops before Molly (a Protestant Mary) and passes the baby to her. He falls, but pulls himself up. Above his head, as he leans against a wooden pillar, is a simple wreath of thorns. Achieving a Christ-like grace, he dies.

This is terribly mawkish, but the sentimentality and the didacticism of the parable are indicative of Hollywood's commonsensical under-standing of what attracts its female audience. Contrasting with this, in the characterisations of the three godfathers and the *mise-en-scène* of the desert and the rough-hewn, dusty town of New Jerusalem, are the conventions of the genre's 'masculine' address. The film's reviews were almost wholly positive. The *Hollywood Reporter* thought it 'GOOD FAMILY FARE WITH HEART APPEAL':

> *Three Godfathers* is good family fare and will make a neat profit in the hinter-lands, where they'll eat up the story of the regeneration of three badmen by the tiny babe they find on the desert. Audiences will shed a tear or two and laugh along and wonder a little why the picture seems so much better than the original'.[17]

Variety agreed with the *Reporter* on the principal audience for the film: '*Three Godfathers* assents to get its share of the grosses in nabe (neighbourhood) and family theatres. It constitutes a strong film for double-billing but should prove big enough to stand alone if only because of presence of Lewis Stone and Chester Morris. For secondary interest it has Irene Hervey, Walter Brennan and Sidney Toler.'[18] *Film Daily* contradicted the *Motion Picture Herald*'s claim about this not being a Western: 'Very good drama of Western type', but qualified this by adding, 'with exceptional cast and production values'.[19] *Variety*'s preview took the same position on the film's generic transcendence: 'Metro jumps back into Westerns with *Three Godfathers*, an old-timer, from the book by Peter B. Kyne, but Chester Morris, Lewis Stone and Walter Brennan yanked up its boot straps and almost pluck it out of the class'.[20] Finally, *Motion Picture Daily* believed this tale of three outlaws 'develops as an interesting character study motivated by a heart gripping theme after starting as an average action feature'. It concludes the picture 'can best be sold from the hard angle'.[21]

Whether the *Motion Picture Herald* was right in suggesting the film should be pitched to the female trade, or the *Motion Picture Daily* in recommending it be sold principally to a male audience, is less important than recognising that the film could be pitched to both genders. Indeed, as the *Hollywood Reporter* noted, it could be sold to all the family, an effect achieved by centring the story on the redemption of the men through the agency of the baby. But this was not a device that could be endlessly replicated, since its novelty had limited appeal.[22] As the 1930/31 cycle had demonstrated, A-feature Westerns had seldom been able to integrate romance successfully with their more 'elemental' fare. The films of the 1936/37 season were, however, constructed within the altered context of Autry's success, which exacerbated pressures to find a solution to this 'problem'. The following studies of Hollywood's productions reveal a variety of narrative devices to introduce a credible romantic courtship to stories of the West.

Annie Oakley, which *Motion Picture Herald* thought combined 'the lure and glamour of the Big Top with the thrill and adventure of the Wild and Woolly West', had gained a broad audience by giving centre stage to the female lead (Barbara Stanwyck), and then using the historical and showbusiness backdrop of Buffalo Bill's Wild West to play out a series of romantic intrigues, suffused with light comedy and a number of suspenseful incidents.[23] The film deals with the frontier not in the Western sense but as a fact of rural life. Oakley is poor white trash who uses her skills at shooting to lift her and her family across the divide and into American civilisation, personified, without intended irony, by Buffalo Bill's Wild West. This was a fantasy of the Wild West wiping clean the past reality of rural poverty. Make the hero a man of the West, however, like Richard Dix's character in *The Arizonian*, and the problem of courtship and the cowboy encountered in 1930/31 A-feature Westerns occurs again. *The Arizonian* was, like *Three Godfathers*, initially defined by what it was not: '*The Arizonian* is not a cowboy picture. It's a melodrama of the West, timed in a theatrical way to one of the new country's most interesting periods.'[24]

The story is based on the exploits of Wyatt Earp and Doc Holliday, with Dix playing his usual role of straight-nosed, square-jawed, righteous lawmaker Clay Tallant. His arrival in Silver City coincides with the attempt by the villain, sheriff Jake Mannen (Louis Calhern), to win the body, if not the heart, of the English songbird Kitty Rivers (Margot Grahame), who performs at the concert saloon he owns. Standing between Mannen and her is Clay's brother, a shy retiring boy/man. As Clay begins to clean up the town, his feelings for the songbird grow, as hers do for him. Being an honourable man, he refuses to go the last mile and break his brother's heart, but a kiss goodbye is witnessed by the brother and is taken the wrong way. Clay may have won the girl and tamed the town but he has lost his brother. Events conspire to resolve the problem, however. Mannen, who has the judge in his pocket, makes one last attempt to regain control. Clay, his brother and Tex Randolph (Preston Foster)—Doc Holliday to Clay's Wyatt Earp—are locked in the jail, which is then set on fire. In a film that has a number of wonderful visual details to hold interest, the best by far is when the three have escaped their fiery prison and walk slowly into a wall of smoke blasting their guns at an unseen enemy who blasts back from the other side. When the smoke clears only Clay is left alive.

As played by Dix, Clay's straight-backed asceticism wrecks the love scenes. His lack of sexual charisma is compensated by his masculine self-assurance, but this in turn leads him to profess a philosophy of misogyny (a considerable obstacle to put before the heroine, though she never mounts a credible challenge to this arch-patriarch). Like the English woman in *Billy the Kid* (1931), she is shown to be the very picture of maidenly purity; how else could it be if she is to be a suitable partner for the hero, even if this is qualified by her position as a performer? Though they make suitable companions, this ascetic hero and virginal maiden make a poor romantic couple because there is no *frisson* in their relationship. Nonetheless, the film offers a number of

12. *Ramona*
Loretta Young, Don Ameche and his wig

other elements to compensate for the lack of romance, not least the concert saloon performances that it opens with, including the ghost scene from *Hamlet*, the gunplay, and a finely wrought *mise-en-scène*.

In contrast to Dix's stoic misogyny, *Ramona* has insipid male leads. Don Ameche's discomfort in the role is compounded by a wig which gives him the appearance of a mediaeval extra in Will Rogers' *A Connecticut Yankee*. Helen Hunt Jackson's romance, first published in

1884, had been adapted for the screen on three previous occasions. The novel was her attempt to popularise her claim in *A Century of Dishonor* (1881) that the government had persistently mistreated Indians. Set in California during the 1870s, the film opens with a tranquil image of a pastoral California, which is sustained for its first half. Here Mexicans and Indians live and work side by side. Ramona, an adopted child of the Rancho's matriarch, is in love with her step-brother and he with her, but the mother will not allow marriage because of Ramona's bloodline. Ramona is the daughter of the matriarch's brother-in-law, a Scotsman who had a brief affair with an Indian maiden. When her step-brother is injured in a horse race, Ramona falls in love with his friend (Don Ameche), the chief of the Indians who visit the Rancho each year to shear the sheep. The matriarch will not allow this marriage either. Marrying an Indian would bring disgrace to the family name. Eventually the couple elope, marry and have a baby. They live a peaceful life until Americans arrive. Dispossessed of their land, they take to the open road in search of a home. Rain and cold force them to seek shelter at a humble homestead, where a contrasting matriarch (Jane Darwell) welcomes them as fellow Christians. The baby falls sick. Its father rides to town for a doctor, but fever is spreading through the town and the doctor cannot leave. The father races back to the homestead with medicine, but his horse becomes lame. Borrowing a horse from a farmer without permission, he finishes his journey; the medicine saves the child, but the farmer tracks him down and shoots him. After the funeral Ramona is reunited with her old family.

As in *Three Godfathers*, biblical symbolism is used with a heavy hand in order to humanise and Anglicise Ramona and her husband. The play for sympathy for the plight of these Mission Indians is, however, less important to the film's appeal than the melodramatic devices it calls forth: the impossible decision Ramona must make between obeying her mother's wishes and choosing the man she is to love; the disruption of the pastoral ideal with the arrival of the Americans; the plight of her baby; the death of her husband; and her final reconciliation with her mother and brother. Coupled with the Griffithian race to save the child in the final reel (Griffith had filmed the first adaptation in 1910), these melodramatic devices make the film potentially compelling. Designed as a star vehicle for Loretta Young and Don Ameche, shot in Technicolor with musical interludes, a large cast and panoramic landscapes, it was 20th Century-Fox's big prestigious production of the season. While the film may have appealed to an audience with a taste for romance, it failed to hold an

13. *The Plainsman*
A love that is barely spoken, Calamity Jane (Jean Arthur) and Wild Bill
Hickok (Gary Cooper)

appeal for what the industry called the 'masculine trade'. Don Ameche
may sing, dance and ride well, but in this role he is a poor example of
vigorous masculinity. To gain sympathy for the Indians, the story calls
for him to be a victim, not a hero. Visually, his inadequacy is compounded when he is juxtaposed to the Native American actor Chief
Thunder Cloud. Next to the hard chiselled features of Thunder Cloud,
Ameche looks like a clown.

Paramount's *The Plainsman* had greater success at the box office
than *Ramona*, making it into *Variety*'s top ten box-office films of the
year. Rather than highlight romance, the film represses it, and the acts
of repression form the heart of the story. The romance between Wild
Bill Hickok (Gary Cooper) and Calamity Jane (Jean Arthur) is contained by the theme of national regeneration. The film begins with
Lincoln discussing the ravages of war and his fears of unemployment
awaiting the returning soldiers, and finishes with images of abundant
wheat fields and a superimposed view of Custer and Wild Bill riding in
front of the Stars and Stripes. Running over these images is a text
crawl: 'It shall be as it was in the past . . . Not with dreams, but with

strength and with courage, shall a nation be molded at last.' This overt politicisation of the frontier narrative led the film's reviewer in the left-wing British journal *New Statesman* to remark: 'Its moral is interesting, though presumably accidental. The Washington government sends its demobilised soldiers to settle in the West and then sells the Indians rifles to blot them out with. One might expect this from Russia. From Tory Hollywood it is a bit of a shock.'[25] But most reviews, American and British, tended to overlook the political themes and concentrated on the adventure, action and endlessly stalled romance. Paramount's exploitation of the film concentrated on the film's 'authenticity', suggesting that 'the recreation of the famous Indian scout as a central character obviously provides a great exploitation angle'.[26]

Wild Bill's mistrust and oft-spoken dislike of women is contradicted by the picture he carries in his pocket watch of himself and Calamity, and by the lengths to which he goes to protect her, all the while denying that he cares for her. Calamity is Wild Bill's perfect partner, refusing to act as a domesticating agent, in contrast to the role with which Buffalo Bill's wife is lumbered. Calamity's tomboyish charms only have a legitimate claim while the frontier still exists, however; they cannot survive civilisation, where she will be forced to conform and become like Cody's wife. Similarly, Wild Bill's intolerance of domesticity signals his impending end once the savages, both Indian and white, have been brought to book. Nevertheless, it is this tension between the conformity to standard notions of love publicly announced through marriage, and the open ended, barely spoken, repressed private love shared by Calamity and Wild Bill, that holds together the film's episodic narrative, which ranges from the end of the Civil War to Custer's defeat at Little Big Horn. Because the repressed love story is the film's central theme, there is a genuine sense of loss at its closure, when Wild Bill dies in Calamity's arms.

In a much-touted contemporary quotation, Graham Greene described *The Plainsman* as 'certainly the finest Western since *The Virginian*: perhaps it is the finest Western in the history of the film'.[27] He also rather enjoyed *The Gay Desperado* (Pickford-Lasky, 1936), one of two films produced for United Artists to trumpet the talents of the Italian opera singer Nino Martini, with the other half of the romantic couple played by Ida Lupino. It is a light operetta given a South of the Border setting. 'There are moods', wrote Greene:

when one almost believes, remembering the great Westerns, from *The Virginian* to *The Texas Rangers*, and the classical Russian films, from *October* to *Storm Over Asia*, that the cinema is only about its proper business if it is in the open air, in natural surroundings . . . These scenes, at any rate, the theatre cannot reproduce.

The American outdoors has been one of the key elements in defining what was exceptional about American movies since the 1910s.[28] The *Hollywood Reporter* noted that until 1938, Great Britain accounted for 35 per cent of the total gross companies could expect from their Western productions.[29] The spectacle offered by America's indigenous landscapes was one of the Western's significant selling points in foreign markets, and no doubt, despite blasé domestic reviewers, it was also important to an American audience.

The Gay Desperado's romance is played out in the open amongst the cactus and against the vast star-filled sky. As a love story it is predictable. A young American society girl is kidnapped by Mexican bandits and falls in love with the singer who has been forced to join this band of incompetent cut-throats. Neither part of the romantic couple belong in this world of lunatic horse rides and car chases, gunplay, braggadocio and buffoonery, where urban American gangsters tough it out with grinning banditos. After watching gangster movies, the banditos comically decide to modernise their criminal operations. The film parodies the contemporary concern that American movies export a false and depraved idea of American culture. For Graham Greene, however, these are minor diversions from the 'lovely shots of cacti-like cathedral pillars, of galloping horses before old Spanish churches, of sombreros against skyscapes, [which] are like a framework of fine and mannered prose'.[30]

The fact that production companies had difficulty in creating credible romances in Westerns did not stop them producing examples of the genre, albeit in very limited numbers in the mid-1930s. While romance is a significant selling point for a film to be pitched at a diverse rather than limited audience, it would be wrong to see it as an absolutely essential prerequisite. The genre's depiction of American history, action, thrills and the spectacular grandeur of its landscapes still made it an exploitable property. By the evidence of press reviews, this is particularly true of the British audience's regard for the Western. It is rare to read a review of a Western from the 1930s that does not make some reference to the landscape: 'The plains of America were made to gallop over' is how one review described the impact of *The Plainsman*.[31] *Ramona* is characterised by its 'memorable and arresting . . . pictorial beauty. The "new perfected Technicolor" is a joy to the eye. Mountains, sky, plains, wheatfields, farmyards are wonderfully displayed.'[32] A review of *Robin Hood of El Dorado* notes that 'the natural settings are good and the film is beautifully photographed'.[33] In *Three Godfathers*, 'The desert photography is very convincing'.[34] In *The Texas Rangers*, 'The virtues of the film are its excellent outdoor photography'.[35] The landscape in this latter film, along with the film's historical authenticity and action-romance, was singled out in the guidance notes written for British film exhibitors, which described it as 'placing a romantic, action-filled plot against a background as vast as the entire outdoors and as historically accurate as research could make it'.[36] Paramount not only sold its prestigious Western productions, but also its series Westerns, around landscape:

> The generous use of the wide open spaces in *Three on the Trail*, latest of the 'Hopalong Cassidy' Westerns . . . proves that the 'old West' still exists—at least scenically. Filmed in the High Sierras near Lone Pine and Kernville, Cal., some four hundred miles from Hollywood, the natural pictorial beauty of the setting forms a perfectly fitting background for one of the most dramatic Western stories ever to reach the screen. Towering hills, mountain streams tumbling over rocky cliffs, and giant trees all play their parts in adding to the beauty of the setting.

The exhibitor would feed this 'review', which is half as long again, to the local British press. The emphasis on the film's topography indicates how important scenic views of the American West were for foreign audiences. The latter half of the 'review' focuses upon the plot and action, concluding with a note on the leading female who 'brings a romantic touch to this thrilling story of the Old West', before ending on the sidekick, 'a lovable old boaster, who "hates wimmin like pizen"'.[37]

In *The Texas Rangers,* Paramount used three male stars who had hitherto been almost exclusively confined to playing urban characters: Fred MacMurray, a light comedian, Jack Oakie, formerly a vaudeville comedian, and Lloyd Nolan, a character actor who specialised in corrupt businessmen and gangsters. Oakie had played Clark Gable's sidekick in *Call of the Wild* (1935): Paramount publicity announced that MacMurray and Oakie 'head the cast in roles entirely new to both of them, yet roles to which they give a convincing reality'.[38] The studio hoped that the stars would bring a 'new' audience to Westerns (though at no point in the publicity is the film called a 'Western') and that the actors' appeal would concomitantly be broadened to include an audience that disliked urban dramas. Oakie's character draws upon the series Western's sidekick's persona. He sings a number of songs, most notably 'Dying Cowboy' and a parody of 'Oh Susanna!'. His tragic and heroic death toward the end of the film, however, differentiates him from the series Western sidekick, just as the film's historic scope also helps to differentiate it from those produced by independent studios.

To avoid direct comparison with series Westerns, the major studios reconfigured the general public's image of the cowboy. Read through trade discourses on series Westerns or in Hollywood's use of the figure in non-Western A-features, the cowboy is either a naive innocent or a mush-mouthed fool. In *Boy Meets Girl* (Warner Bros., 1938) and *The Shopworn Angel* (MGM, 1938) these constructions of the cowboy are met head on. In the former, James Cagney and Pat O'Brien play two bored Hollywood scriptwriters whose latest job is to write a story for a Western series starring the intellectually challenged Larry Toms, played, self-reflectively, by Warner Bros.' singing cowboy, Dick Foran. Toms desperately needs a good script so that the studio will renew his contract, but Law (Cagney) and Benson (O'Brien) won't play ball. Toms, now almost pleading, says: 'Just because I don't get Dick Powell's fan mail don't mean I ain't got a following. Well, a lot of the people who want to write to me just ain't learned how to write.' To which Law responds: 'Injustice has been done, we've been lacking in the proper respect for the idol of illiteracy'. This idea is underscored by visually equating Toms with a monkey. Eventually, Law and Benson develop a harebrained story—a parody of *Three Godfathers*—which hits big with the public, gaining Toms a new female audience.

The merciless fun that the story has at the expense of series Western cowboys and Hollywood's notions of authenticity had already been touched on in an earlier Cagney vehicle, *Lady Killer* (Warner Bros., 1933), where Cagney plays, for laughs, a down-at-heel mobster who finds work as a cowboy extra, one of the many preposterous roles given to the character in his rise to stardom. To some extent, series Westerns had already anticipated this construction of the cowboy-as-fool, but had displaced it on to the figure of the sidekick. As Warner Bros.' singing cowboy, Foran was anything but a fool. Nevertheless, the cowboy as a figure of ridicule dominated major studio productions for a metropolitan audience. In *Gold Diggers of 1933* (Warner Bros., 1933) a group of Jewish New Yorkers who are dressed like cowboys turn up for an audition as 'the Kentucky Hillbillies'. 'You know your "Your Old Kentucky Home"?' asks the producer. 'You bet'. 'Then go back to it. Your mammy's waiting for you.' In the Sonja Henie vehicle *Thin Ice* (20th Century-Fox, 1935), Joan Davis's comic sketch has her make play with Alpine, Hillbilly and cowboy yodelling. In *Stage Door* (RKO, 1937) the theatrical aspirants create a contrast between high culture, represented by Shakespeare, and low culture, represented by a cacophony of yodelling. *In Caliente* (Warner Bros., 1935) has an Irish Broadway singer transform himself into a singing Caballero and features a female Mexican yodeller. *Stand Up and Cheer* (20th Century-Fox, 1934) a 'Fox Follies' featuring, among others, Will Rogers and Shirley Temple, neatly collapses female Western wear and hillbilly clothes with Hollywood glamour in a song and dance number that celebrates and parodies the 'Broadway Hillbilly'. In these films the cowboy was a hick and the hick was a cowboy. In *That Certain Woman* (Warner Bros., 1937) Bette Davis's character asks her four-year-old son to 'yodel for the lady', which suggests that yodelling was no more than a juvenile accomplishment.

Alternatively, the cowboy as innocent could be easily incorporated without ridicule into an American identity. In *The Shopworn Angel*, James Stewart's character, Bill, is fresh off a Texas ranch, a world where cars still make way for people and horses. While waiting for his regiment to be shipped off to fight in the trenches of France, he meets the 'lady' of his dreams in New York. When the hard-bitten New York socialites, played by Margaret Sullavan and Walter Pidgeon, pit their cynical and world-weary view of life—'what's the percentage?'—against Bill's guileless and honest patriotism, it is they who must change and embrace a sense of social responsibility. James Stewart's Texas cowboy is not dumb, he is simply outside the corrupt world of the city. Only through him is Sullavan's character able to see the stars that shine between the New York skyline, to see beyond the percentage coming to her in any and all human transactions. He embodies what America once was and now must become again as it faces the test of war in Europe (in 1916 and in 1938). Jimmy Stewart, 'Hollywood's most promising juvenile' as one contemporary star profile called him, would take this character with him when he played opposite Marlene Dietrich's jaded Frenchy in *Destry Rides Again* (1939).

The Cowboy and the Lady (Goldwyn, 1938), which travels similar territory to *Shopworn Angel*, makes greater play of the cowboy as American innocent. Stretch (Gary Cooper) is the Montana cowboy who joins a rodeo in the hope of finding a wife to complete his dream ranch. While in Florida he meets and falls in love with society girl Mary Smith (Merle Oberon), whom he believes is a lady's maid. They marry in double-quick time but are soon separated, as she must return to help her father host a dinner at which he hopes to gain the support of Henderson (Berton Churchill), a king-maker, in a bid to gain his party's nomination for President. Stretch, still ignorant of his wife's real family, bursts in on the dinner party. He is invited to sit at the table to offer his opinion on whether Henderson should back Judge Smith. The patronising attitude of the dinner guests, who mix up Montana with Texas and Mounties with cowboys, soon gets to Stretch and he delivers a fine example of populist rhetoric that leaves all stunned, if not humbled:

> In the first place I don't see where you get off picking anybody for President. If you had the decency to treat a person like a human being, instead of asking people to sit down at your table so you can laugh at 'em. Maybe you wanna go out and find out what they think, see what their needs are and what you can do to help them. That's all that's gonna count in the long run. If Judge Smith, there, wants to be President he ain't gonna get very far looking down his nose at people, or thinking he is better than they are. Abraham Lincoln didn't have to do that, and he turned out to be a pretty good President.

He finishes by inviting them all out to his ranch, so they can learn some manners and discover for themselves how honest people live. At the story's close he is reconciled with Mary and her father. Though the film was not a big box-office success, it still managed to garner plenty of publicity in the fan magazines and helped towards refamiliarising mainstream audiences with the figure of the noble cowboy. The film downplays action and there is no criminal intrigue; everything revolves around the on/off romance between Cooper's and Oberon's characters. In its forsaking of gunplay for romance it incorporates songs familiar from singing cowboys' repertoires and introduces one-time New York nightclub singer Fuzzy Knight as a sidekick who, with Walter Brennan, acts as comic relief—creating with Cooper an up-market replication of 'trio' Westerns. Fuzzy gets to sing a number of cowboy songs and ends the film playing a swing tune 'Rootie Tootie' on a pump organ. He was soon to be fully employed in roles similar to Smiley Burnette's in Tex Ritter Westerns, amongst others.

The guileless cowboy and the socialite girl were an old Hollywood formula. Cooper had played the role before alongside Carole Lombard in *I Take This Woman* (Paramount, 1931), which in turn reworked the theme used a year earlier in *Montana Moon* (1930), where a jazz baby, played by Joan Crawford, falls in love with a Texas cowboy (John Mack Brown). Brown's character may have an accent that drips molasses and grits, he may own little beyond his horse and a change of hats, but he knows the value of a hard-day's graft, and most importantly he knows what is right and wrong. He eventually calls a halt to his wife's debauched and hollow friendship with 'the kids', her associates from the East who lack any sense of moral propriety. Taking the girl out of the city and putting her into the West (or at least into a rural environment) was a sure-fire means of female redemption. This happens in most of Mae West's post—*She Done Him Wrong* films and notably in *It Happened One Night* (Columbia, 1934). As in *Shopworn Angel,* having the West come to the woman also allowed for her personal transformation. On the other hand, taking the urban male and transforming him into a cowboy had the effect of countering questions of urban masculine effeminacy.

In films such as *The Virginian*, *The Plainsman* and *The Cowboy and the Lady*, Gary Cooper had shown that it was possible to incorporate romance and Westerns, but Cooper was relatively unusual in Hollywood's pantheon of male stars, appealing equally to a female and male audience. A contemporary reviewer summed up Cooper's appeal when he described him as having a 'whimsical masculinity'.[39] If Westerns were to succeed with a diverse audience, Hollywood would need to find a means of broadening their appeal. In *Shopworn Angel*, James Stewart had partly shown the way (the film was a remake of a 1929 star vehicle designed around Gary Cooper), as had the leads in *Three Godfathers*, managing to negotiate the sentimental and the hard-bitten in a manner that had escaped Don Ameche's character in *Ramona*. Moreover, *Three Godfathers* showed what could be achieved by constructing Westerns around an ensemble of complementary and contrasting characters, a structure that would later be successfully exploited in *Stagecoach*. In *Annie Oakley* and *The Plainsman* Barbara Stanwyck and Jean Arthur showed that there was a place in Westerns for women who did not conform to domestic stereotypes, and Loretta Young's *Ramona* suggested that the West was a conducive setting for romantic intrigue. *The Texas Rangers* revealed the possibility of broadening the appeal of actors who specialised in romantic or urban roles by featuring them in outdoor adventure dramas. In the following chapter, I argue that the box-office success of the 1939/40 cycle of Westerns was in large part due to the major studios learning from the marketing, casting, narrative and dramatic successes and failures it had with the genre during the preceding ten years.

Meanwhile, Republic was becoming synonymous with high-quality Western products. While its producers exploited this reputation, it was also found to be a handicap when they attempted to compete in the class A-feature market in the late 1930s and early 1940s. Noting Republic's change in the title of *Wagons Westward* to *Man of Conquest* (1939), the *Hollywood Reporter* wrote: 'Consensus was that Republic's reputation as a Western picture producer might handicap "Wagons" causing it to be classed "just another Western" '.[40] With the consolidation of a number of Poverty Row studios under the banner of Republic, the changed fortune of series Westerns coincided with renewed interest in the genre by some of the larger studios. By 1939, when the major studios began to consolidate their relatively novel production of A-feature Westerns, Republic found it no longer dominated the field.

It was in the 1939/40 season that the Western, according to André Bazin, reached 'a definitive stage of perfection'.[41] The Westerns Bazin canonised alongside his formulation of *Stagecoach* (United Artists, 1939) as *the* classic Western remain crucial to an understanding of the genre. Yet attempts to explain why these films appeared at this particular juncture in American history have been at best impressionistic and fragmentary. In *The Crowded Prairie* (1997), Michael Coyne works from the simple presumption that 'the time was evidently ripe for the Western to take its place as a major Hollywood genre'.[42] This is a wholly inadequate conceptualisation, but it is also a commonplace in histories of the genre.

In *The BFI Companion to the Western* (1988), Ed Buscombe notes that 'between the mid-1920s and the late 1950s . . . Westerns . . . comprise(d) between a fifth and a quarter of all films made in Hollywood'.[43] Buscombe qualifies this extraordinary statistic by noting that all but a few Westerns were small-scale productions: 'Indeed, big budget or so-called A-feature Westerns . . . were a rarity. Of the 1,336 Westerns made by all producers between 1930 and 1941, only 66, or a mere 5 per cent, could be classed as A-features.'[44] Thirty-one of these A-features fall within the years 1939–41. Buscombe argues that 'There can be no simple explanation of why so few A-Westerns should have been produced in the middle years of the 1930s'. He outlines and dismisses the two most commonly offered determinants: the introduction of sound (fairly rapidly overcome); and the demand for a 'realist' response to the problems raised by the Depression and the rise of fascism in Europe (which he disqualifies by the evident popularity of 'escapist' entertainment such as Busby Berkeley spectaculars and the screwball comedy). He then adds his own determinant: the failure in 1930/31 of two prestige Westerns, *The Big Trail* (Fox, 1930) and *Cimarron* (RKO, 1931). 'Eventually', he summarises, 'things picked up; not solely as legend has it, because of the success of *Stagecoach* in 1939, though that undoubtedly helped'.[45]

With the material available to him, Buscombe falls short of offering a full explanation for the Western's revival. The return to Western production should be seen as part of an industry-wide response to declining box-office receipts during the 1937/38 season, led by exhibitors' demands for better quality product along the lines of *The Adventures of Robin Hood* and *Test Pilot*, two unqualified successes. Both films suggested to the studios that a return to 'outdoor dramas' might boost attendance. Furthermore, the industry's monopolistic practices were again under threat from government intervention which focused on the restraint of trade implied in blind and block booking and on the inability of 'innovative' independent producers to secure distribution and exhibition for their pictures.

According to Giuliana Muscio in *Hollywood's New Deal* (1997) 'pressure groups' promoted an image of the major studios as holding not only economic monopoly over the industry, but also monopolies of production and discourse which exercised 'decidedly "un-American" control over the thought of the entire nation'.[46] The studios sought to counter government action by avowedly shifting production away from properties thought to have little interest to audiences outside the major metropolitan centres, such as sophisticated urban dramas and screwball comedies, and towards outdoor and action pictures.

By privileging Westerns within their production schedules, the major studios hoped to win back the goodwill of independent ex-hibitors who felt their audience had been ill-served. The studios also meant to keep their metropolitan theatres busy, and to do this they had to sell Westerns to an audience they suspected was antipathetic to the genre. In particular, they gave these films all the attendant glamour and promotion that Hollywood usually reserved for more up-market properties. Creating female interest in Westerns was a major concern in the publicity that surrounded these films. This was achieved principally through casting the romantic male leads of the day—Robert Taylor, Tyrone Power, Errol Flynn, Nelson Eddy, Jimmy Cagney,

James Stewart, Henry Fonda, Joel McCrea, Clark Gable, Gary Cooper, Robert Young, Spencer Tracy, Franchot Tone—and ensuring that there was enough love interest in the stories to seduce those who had previously had no interest in the genre. In keeping with their aim of pleasing a wide and diverse audience, Westerns produced in this period offer significant innovations in settings, character types and, in particular, the roles given to women. Series Westerns had a substantial influence on these films both in terms of the incorporation of specific elements, such as the sidekick, and more generally in terms of their theme of the home under threat—something of an ur-text in films since the days of Griffith, but enlivened in the context of the Depresssion by the suggestion that the principal threat is economic dispossession. A-feature Westerns also sought to distance themselves from the negative connotations of series Westerns and their implied audience of lower-class men and boys, however. They did this through high production values, and also through the marketing of Westerns as both a more authentic *and* romantic vision of American history.

Intersecting with the independent exhibitors' concerns around restraint of trade were governmental and pressure group claims that, through self-censorship, Hollywood consolidated its monopolistic control over production content. In its attempts to break up Hollywood's stranglehold over the industry, the Department of Justice sought to prove that the Production Code Administration, as Richard Maltby has noted, used the Code to exercise 'a practical censorship over the entire industry, restricting the production of pictures treating controversial subjects and hindering the development of innovative approaches to drama or narrative by companies that might use innovation as a way of challenging the majors' monopoly power'.[47] Westerns were uniquely positioned to circumvent such accusations about the monopolistic effects of the Production Code while remaining under its authority. By this I mean that Westerns were the most amenable (and safest) platform for introducing a more forthright discussion of contemporary adult concerns in the realms of both politics and the representation of sexuality.[48]

Lea Jacobs has argued that self-regulation in the 1930s, rather than quasi-legally enforcing producers to cower to its demands, was 'above all a way of figuring out how stories deemed potentially offensive could be rewritten to make them acceptable'.[49] Controversial subject matter was not outlawed by the industry and its censors but 'treated as problems of narrative and form'. Filmmakers intentionally sought to construct key dramatic moments that potentially violated the

Production Code through what Jacobs has called an 'instability of meaning'[50], that is, the intentional creation of ambiguity. However, this needed to be set against an equal need on the part of the filmmakers to *reduce* ambiguity, so that a film remained both accessible and comprehensible to as wide an audience as possible. These are processes Jacobs usefully terms the industry's 'indirect modes of representation'.[51]

As Maltby has argued, this meant that the studios had to develop a system of representational conventions which allowed films to play to a heterogeneous audience without alienating any particular segment. Quoting Colonel Jason S. Joy (the director of the Studio Relations Committee), Maltby suggests that these representational conventions enabled conclusions to be 'drawn by the sophisticated mind, but would mean nothing to the unsophisticated and inexperienced'.[52] As allegories, Westerns were putatively 'accounted for' in terms of presupposed meanings: if these meanings subsequently proved controversial or embarrassing to the industry, a Western's historical 'authenticity' could be cited as alibi. In extremity, Westerns could be both innocuous historical adventures *and* politically loaded allegorical tracts that could speak effectively to the issues of the day. More usually, they represented a vivid and exciting visualisation of American history which spoke tacitly to contemporary tensions and concerns: Westerns proved to be particularly adaptable story forms for addressing internal and global conflicts.

5

Democratic Art
Westerns 1939–1941

For critics and reviewers, the renaissance of the Western at the end of the decade was greeted as a return to a more democratic and American form of picture making. In particular, the plaudits garnered by *Stagecoach* (1939) suggest that reviewers had wearied of the 'sophisticated' subjects that they perceived had come to dominate American cinema from the mid to late 1930s. The *Moving Picture Daily* review encapsulated this idea in its nostalgia for a pre-self-conscious cinema, which lay at the heart of why it liked Ford's film:

> This, ladies and gentlemen of the box office, is a Western after your own hearts, the kind with which Tom Mix, Bill Hart and Broncho Billy Anderson used to please all the people all the time, but beneficiary of all improvements the art-industry has accumulated since those pioneer delineators of the American pioneers rode the screen. This is, without question, the biggest and best such Western Hollywood has turned out since the screen became self-conscious.[1]

This point was echoed by the *National Board of Review* that rated the film 'exceptional'. *Stagecoach* 'brings things that are eternally delightful back out of the youth of the movies, with a freshness and vigor of something newly created'.[2] The *Film Daily* review emphasised the 'humanising' aspect of the screenplay and performances against Hollywood dramas of characters who live a charmed and otherworldly life among the urban elite:

A tempest film that stands out as one of the greatest human-action dramas. Might stand as one of the grandest outdoor pictures ever to reach the screen. It is a lusty, gutsy story of pioneer days, covering the post Civil War period in the West. It has one of the strongest groupings of really fine characterisations ever to be brought together in one picture. It has a story shot through with great thrills and action scenes and breathless suspense, and overall a vastly moving story of human beings facing their individual problems with courage and grim fortitude. It catches the spirit of the pioneering West and you feel every minute you watch these people are real, and that the things that they are doing are happening in real life before your eyes. And that's a feeling that few pictures can give.[3]

In the *New York Times*, Frank S. Nugent focused his admiration for the film on its rejection of formal artifice and its return to the 'grand old school' of filmmaking:

In one superbly expansive gesture which we (and the Music Hall) can call *Stagecoach*, John Ford has swept aside ten years of artifice and talkie compromise and has made a motion picture that sings the song of camera. It moves and how beautifully it moves across the plains of Arizona, skirting the sky reaching the Mesas of Monument Valley, beneath the piled up cloud banks that every photographer dreams about, and through all the old fashioned, but never really outdated, periods of prairie travel in the scalp raising 70s, when Geronimo's Apaches were on the war path. Here, in a sentence, is a movie of the grand old school, a genuine rib-thumper and a beautiful sight to see.[4]

The *New York Herald-Tribune* was particularly pleased by the democratic casting of the film with its 'no star cast':

The great director-writer team of John Ford and Dudley Nichols has turned out a stunning motion picture in *Stagecoach*. It is a glorified Western, if you like making melodramatic capital with skirmishes with Indians, the last minute rescue by the United States cavalry and the frontier town shootings, but it is a superlative example of its particular screen form. In Mr Nichols' taut scenario, acting material has been vitalised by striking situations and peopled with real characters. The no star cast has a balanced authority which is not often to be found in the performance of a photoplay. Furthermore Mr Ford has staged the offering with such visual beauty and dramatic power that it would have been notable without the foregoing benefactions.[5]

The *Hollywood Reporter* echoed these sentiments: 'One swelligant Western that even the carriage trade will go for. A whale of a good story that has brilliant direction, writing and action. No stars for come ons, but an all star cast of players that does itself proud. Play it and play it heavily, and give a good Western a chance to pay through the box office.'[6]

These reviews are celebrating Hollywood's rediscovery of an elemental cinema that caught again the dramatic potential of open spaces, filled by frantic movement through and across the screen; of obstacles and conflicts met and overcome; of characters who have the potential to redeem themselves, who point out the innate goodness in man rather than his potential for evil; of a world where desire does not lead to the hero's and heroine's destruction, which is not essentially corrupt, diseased, despoiled and perverted. This is what *Stagecoach* screenwriter Dudley Nichols had hoped to achieve. In an article written just prior to *Stagecoach*'s release, he set out his and Ford's intentions: 'we sought for the old Western technique which they forgot when sound came in . . . It is really going back to first principles. That is what we tried to do in this picture.'[7] Westerns in general, and *Stagecoach* in particular, reaffirm America's institutions and ideas of individualism. The audience is taken back to times less complicated, where they are able to thrill again at the spectacle of American cinema: 'Under John Ford's clever and masterly direction the audience at the Music Hall is transported back to the pioneer days of the old west and then taken for a ride. And what a ride!'[8] 'Like any first-rate movie, *Stagecoach* is something to see and not to write about. Only in movies can the spectator be snatched along with what he is watching, always physically close, with all his most vivid senses, to the heart of the action. This movie does that.'[9] To paraphrase Frank Nugent, its reviewers saw *Stagecoach* as representing a cinema that sings the song of America. But this was the effect, not the cause of the Western's renaissance.

OUTDOOR PICTURES LEAD, SAYS JOHN FORD.
John Ford, director, who recently completed *Stagecoach* for Walter Wanger, visiting in N.Y. last week, made the observation that 'outdoor films with an action motif are staging a comeback and they will dominate 1939 production. Westerns are once more rising in popularity.'[10]

The 1937/38 season had seen a general fall in box-office takings. Hollywood's response, at least publicly, was to shift production away from sophisticated urban comedies and musicals and hope for an upswing in returns at the box office with its switch to outdoor dramas. 'HOLLYWOOD HOT FOR ACTION PIX' read the headline in an April 1938 edition of the *Hollywood Reporter*: 'All Studios Now Turning To Virile Outdoor Drama As Hypodermic For Box Office':

> Spurred by public demand at the box office for outdoor action dramas, Hollywood is turning its production facilities to making pictures of this type, all the way from $7000 quickie Westerns to million-dollar Technicolor classics, in the heaviest market offensive of its kind ever attempted.

The article outlines both the majors' and independents' future productions, making much of what it considers to be 'dressed up Westerns' like *The Adventures of Marco Polo* and *The Adventures of Robin Hood*. It concludes: 'All in All, the Westerns (or what you might call such) have it. More than 300 are planned for the year. The cowboy is in the saddle, and thar's gold in them thar saddle bags.'[11]

The following month, the journal reported on Warners' sales convention: 'Gradwell Sears stated that action will be stressed in all films. "What has been wrong with a good many pictures in the past few years has been lack of action" he said, "Moving pictures, in their very nature, must move . . . Our sales slogan is: Warner Brothers [*sic*] will give you Action in 1938–39." '[12] The success of *Test Pilot* and *Robin Hood* at the tag end of the 1937/38 season was seen as the main reason for dropping 'anything that smacks of the parlor and society drama'. Exhibitors' complaints about 'weak screen fare' were blamed on adaptations, presumably referring to sophisticated novels with urban settings. The turn to outdoor pictures was also, according to the *Hollywood Reporter*, a turn to original screenplays, though this is not supported by evidence. Many of the films produced in the 1939/40 season still relied on pre-sold properties, most notably *Gone With the Wind*. The trend in action films was, however, confirmed in January 1939 in a report in the *Motion Picture Herald*: 'Hollywood's 39–40 season plans fewer B's, more action . . . Action pictures will be emphasised. Not one Glamour-Girl Musical or Screwball comedy indicated thus far.'[13]

The picture of Hollywood's production plans represented here— downscaling of B productions, the emphasis on outdoor action dramas, the plugging of original screenplays, and the rejection of society dramas and comedies—was intended to meet the demands of exhibitors, whose protests (in particular around blind and block booking) it needed to forestall if it was to fight off government antitrust litigation. As in the late 1920s and early 1930s, the production of high-profile Westerns was one means, amongst others, that Hollywood used to placate exhibitors outside the large metropolitan centres. The production of Westerns was deployed not just to ease the anger of disaffected exhibitors by giving them what they demanded. My analysis of primary material suggests this was also part of a wider industry response to the changing international and domestic political environment.

As the new year began, the pages of the exhibitors' trade magazine *Motion Picture Herald* continued to chart the shift to large-scale production of Western films or, as the major studios called them, 'Outdoor Pictures'. This trend did not go by without comment, yet neither was it seen as particularly remarkable. In part this was due to the wider industry-led debate (within which much of the discussion of the new Westerns is found) on how Hollywood should respond to the escalating conflicts in Europe and Asia. This debate was given a public profile in the autumn of 1938 with a speech on patriotism by Harry Warner. The speech was part of a concerted effort by Warner Bros. to promote a series of historical two-reelers as their initial contribution to Hollywood's 'Americanism' movement. In January, RKO Pathé announced it was also 'join[ing] the move toward the treatment of "Americanism" in films' and was producing a 'series of educational and patriotic shorts designed to combat Communist and Nazi propaganda in the States'.[14] 'Americanism' in Hollywood parlance was the active promotion, through its films and other channels available to it, of American themes. In January 1939 the *New York Times* carried the following report on one of Jack Warner's speeches:

> 'Defence of American democracy has been left almost entirely to the press,' J.L. Warner said this week. 'Through our medium we can reach from 40,000,000 to 70,000,000 with a single picture . . . We know from personal experience the value of American philosophy. We are descendants of immigrants and we know why our fathers came to America . . . We believe that anyone who is anti-semitic, anti-catholic, anti-protestant or anti-anything that has gone into building this country is anti-American. The visual power of the screen is tremendous and we propose to use it to acquaint Americans with their heritage.'[15]

How was Hollywood to deal with a market that was becoming increasingly politicised, both internationally and on the domestic scene? How could it manage, in the words of one contemporary commentator, Douglas W. Churchill in the *New York Times*, to revise 'its attitude that the screen should strive to please all and offend none' without damaging itself at the box office?[16]

Richard Maltby has argued that 'the overwhelming majority of [Hollywood's] political activity was immediately defensive in nature . . . for the primary purpose of sustaining the profitability of the industry's enterprises'.[17] During 1938 and early 1939, in the pages of *Motion Picture Herald* and the *New York Times*, the independent producer Walter Wanger asked for latitude to produce films that were 'free to mirror all the pulsating vitality of modern life. When a free screen replaces our present set up we will give proper service to democracy.' Wanger, who tirelessly promoted himself to the media as a radical in a world of conservatives, was not the only industry voice arguing for a change in policy, but he was certainly the loudest.[18] His argument was answered by Martin Quigley, publisher of *Motion Picture Herald* and one of the original architects of the Production Code. Quigley vociferously maintained that any attempt to deal overtly with contemporary world affairs would divide audiences and hit box-office returns. In a February 1939 editorial in *Motion Picture Herald*, Terry Ramsaye acted as a broker between these dissenting voices:

> PROGRESS and PROBLEMS: the wider angle of the screen materials of tomorrow
> The waning of the foreign market, from Berlin to Baghdad, and the rising tides of consciousness at home tend to bring an equivalent state of consumer non-acceptance for the screen.
> A consequence among the many manifestations, is a tendency, in view of the dwindling of the appeals and profits of internationalism, to turn to an acute, maybe too acute, nationalism.
> There's a wise old saying: 'easy does it'.[19]

Productions were, however, already outstripping this debate. A week later the *Motion Picture Herald* charted the inexorable rise of films with a nationalistic slant:

> Of all the trends towards types contemplated for 1939–40, 'Americanism' is the most outstanding, numerically at least.
> Growing out of the long threatened international strife, 'Americanism' and 'patriotism' were made subjects of motion

picture treatment as long ago as last Fall. Now deeply embedded in film fabrication, the theme is certain to continue well into the new year.[20]

The article cited forty-three feature and eighty-four short subjects on 'Americanism' that were either in release or planned for the coming season. Hollywood would negotiate the volatile arena of world affairs through the deployment of 'Americanism'. In its turn to insular concerns, Hollywood hoped to appeal to both isolationist and interventionist sympathisers and to placate its remaining foreign markets by apparently offering its product as being free of any geopolitical alignments.

In March, Will H. Hays offered his commentary and qualified blessing on the theme of 'Americanism' in his annual report to the industry. It represented a major shift from the previous year's report, which had heavily cautioned against the production of partisan films that could upset both American pressure groups and the remaining international trading partners: 'The function of the entertainment screen is to entertain . . . There is no other criterion.'[21] Hays' *volte face* can be read in the following quotation from the 1939 report:

> Through the exhibition of American pictures on the screens of the world, our country maintains a great communications service to many peoples with whom we wish to be at peace. Government-controlled news services may misrepresent our democratic ideals. Government or controlled broadcasting may bleat out distortions of our policies, but American pictures, even when censored by foreign agencies, necessarily carry their own refutations of the alleged failures of our ideals, our policies, our efforts and our system. In this lies our continuing responsibility for the production and distribution of such films abroad as will give a balanced picture of American life.[22]

The report was widely commented on in the trade press and in the daily broadsheets, but as Maltby has argued, this new-found support for a more 'vital' entertainment had less to do with anti-Nazi and anti-Communist sentiments than with the need to address the MPPDA's 'immediate political and legal situation, in which the censorship of the movies—as opposed to movie content—was in danger of becoming the issue'.[23] It was an attempt to forestall antitrust litigation which would use the Association's regulation of movie subjects as evidence of the industry's monopolistic practices. Maltby notes:

the need to contain the jurisdiction of the Production Code in order not to embroil the MPPDA in a violation of the anti-trust laws had what was on the face of it an unlikely effect on the content of motion pictures, encouraging, or at least acquiescing in their use of more politically controversial content as a means of demonstrating that the 'freedom of the screen' was not hampered by the operations of the PCA, and that in this respect the Neely Bill to prohibit block booking and blind buying was unnecessary.[24]

Hays' appeal for a 'balanced picture of American life' was an appeal to moderation. He recognised that 'there is nothing incompatible between the best interests of the box office and the kind of entertainment that raises the level of audience appreciation'. He also observed, however, that in *Snow White and the Seven Dwarfs* 'no isms whatever were discussed . . . and the millions who hailed it did not seem to miss its lack of social significance'.[25] But what was socially significant and which films (apart from *Snow White*) were free of 'isms'? In his bid to get Hollywood producing 'progressive' pictures in defence of democracy, Walter Wanger had made the point that 'Gilbert and Sullivan operettas were as much propaganda as they were entertainment when they were written'.[26] And as Paramount producer Albert Lewin noted, the 'Knights of the Round Table . . . would have certain political implications, which grown ups will realise . . . an affirmation of democratic and Anglo Saxon patriotism'.[27] Hollywood historian Ruth Vasey has recorded how Wolfgang Reinhardt, while working on the script for *Juarez* (Warner Bros., 1939), 'frankly intended that "every child must be able to realize that Napoleon, in his Mexican adventure, is none other than Mussolini plus Hitler in their Spanish adventure"'.[28]

It was, then, to historical allegory that the industry turned, and it did so specifically through Westerns. The Western as allegory was picked up in a number of commentaries on the genre's renaissance. In April 1939, the *New York Times* published a feature article on the phenomenon:

> The current cycle, touching high with *Stagecoach* . . . has rung a few changes on the old mess-house chimes . . . *Let Freedom Ring* rang up the score for democracy. Others like *Stand Up and Fight*, *Oklahoma Kid* and *Dodge City*, have made a few topical gestures . . . This renaissance is due in part to natural causes, such as the inevitable cycle that follows a successful picture, and, in some measure, to Hollywood's rediscovery of America. While the industry is busy with propaganda pictures designed to create a

national consciousness, the Western is employed as the logical medium in which to expound the American philosophy and to show that right thinking, clean living and a devotion to duty are the ingredients necessary to success. That some of the outdoor pictures will make no attempt to conceal this propaganda goes without saying: most however, will strive for adroitness and preach in general terms and by inference.[29]

Time magazine went even further in making sense of Hollywood's new-found patriotism, beginning its review of *Let Freedom Ring* with the following insights:

The latest Hollywood discovery of box office lures is the value of Americanism. Flag waving of the George Cohan variety has always been a box office standby, but the cinema's new patriotism goes deeper into the last refuge, it stems from 1) a sudden awareness that in failing to capitalise the forces which produced the New Deal, John L. Lewis [President of the United Mine Workers and one of the chief architects of the Congress of Industrial Organisations that unionised unskilled labour] and the Wagner Act [guaranteed labour's right to organise and to collective bargaining], the cinema has missed a golden opportunity; and 2) the general eagerness of producers to forestall a wave of U.S. anti-semitism, which they greatly dread.[30]

The major Hollywood studios may not have dealt particularly cogently and coherently with the New Deal and workers' rights, or at least not as overtly as Republic Pictures with its John Wayne and Gene Autry series Westerns discussed in an earlier chapter, but they took these issues on board to a greater extent with their new Westerns.[31] Equally, fighting homegrown anti-semitism may have been one of Hollywood's motivations for dealing with American subjects, and it is certainly explicit in Jack Warner's speech quoted earlier, but other publicity around the topic gave this patriotism a much broader and indeed international remit.

In April 1939 *Motion Picture* magazine published an appeal, under the heading 'LET FREEDOM RING', by 'fifty-six of Hollywood's most prominent personalities' for 'a new declaration of democratic independence'. In an open petition, they urged the President and Congress to end all economic connections between America and Germany. Calling on the Declaration of Independence as their guide, they accused 'the leaders of Nazi Germany, as a ruler was accused in

1776, of a "design to reduce the world under absolute despotism" '.[32] This petition, and the following month's article 'Hollywood Declares War on the Dictators', represented something of a political fissure in the magazine's usual coverage of new releases and the loves and lives of Hollywood's stars.[33] The article begins by setting out the notable events in Hollywood during the early months of the year—the ending of the search for Scarlett O'Hara, Nelson Eddy's marriage, Clark Gable's divorce—and then adds:

> All of these events have been more or less surprising to a large portion of the population. They have been news. But—ten years from now, or even one year from now, who will care? They won't change the course of history one iota. But something else has happened in Hollywood since January first that *will* make 1939 remembered. Hollywood has declared war on the dictators. Hollywood has finally realized something that the dictators have known for a long time: Democracy won't vanish from the earth until it vanishes from America. And American movies can awaken people to the attractions of the right to life, liberty and the pursuit of happiness'.[34]

Noting Hollywood's prior attempts to placate the dictators, the article continues to explain why 'Hollywood's remaining audience isn't easily entertained. Especially by the same old story about boy-meets-girl, boy-pursues-girl, boy-wins-girl'. It wants 'movies, like the newspapers and radio, to keep up with the excitement of the times. It wants the movies to say something vigorous about the things that matter more to free people today than ever before.'[35] The piece concludes with a long survey of the films, either in release or imminent, which exploit Hollywood's 'rediscovery of America':

> Until the spring of 1939, no producer ever thought of asking audiences to stand up during a picture. But during *Let Freedom Ring*, audiences not only stand up, but cheer, hearing Nelson Eddy sing, 'My Country 'tis of thee, Sweet land of liberty . . .' M-G-M's *Northwest Passage*, like Paramount's *Union Pacific*, Warners' *Dodge City*, 20th Century-Fox's *Panama Canal* and Selznick's *Gone With the Wind*, will reawaken America's never-say-die spirit.[36]

This kind of didactic coverage in the fan press meant that, as an allegory for the state of democracy, and by extension for the state of

America at the turn of the decade, the Western would be recognised by an audience who consumed subsidiary forms of discourse on the movies. To this end, Hollywood worked with instantly recognisable historical subjects—the Oklahoma land rush, the taming of frontier towns, the coming of the railroads, Indian attacks, pioneers, covered wagons, and historical figures like Jesse James.

The use of allegory allowed for sufficient ambiguity around a given film's meanings. Making it sufficiently obtuse, Hollywood could always deny calling too strongly for American involvement in the war in Europe—whatever the sentiments of individual filmmakers. In a series of small advertisements running through a March issue of *Motion Picture Herald*, Republic Pictures marketed the Richard Dix Western *Man of Conquest* through the now firmly established rhetoric of Americanism. The lead copy used a rhetorical slogan that linked the film to the isolationist America First movement ('America—First, Last—Always!'). Under this appeared dialogue quotations from the film's hero Sam Houston which qualify apparently overt support for isolation:

> 'You're afraid to go to war, that's all—and it ain't nothing to be ashamed of. The man that says he's not afraid to face gun-fire is a liar and a fool'.

> 'But ther [sic] are things Americans have always been afraid of—things they've hated worse than gun-fire an' one them's dictatorship'.[37]

By referring to both the America First movement and defence against dictators, the promotion of the film managed to align itself with both isolationist and interventionist sentiments. The same attempt to placate the contradictory positions of isolationist and interventionist platforms is evident in *Let Freedom Ring*. The *Motion Picture Daily* concludes its review: 'Eddy delivers his "America First Last and Always" narration, Miss Bruce begins "America", everyone joins the chorus and the villain slides out of the picture'.[38] Jim Wade's (Nelson Eddy) triumphalist speech at the end of the film may espouse an America First platform but the major thrust of the narrative is concerned with the overthrowing of powerful dictatorial forces in the shape of the railroad owners who would turn their workers (all recent immigrants from Europe) into virtual slaves, and who have, by tyrannical methods, confiscated the land belonging to small farmers.

14. *Let Freedom Ring*
Nelson Eddy's character organises the railroad workers to stand
against their employer's tyranny (note the ethnic stereotyping of
the workers)

Jim Wade fights back by setting up an underground newspaper
through which he organises the farmers and 'Americanises' the railroad
workers. The championing of free speech becomes the means by which
the implacable contradiction between interventionist and isolationist
camps is tenuously resolved, an idea echoed in *Man of Conquest*:

> Up in Washington you said we'd buried freedom under a pile of
> dirty politics, you tell Sam Houston to just remember America is
> still the land of the free, and there is many a brow beaten people
> who would trade their dictatorships in a minute for a good dose of
> our dirty politics. Not that our brand of freedom ain't got its
> faults, couldn't help it being run by ornery humans like
> Congressmen and you and me, but I reckon the United States is
> still the only place where a man can cuss the President out loud
> and all the President can do is cuss back, or else go fishing, that's
> what I call democracy.

In review, Hollywood's engagement with issues around the defence of democracy and Americanism foregrounded the Westerns' adaptability as national and political allegory; the production emphasis on outdoor and action pictures, though, might better be read as responding to the need to placate exhibitors in order to nullify government litigation. Between them, these strategies would count for little if Hollywood could not overcome the general perception that A-feature Westerns lacked appeal to a large sector of the cinema public—the female audience. It sought to do this by casting male stars with a proven appeal to women and by highlighting women's roles within these productions.

Casting the Western

> Last summer [Joe Pasternak—producer] looked at Gene Autry's fan mail and took heed.
>
> (*Picture Play*, February 1940[39])

In a January 1939 review of the George O'Brien picture *Arizona Legion*, the writer doubted that the forthcoming slew of 'outdoor pictures' from the major studios would have much to offer above the usual series Western fare:

> In the next few months Hollywood will supply theatres with many stirring outdoor pictures: *Stand Up and Fight, Song of the West, Union Pacific, Wagons Westward, Gunga Din, Jesse James, Oklahoma Kid, Dodge City* to name a few. Four or five more pictures like *Arizona Legion* could be made for the cost of any of those mentioned, yet their substance will be that which is the substance of the O'Brien production.[40]

One of the principal means that the studios used to overcome this kind of negative perception was to cast the leading male stars of the day, a lesson they had learnt from their promotion of *Cimarron, The Big Trail* and *Billy the Kid* at the beginning of the decade. Translating and adapting a star's persona to fit the equally promotable notions of historical authenticity and verisimilitude, however, raised some not wholly supportive comments from the trades and general media alike. Frank S. Nugent in the *New York Times* expressed his dismay at the thought of Tyrone Power, Robert Taylor and Nelson Eddy as cowboys:

It isn't quite so great a shock to find Jimmy Cagney doubling as the *The Oklahoma Kid*, with Humphrey Bogart's villainous assistance. Joel McCrea has been so many things we won't mind his presence in Mr. De Mille's *Union Pacific*. Richard Dix of *Man of Conquest*, a biography of San Houston of Texas, is not entirely unacquainted with horseflesh. But Errol Flynn, in spite of his training in piracy, Robin Hood-ing and being a perfect specimen, is going to look mighty strange on a bronch's [*sic*] back in *Dodge City*. And it probably won't be long before we meet Clark Gable in the old Bloody Gulch saloon or spot Shirley Temple as the girlhood of Calamity Jane.[41]

Shirley Temple would make her Western debut in the pro-British *Susannah of the Mounties* (20th Century-Fox, 1939) and Clark Gable made his first appearance in the outdoor cycle (not counting *Gone With the Wind*) in the roughneck drama *Boom Town* (Paramount, 1940). The Western roles for Eddy, Power and Taylor were designed to increase their box-office appeal, which was seen to be limited to a feminine audience: 'By this picture [*Stand Up and Fight*] MGM hopes for all time to remove the stigma of "pretty boy" from Taylor's name, thus surrendering the field to Tyrone Power'.[42] Reviewing *Stand Up and Fight*, *Motion Picture Herald* noted its emphasis on the fights between Taylor's and Wallace Beery's characters, and observed: 'After this terrific beating, he [Taylor] should be jake with the masculine trade'.[43] *Stand Up and Fight* was sold as an 'adventure-romance', which was echoed in the film's advertising copy : 'THEY BUILT A NEW AMERICA WITH GLORY AND GUNS . . . THEY WERE <u>MEN</u> THAT WOMEN COULD LOVE.'[44] *Motion Picture* magazine, however, was not so happy with Taylor's change of roles:

> He's pretty so what? Besides you don't have to take Taylor on his 'face value.' He has proven himself an actor and when people go to the movies there are only two things they want—good characterizations and a good story. But, Metro, determined to make a he-man of Taylor scouted around until they hit on Forbes Parkhill's [novel] *Stand Up and Fight* as the vehicle to sell the new Taylor . . . The story has action and suspense and love interest, too, but we'd rather have Taylor minus the bloody nose. The gentleman-lover role is far more becoming and natural to Bob.[45]

A similar response to the 'toughening up' of Power was recorded in the letter pages of the June issue of *Motion Picture* magazine. An open

15. *Stand Up and Fight*
'Jake with the masculine trade'—Robert Taylor and Wallace Beery

letter to Tyrone Power from a fan bemoaned the fact that he played an outlaw: 'I have been disappointed and sad that the studio would make such a mistake as casting you in *Jesse James*. You were very good in it as far as acting goes but Jesse James was a scoundrel and you made him a hero.'[46] The writer finished by hoping that Power would return to the kind of roles he played in *Alexander's Ragtime Band* and *Love is News*.

This letter was, however, later balanced by a Southern reader's appreciation of Henry Fonda's characterisation as Frank James: 'We of the deep South appreciate more and more the excellent work of Henry Fonda. Whether he was born in the South or elsewhere matters little, for Hank has that unusual quality other actors lack—the quality to portray accurately the kind of people we come in contact with daily. He's typically Southern—from his natural drawl to his easy-going home-folksy personality.'[47] *Stand Up and Fight* and *Jesse James* broadened the range of roles available to Taylor and Power, exemplified by their characterisation of gangsters in, respectively, *Johnny Eager* (1941) and *Johnny Apollo* (1940). Taylor's ability to play outlaws was confirmed when he was cast in the title role of *Billy the Kid*. On the other hand, operating as a high-class Gene Autry, Nelson Eddy gained little masculine credibility from his flirtation with the genre.

Westerns not only offered the possibility of an image of unassailable masculinity for its pretty-boy male leads, but also an arena in which they could grow old gracefully. In the 1920s and early to mid-1930s, middle age was not seen as a disability in playing the male lead in Westerns: 'A he-man is a he-man and must remain so. And if he doesn't slip, his screen life is far longer than that of the less elemental players.'[48] The genre therefore became one means to elongate the screen careers of Hollywood's romantic male stars. It may not have been a pressing problem for Taylor, Power and Flynn who were 28, 26 and 30 years old respectively in 1939, but it was becoming acute for Gary Cooper, who was 39 when he made *The Westerner* (United Artists, 1940), and, as Robert Sklar has noted, it was a cause for real anxiety for Warner Bros. in the immediate post-war years with regard to Cagney and Bogart.[49]

For Nugent, Cagney and Bogart posed less of a shock in their role as cowboys because there was no perceived lack of testosterone on their part. There was, however, a bigger problem in adapting their 'city boy' personae to a Western milieu. In *The Oklahoma Kid* (Warner Bros., 1939) the story begins with the opening of the Cherokee Strip to settlers and some fine visionary words from one of the would-be founders of Tulsa City:

> All around are thousands of acres of the richest land in Oklahoma and it will all be peopled by this time tomorrow, by folks that'll need doctors, lawyers, merchants. It's a new start for all of us. But it's gonna mean a lot of hard work and it's gonna mean sticking together for the common good.

16. *Oklahoma Kid*
Transplanted 'city kids'—Humphrey Bogart and James Cagney

The irony of this speech, and an earlier one about Oklahoma having the finest farming land in the country, delivered by the President, would not have been missed by a contemporary audience used to seeing newsreels of Oklahoma transformed into a dust bowl. But the film has no truck whatsoever with farmers, concentrating instead on a city built on a compromise with crime. The good citizens are forced to fight a battle that they cannot possibly win against the forces of evil, led by a malevolent Whip McCord (Humphrey Bogart). McCord and his men turn with surprising haste from outlaws into 'The McCord Corporation', and the film manages to exploit Bogart's gangster credentials to suggest a malign capitalism which has corrupted the agrarian dream implied in the founder's opening speech.

The man in the middle is the Oklahoma Kid (James Cagney). Cagney is his usual charismatic self and plays the role with his tongue firmly in his cheek. The trade press advertising for the film offers the kind of authenticity and novelty upon which the other films in the cycle were marketed. Copy lines alongside a photograph of two-gun Cagney, legs astride, exclaim: 'He Means Business' and 'Never before a

17. *Jesse James*
'A different kind of hold-up' Jesse (Tyrone Power) and Zee James
(Nancy Kelly)

frontier epic like this . . . because there never was a star like this to play it!' Nevertheless, *Motion Picture* magazine, no doubt with its tongue also in its cheek, still managed to emphasise the romantic element in the film, provided by Rosemary Lane: 'the romance is brought forth in interludes the minute the gun-fire ceases'.[50] For the *Film Daily* eviewer these distinctions did not amount to much. He saw the *Oklahoma Kid* as simply a Western: 'They are selling [*Oklahoma Kid*] as a frontier epic, and if you put it down as a glorified Western, with the added attraction of a name like Cagney's, that would be about the right classification'.[51] Cagney's parodic performance was one way of introducing male stars to the genre. Romantic male leads like Tyrone Power and Robert Taylor played the role of the cowboy with rather more conviction.

In advertising and other promotional gambits, the studios took care to highlight the romantic elements in these films. The promotional stills for the big Western productions used in fan magazines such as *Motion Picture* (aimed almost wholly at a female readership) usually featured both the male and female leads lovingly clasping one another. Under the lead copy 'A DIFFERENT KIND OF HOLD-UP FOR JESSE JAMES', a photograph showed Tyrone Power and Nancy Kelly in a lovers' embrace.[52] The image was repeated in the advertisement for the film in the same issue. The copy read: 'He was hunted; but he was human! And there was one—gentle yet dauntless—who flung her life away—into his arms.'[53] The magazine's review in the following issue stressed that 'This isn't just another saga of the West but a meaty, dramatic story that will appeal to all audiences'.[54]

The A-feature Western's focus on romantic engagement meant that the women in these films were given a prominent role. Indeed it is arguable that their concerns were dominant. Within the narratives, much is made of the suffering and sacrifice that the women go through in order to establish a safe and permanent community. In *Jesse James* the audience is constantly reminded of the suffering caused to Jesse's wife Zee by his absence and increasingly criminal lifestyle. *Drums Along the Mohawk* opens with the marriage of Gilbert (Henry Fonda) and Lana Martin (Claudette Colbert). The splendour and comfort of her premarital lifestyle are immediately contrasted with the primitive circumstances of Gil's farm. The film revolves around Lana's problems. Gil is given a stick by the Indian Blueback to beat her with, but he never has recourse to its use as it becomes evident that it is her strength which will see them through the difficulties ahead. Olivia de Havilland's character in *Dodge City* similarly struggles with frontier life, revealing an ability to endure and showing herself to be a worthy match for the film's hero. Like *Dodge City, Frontier Marshal* (20th Century-Fox, 1939), based on the Wyatt Earp story by Stuart N. Lake, is ostensibly about the taming of a frontier town, but it gives an equal emphasis to the two female leads who vie for the love of Doc Halliday.

18. *Arizona*
Phoebe Titus (Jean Arthur): 'what a woman, nothing but iron from
top-knot to gizzard'

Like de Havilland's character, Sarah (Nancy Kelly) is an outsider who
shows herself to be equal to the demands of the frontier, while in the
closing scene the archetypal saloon girl Jerry (Binnie Barnes) shoots
the film's villain after he gets away from the hero. As the daughter of a
railroad navvy, Barbara Stanwyck dominates most of the scenes in

Union Pacific. Blake Cantrill (Taylor) in *Stand Up and Fight* is matched against the Boston beauty Susan (Florence Rice) who owns and eventually runs a frontier haulage company. Before Taylor's character is transformed into a frontiersman, Susan confronts him: 'All you can think about is preening the few shining feathers you have left and walking up to the newest girl in town—well if you're a cross-section of the Southern gentleman then I'm sorrier for the South than I am for you'. Cantrill responds, 'Ladies don't talk to men like that down here. We've made them a pretty charming place and they keep it, you understand . . . neither you nor any other lady is going to tell me what to do.' But she does. Her actions lead to his transformation; he must meet *her* exacting demands.

The paragon of this female character is found in the figure of Miss Phoebe Titus (Jean Arthur) in *Arizona* (Columbia, 1940): 'What a woman, nothing but iron from top-knot to gizzard' as she is described towards the end of the picture. This is Jean Arthur's film, and she receives the sole star billing. *Variety* noted that she 'dominates throughout with strongly convincing performance of a pioneer girl, shading character believably from hardness in dealing with men to softening with romance with Holden'.[55] Apart from a few minor expository scenes, she is constantly on view. The picture is an intimate romance masquerading as an epic. Phoebe is the only American woman in antebellum Tucson. To make her living she bakes pies—an idea of the domestic woman that is parodied throughout the film—but she dreams of owning the best cattle ranch in the territory. In some respects Arthur's role is an extension of the Calamity Jane character she played in *The Plainsman*. She is introduced facing down two men who have stolen her savings. She asks and needs no help from anyone: 'I don't ask or get favours for being what I was born'. She sets up a freighting business, and in her drive to get the ranch she meets the villainous entreaties of both Indians and white men with equal vigour and skill. Her romance with the drifter Pete (William Holden) is carried out entirely on her own terms, and although she spends most of the film in pants, there is absolutely no question of her transgressing her gender. Pete's eventual confrontation with the villain does not constitute a diminution or subordination of her preeminence, but a final test for the man she has chosen to prove his worth. The gunfight is not shown; rather, the film stays with her as she awaits the outcome. Given the context of much of the critical writing on representations of women in Westerns, Arthur's character is an extraordinary realisation, but within the context of the 1939/40 cycle of Westerns which give

19. *Destry Rides Again*
The film's cast pose in front of the ornate and grand bar in the
Last Chance saloon

equal space to female and male roles it is only relatively remarkable. In *Belle Starr—The Bandit Queen* (20th Century-Fox, 1941), starring Gene Tierney, even the figure of the outlaw would be played by a woman.

In *Destry Rides Again*, the dramatic tension is supplied by swinging backwards and forwards between competing versions of the masculine and feminine ideal. The resolution of the conflict between Destry (James Stewart) and the villainous Kent (Brian Donlevy) is brought about not only through Destry's eventual move towards violent confrontation, but also through the townswomen's move to become the major force in clearing out the corrupt. As the gingham horde march on the Last Chance saloon with farm implements raised high, they appear, at least temporarily, to be a wholly unstoppable force. With order restored, Boris, a Russian immigrant and one of Destry's barely competent deputies, can finally stamp his authority over his wife, a woman who had called him by her first husband's name, Callahan. Boris now reclaims his rightful name and throws out the portrait of Callahan that hung above his and his wife's bed, replacing it with a picture of himself in a ten-gallon hat; he is born again as cowboy and American.

Boris's Americanisation was rhymed in the publicity that surrounded the film, particularly in interviews with Marlene Dietrich. In one case a reporter feigned incredulity upon hearing Marlene Dietrich and Joe Pasternak share reminiscences of reading in their youth the German author Karl May's Western stories. Much mirth was produced by the stories' inaccuracies:

> 'Look at that Indian on the cover', chuckled [Charles] Winninger. 'He looks like Ernst Lubitsch. 'That is Winnetou, the big chief', Pasternak explained . . . 'Listen to this'. Then he read '. . . Die Augen des Indianer's spruehten vor Freude. "Sharley!" murmelte er'. ' "Sharley!" What is this—a Baron Munchhausen story?' exclaimed Brian Donleavy. 'That "Sharley" sounds like a Jack Pearl script'.

The report continues, noting on the way that May, who died before 1914, 'didn't live to see his German boys picked off in the war by the dead-shot American cowboys and Indians they had read about in his books'. In its promotion of the film and those involved in its making, the article is tacitly acknowledging the international fascination with Westerns, while confirming their American specificity and their assimilationist potential: 'When I read *The Black Mustang* I was worse than the kids now with "Hi-yo, Silver". I wanted to take the first boat over here and be a cowboy'. says Pasternak. 'So did I', smiled Miss Dietrich, 'And here I am in a Western at last'. The article concludes on a note about the historical accuracy of the film in contradistinction to German Westerns: 'Marlene's first essay in early Americana was as scrupulously documented as a baccalaureate thesis'.[56]

Initially, *Destry Rides Again* was to be a more or less straight adaptation of the Max Brand novel. The synopsis of the story logged with the PCA on 22 December 1938 already indicates James Stewart in the title role, but by 2 September 1939 the script had been completely rewritten to accommodate Dietrich. A new title was proposed, *The Man from Montana*, echoing the title of the biography of isolationist Senator Burton K. Wheeler, the book on which *Mr Smith Goes to Washington* (Columbia, 1939), starring James Stewart, was loosely based.[57] This title appears to have been only a passing gesture, however, and the film went into production a week later under its original title. Any viewer familiar with the best-selling Max Brand book or its earlier Tom Mix adaptation would have had their expectations as confounded as the inhabitants of Bottleneck, who expect a taciturn, super-lawman and instead get an unassuming homespun philosopher in the mould of Will Rogers.[58]

Dietrich's star persona as a European vamp is reworked in *Destry* through casting her as Frenchy, a fallen high-class Creole (someone of indeterminate ethnic origins) prostitute from New Orleans. She brings to Westerns an overt sexuality that is usually coded in terms of European decadence, but is here held within an American arena: 'Marlene Dietrich is straight from the old West . . . and we mean Mae!' as one bit of advertising copy put it. *Variety* noted that 'this is a deglamorised Dietrich in extreme opposition to her more recent roles . . . Miss Dietrich seems more natural and alluring in this dynamic part as a dance hall queen than in all the languid siren roles she has ever played.'[59] Frank S. Nugent in the *New York Times* makes a similar point: 'Typecasting, the bane of the film industry, has rarely been more successfully pied than by producer Joe Pasternak in his *Destry Rides Again* . . . with a sweep of his Hungarian fist he has taken Marlene Dietrich off her high horse and placed her in a horse opera and has converted James Stewart last seen as Washington's Mr Smith into a hard-hitting son of an old sagebrush sheriff.'[60] The casting of *Destry Rides Again* is also brought to the fore in the *New York Herald*: 'Here is a part which is not far distant from the one she played in *Blue Angel*. It should convince anyone that Hollywood made a bad mistake by trying to change her into a sophisticated glamor girl.'[61] According to the *Motion Picture Herald*: 'Miss Dietrich plays a barroom entertainer gyp-artist and the girl pal of the town badmen that nobody has played in years, if ever, and only Mae West might. The knockabout fight by Miss Dietrich and Una Merkel so widely publicised in the cinema columns is wilder, hotter and longer than they said it was, nothing since Pola Negri's passion has approached it'.[62]

In these reviews, all of which were smitten with the film in general and Dietrich in particular, much was made of the distance placed between Dietrich's recent depictions of sophisticated and otherworldly sexuality and this new more earthy and worldly representation of her sexual allure.[63] This idea was summed up in the coarse and bawdy line from the film which accompanies the image of Frenchy slipping money between her breasts: 'Thar's gold in them thar hills'. The PCA had demanded the elimination of this bit of dialogue, but it remained in the early release prints. Both literally and figuratively, the Last Chance saloon was a long way from the character and social milieu that

Dietrich inhabited in *Angel* (Ernst Lubitsch, 1937), a point obviously recognised by the filmmakers when they changed the character's name from 'Angel' in initial drafts of the script to 'Frenchy'.[64]

The Americanisation of Dietrich had a much more serious side, however. In an editorial on the Americanisation of Hollywood's pictures in *Motion Picture* magazine, Larry Reid writes:

> haven't we had enough of foreign star importations? No American star would be accepted on a foreign screen unless this star spoke its language perfectly. Over here we consider it cute if the foreigner speaks English with an accent. We call it charm. Over there an American accenter would be called an ignoramus. Take away the foreigner's accent on our screen and their combined talents wouldn't loom as large as the tip of Bette Davis' little finger. So long as Hollywood is going American it should send the majority of its 'furriners' packing—and concentrate on discovering new American faces.[65]

With this kind of xenophobia in the air there was obviously a need for the studios to protect their investment in foreign talent, through a process of Americanisation. In August 1940, the *New York Times* reported on Fritz Lang's recently acquired American citizenship and the opening of *The Return of Frank James*: 'Fritz Lang, U.S. Citizen Celebrates by Making a Horse Opera'. In some respects the article was little more than a novel way to promote the film—a PR conceit to produce news copy. Like much of the publicity surrounding the major Western productions of 1939/40, it emphasised both the filmmaker's credentials in turning in an authentic portrayal of the Old West ('he has become more of an authority on Indian lore and the tales of the old Western frontier than most of the American-born directors in Hollywood') and its high production values ('In one of the chase sequences involving only four actors, more than eighty technicians had to be on hand for filming'). More revealingly, it suggested how accustomed commentators had become to the presence of Westerns in Hollywood's production schedules and how central the genre now was to cinematic discussions of the state of the Republic: 'In the year that he became a citizen Mr. Lang turned to a theme as indigenously American as corner drug stores or tiled bathrooms—the Western horse-opera'.[66]

Like Dietrich and Lang, Errol Flynn used Westerns to equip himself with an American identity, just as he had originally used an Irish persona to cover up his Australian birthplace, allowing him to flit between Irish (*Captain Blood*, Warner Bros., 1935) and English (*The Adventures of Robin Hood*) characterisations, depending on the needs of the story. At the beginning of *Dodge City*, his character is introduced as an ex-British officer, a Civil War veteran *and* an Irishman. In an echo of the Irish character he played in *Captain Blood,* the film retains the signifying mangled grammar and repeated use of the phrase 'faith now'. His cultural sophistication (represented by a number of references to Shakespeare) is levelled somewhat by his two sidekicks, played by Alan Hale and Guinn 'Big Boy' Williams, who represent his coarser side. By the end of the film, Flynn has become a Westerner and an assimilated American. In *Virginia City* (Warner Bros., 1940), his character is again an Irishman who fought for the British Empire and in the American army, this time on the side of the Union. In *Santa Fé Trail* (Warner Bros., 1940), however, he played the Confederate J.E.B. Stuart, a role he followed with his portrayal of George Armstrong Custer in *They Died With Their Boots On* (Warner Bros., 1941). Flynn had finally lost his Australian-Irish roots and become an American.

The successful deployment of top rank male stars, the seamless interpolation of romance and the significant roles given to women account in great part for the 1939/40 cycle's triumph at the box office. Hollywood had, however, not only to find ways of adapting its stars to the genre; it also had to adapt the genre to their personae. In *Destry Rides Again*, Marlene Dietrich brought both an erotic and exotic quality to Westerns, aspects that helped to distinguish A-features from the homely, asexual series Western. But A-feature Westerns also took sustenance from lowly series Westerns, and their paths were not wholly separate. As series Westerns, in the guise of Gene Autry's films, sought an ever wider audience, A-feature Westerns also set out to capture an audience that Hollywood had barely considered. With the closing of international markets, the need to placate independent exhibitors and the rise in employment (and disposable income) brought about by the lifting of the Depression, the neighbourhood, small-town and rural markets took on new significance.

Drinking, Prostitution and the Concert Saloon

A-feature Westerns conspicuously played up elements that had been more or less taboo in series Westerns. Particularly pronounced was the dramatic space offered by the bar room and concert saloon, where drinking, gambling, sex and violence were pushed to the fore. In a puffed-up 1935 article on series Westerns aimed at amusing its 'sophisticated' readership, the *New York Times* presented the genre as some strange species enjoyed by alien audiences:

> there is a large section of America and an even larger faction abroad that demand and pay to see the same Two-Gun. These followers of the exponents of the Great, Clean West take their cowboy epics seriously . . . they feel that Western stars, whose lives have been devoted to succouring maidens in distress and lacing their tormentors, are out of place in sordid establishments in which the stuff is sold that stunts the growth and destroys the moral fibre.[67]

The piece was written around Universal's edict that George O'Brien's films should no longer have bar room scenes. In fact, drinking and bar rooms already had a very limited dramatic and spatial role in series Westerns. If a scene is shot in a barroom in Autry's Westerns it is noticeable that he refuses to drink. If John Wayne is shown drunk, as in *The Man From Monterey*, it is as a ruse to fool the villains, or else there is a fadeout as he raises a drink to his mouth, as in *Rainbow Valley* (Lone Star/Monogram, 1935). Generally, however, bar rooms and drinking are conspicuous by their absence. There is a scene set in a cantina in the George O'Brien series Western for RKO, *The Fighting Gringo* (1939), but like Autry he does not drink; instead he does battle with around twenty Mexicans.[68]

The concert saloon was one of the key novelties offered by the 1939/40 Western. While saloons had been an almost permanent feature of the Western since its filmic inception, the addition of a stageshow did not occur until this season of films. Its dramatic potential had been signalled in a number of extremely popular films that celebrated a particularly rowdy and bawdy image of America's past. The Mae West vehicle *She Done Him Wrong* (Paramount, 1933), set in the Bowery during the 1890s, was followed swiftly by the Wallace Beery, George Raft and Jackie Cooper film *The Bowery* (the first film produced by 20th Century Pictures formed by Darryl F. Zanuck and Joseph M. Schenck after the former left Warner Bros.), which was clearly intended to ride the success and celebrity of *She Done Him Wrong*. Released in October, seven months after the Mae West vehicle, the film draws its story from the same romanticised locale and time period. *She Done Him Wrong* and *The Bowery* popularised and helped fix Hollywood's representation of the concert saloon. Their success at the box office ensured that producers would make further use of this milieu. *Barbary Coast* (Goldwyn, 1935) transported the concert saloon to San Francisco at the height of the gold rush in 1849, and in the same year *Call of the Wild* placed it in the Yukon. *San Francisco* (MGM, 1936) uses it as the chief setting to dramatise the earthquake of 1906. In *In Old Chicago* (20th Century-Fox, 1938), the concert saloon is used to dramatise America's move from anarchic and vulgar beginnings to ordered civilisation, which is achieved after the great fire cleans up the town and its dens of vice. In these films the concert saloon is made to occupy the site of contestation between the forces of lawlessness and reform.

By the early 1940s, with the success of Westerns like *Dodge City* and *Destry Rides Again*, the concert saloon had become part of the iconography of Westerns. In its transition to the West, the concert saloon lost much of its urban specificity, but it remained a sign of America's primitive beginnings. The dances on stage are often little more than variations on 'Ta Ra Ra Boom Der Re' and 'Frankie and Johnny', dance and song sequences in *The Bowery* and *She Done Him Wrong* respectively. The incidental music in these films and the A-feature Westerns discussed here are almost without exception based on the most immediately recognisable minstrel tunes of the nineteenth century: 'Oh Dem Golden Slippers', 'Oh! Susanna', 'Camptown Races', 'Buffalo Gals', and so on. The logical extension of Westerns' play with minstrelsy and the concert saloon is found in John Wayne's appearance in blackface in *The Spoilers* (Universal, 1942).

The concert saloon had first appeared along the Bowery in the 1860s. According to Robert C. Allen's study of burlesque, what distinguished the concert saloon from other performance spaces where alcohol was consumed was the 'incorporation of feminine sexuality as part of the entertainment'. The concert saloon appealed primarily to working-class men who were served their beverages by waiter girls costumed in 'what were for the period, short dresses', with variety acts providing the onstage amusements.[69] The idea of independent women working in a male environment carried implications of prostitution for the period's middle-class moral guardians, and in short time by-laws were passed driving the concert saloon underground. How conscious Hollywood's filmmakers were of this period, or whether they simply 'borrowed' the idea from *She Done Him Wrong* and transposed the concert saloon into the West so that they would have a place for musical and other divertissements of a decidedly vulgar turn, is uncertain. The implication that the saloon girl was a prostitute continued to resonate, however, and much play would be made around this ambiguity.

Though drinking in A-feature Westerns can be seen as a counterpoint to the series Western's temperance, it also has a dramatic role. In *Jesse James* it is used to underscore the hero's moral degeneration. Just before the raid on the Northfield bank and sometime after his wife has left him, Jesse is shown drinking from a jug as his paranoia and hubris begin to affect his gang of outlaws. In *Dodge City*, drinking is used to provide the comedy. Alan Hale's character's attempts at staying on the wagon by attending a temperance meeting are paralleled with Guinn Williams' character's revelries in the adjoining saloon, leading to a spectacular bar room punch-up. Drinking also services much of the comic interplay between Judge Roy Bean and Cole Harding in the early scenes of *The Westerner*. Bean sells a particularly lethal rot-gut whiskey which eats into the bar like acid when it is spilt. The scene the morning after Harding and Bean's drinking competition is beautifully evoked by director William Wyler, his actors, and especially the soundtrack: every noise appearing to send physical shocks through Harding's alcohol-racked body. *Frontier Marshal* uses drinking to underscore Doc Halliday's physical and moral corruption. The comic potential of the drunk and its more serious side are neatly combined in the character of the Doctor (Thomas Mitchell) in *Stagecoach*, one of Ford's saintly drunkards.

Drinking and drunkenness did not pass unnoticed by the PCA. Their files on these films contain multiple references to the 'problem' —'please hold drinking to the necessary minimum' and 'liquor and drinking needs to be modified'. Joseph Breen's and the PCA's position on drinking and drunkenness was clear: it had little to do with any personal support of temperance but a great deal to do with its effect on the box office, as noted in this extract from a letter to Republic Pictures:

> I note in connection with your proposed production *Wagons Westward* that you intend to indicate a scene of Sam Houston getting hopelessly drunk.
>
> . . . I want to take time to tell you that I think this is very unfortunate and it will definitely minimise the box office appeal of your production.
>
> We are constantly being appealed to by patrons and theatre managers to urge upon producers to keep away from scenes of excessive drinking and drunkenness. The general impression

20. *Dodge City*
The saloon: female companionship, gambling, drinking, singing,
dancing, and fighting

seems to prevail—that this opinion comes not from the usual
run of 'cranks' or 'reformers'—that drinking men, and especially
drinking women, provide little entertainment for millions of the
film going public. There is something about scenes of drunkenness, which, in many cases, are revolting to people and I wish you
would consider earnestly our suggestion that you change this piece
of action. I think if you do so, you will help your picture to a more
widespread appeal at the box office.

I understand of course that the point is important as a story
point in the dramatisation of your story, but, aside and apart from
this, I think you are making a serious mistake.[70]

In effect, the PCA acted to contain the excesses that were suggested in
scripts sent in for approval. The PCA files give the impression that
without their recommendations the characters in these Westerns would
have been leaking rot-gut whiskey from every pore as prostitutes relieve
them of what little money they have left after drinking the Southwest
dry.

Nevertheless, the perception in a number of reviews was that there was a pushing back of the PCA's more puritanical control over the representation of adult activities, something the PCA sought both to promote and to disclaim in order to placate both anti-monopoly interests and censor boards. The *Time* magazine review of *Stagecoach* opened with a career overview of 'Walter Wanger (rhymes with ranger)' identifying him as being in the 'forefront for Hollywood's crusade for social consciousness':

> Three years ago he astounded the industry by announcing that he and Mussolini would build a cinema city on the outskirts of Rome, putting Italy into production on a grand scale. When the Hitler–Mussolini axis was formed, the Mussolini–Wanger axis broke. Wanger went on record as Hollywood's number one anti-dictator producer by making *Blockade* and is now leading a move to revise Hollywood's famed Production Code, to permit producers to deal more frankly with controversial themes. In *Stagecoach* producer Wanger's contempt for the Code is manifested by the fact that its heroine Claire Trevor is a prostitute, its hero John Wayne a desperado, and its most likable character, Thomas Mitchell, a rum-pot physician. No social document, *Stagecoach* is merely the record of a journey made by these and several other engaging personages from Tonto to Lordsburg in an era when Geronimo and his Apaches made life on the Arizona frontier more than normally exciting.[71]

In actuality, Wanger, Ford and Nichols worked *with* the PCA, not in contempt of it.

On receipt of the first treatment for the film in late October 1938, Breen noted that the 'present version seems to be in violation of the Production Code in the following respects':

> The characterisation of your sympathetic feminine lead as a prostitute. The triple killing for revenge by your sympathetic male lead. The indication at the end that the sheriff connives in the killing of three men, and the latter assists in the escape of the killer, who is also characterised as an escaped convict. There also seems to be an indication of too much display of liquor and drunkenness in connection with the characterisation of your drunken driver [*sic*]. It would seem, therefore, that a story based upon this treatment would result in a picture which we could not approve under the requirements of the Production Code.

Three days later the filmmakers met with representatives of the PCA and 'agreed tentatively to the following':

> There will be no specific references to prostitution. The girl will merely be characterised as an undesirable woman who regenerates. The present flavor of killing for revenge on the part of the hero will be changed. It is their intention to indicate that he definitely gives up this idea half way through the story; and the end of the story will indicate that it is the three heavies who attack him. We agreed to wait until we receive the script before passing further judgment on this matter'.[72]

In a scene in the early drafts of *Billy the Kid* (1941), Billy's sexual attractiveness is suggested through an exchange of looks and some bawdy dialogue between him and two saloon prostitutes. The most forward of the two, Bessie, tells Billy: 'I get so lonesome sometimes I can taste it'. and 'Honest, baby, you've got the nicest guns', which gets changed in a later draft to 'Honest, baby, you've got the nicest pers'nality'. By the time the film was shown all that was left was the exchange of looks, and Bessie's employment had shifted from prostitute to archetypical saloon girl, with little noticeable difference in her behaviour. Whatever Bessie is, the bar room and the concert saloon are where sex in Westerns is to be found. In *The Westerner*, it is in Judge Roy Bean's obsession with images of Lily Langtrey, which cover all the available surfaces behind the bar. In *Dodge City*, the saloon is where the cowboys find female companionship after completing the cattle drive. In *Frontier Marshal*, Jerry leads a troupe of high-kicking girls through a song and dance routine, in which she sings about the travails of being a working-girl in a spectacle much appreciated by the male punters. In *Destry Rides Again*, the saloon is the public space dominated by Frenchy, where men can escape their haranguing wives and lose their pants. When Mrs Callahan enters this space to reclaim her husband's trousers, she has to do battle with Frenchy. This homo-social space is where men are permitted a coarseness and vulgarity denied them in the domestic space. The entry of the townswomen of Bottleneck into the Last Chance saloon at the close of *Destry* symbolises an end of this 'freedom', but it also establishes a com-plementary change on the domestic front, where men now have a defining role.

As the cycle progressed, there was an increased emphasis on the 'adult' content of these Westerns that would reach a climax of sorts with Howard Hughes's *The Outlaw*. The Clark Gable/Lana Turner vehicle *Honky Tonk* (MGM, 1941) was set almost exclusively in and around the saloon, with much of the dialogue emphasising the sexually charged relationship between the leads which, as Breen pointed out to Louis B. Mayer, tended towards a 'rather blunt sexual suggestiveness'. However, as in the case of *Stagecoach*, but unlike *The Outlaw*, the producers sought to work with the PCA in finding an acceptable middle-ground so as 'to avoid being offensive to mixed audiences'.[73]

The Outlaw: Authenticity and Novelty

> Legend rides the trail with history; truth rides a lonely trail.
> (Cecil B. DeMille, plugging *Union Pacific*[74])

A-feature Westerns would be essentially historical. Even James Cagney's character, the Oklahoma Kid, was partly sold as an authentic recreation of the past. According to studio publicity, the character was 'based upon Billy the Kid and his make-up has been taken from tintypes of that outlaw'.[75] But Cagney's eye make-up was the same as that worn in most of his pictures. History was a marketing tool, an exploitation angle in promoting the film, but it would not, and did not, get in the way of the action and romance. The outlaw figures of Jesse James and Billy the Kid best exemplify this process.

The exploitable value of the name 'Jesse James' had to be negotiated alongside the recognition that his legendary status was based on banditry. In the first instance, Fox sought to contain this difficulty by emphasising the film's historical basis, and then by making the film's representation of this history a selling point, while also promoting the suggestion of the figure's contemporary relevance. In both the film and its promotion, 20th Century-Fox consciously played with the outlaw's ambivalent status, finding him at first a victim to be sympathised with, a man driven to a life of crime by extraordinary circumstances, and then punished for being unable to resolve the conflict in a lawful manner. At the close of the film, Major Cobb, Jesse's most ardent supporter, attempts to mount a justification for his actions:

> There ain't no question about it. Jesse was an outlaw, a bandit, a criminal. Even those that loved him ain't got an answer for that . . . I don't know why, but I don't think even America is ashamed of Jesse James. Maybe it was because he was bold and lawless like we, all of us, like to be sometimes. Maybe it's because we

21. *Oklahoma Kid*
According to studio publicity the outlaw's look was based upon
tintypes of Billy the Kid

understand a little that he wasn't altogether to blame for what his times made him. Maybe it's because for five years he licked the tar out of five states. Or maybe it's because he was so good at what he was doing. I don't know.

When Jesse turns to robbing banks rather than fighting back against the railroads, however, a line has been crossed, and he turns from righteous defender of the exploited into an outright criminal.

Much store was placed on authenticity in the publicity surrounding *Jesse James*: the shooting of exterior scenes in and around Pineville, Missouri, using the residents of McDonald County as extras, having access to the Pinkerton newspaper files on the outlaw. A particular publicity coup was the employment as an advisor to the film of Jesse's granddaughter Jo Frances James, who, as the *Hollywood Reporter* noted without a hint of irony, 'works in the escrow department of the Bank of America'.[76] She would, however, later claim that 'about the only connection which it [*Jesse James*] had with fact was there was once a man called James and he did ride a horse'.[77] An article in the *New York Times* covered the effect that the production of the film had on the local community and its economy. Underlying much of the coverage is the barely spoken recognition that the Depression is still biting: 'Not everyone has been taken off relief in Noel yet, the Mayor's wife said, because at first nobody could believe that the movie people were really coming'.[78] This was a rather neat publicity angle that suggested Hollywood, like Jesse James, offers salvation to the beleaguered community. This is the domestic backdrop to what was essentially Fox's attempt to create an American Robin Hood, both as a way of exploiting the success mustered by Warner Bros. with *The Adventures of Robin Hood*, and as part of the industry-wide trend to find and create American heroes. In a contemporary interview, Henry King, the director, explained: 'what we were trying to do was create a Jesse James who would be worthy of the legend, for we knew that no matter what we or any other creators of fiction did now, the legend would persist. Our effort was to make the legend a better one, morally as well as dramatically.'[79]

Hollywood had made a number of attempts to film the story of Jesse James, all of which had proved to be contentious. *The James Boys in Missouri* (Essanay, 1908) was held up for censure by industry commentators in the trade press:

> the notorious James brothers murdered, robbed and set fire to buildings . . . One can have little admiration for the pains and

time spent in making such films in the first place—the patient training of the actors, the selection of the proper backgrounds, the hiring of horses, furniture, railroad-trains, steamboats, automobiles—anything necessary for the picture; but one can wish heartily that the effort had produced something elevating, or at least harmless, instead of the seeming realism of bloodshed, crime, and brutality.[80]

The James gang had achieved mythic status through dime novel portrayals. Between 1901 and 1903 alone nearly 300 stories about the gang were published. Matthew Solomon has recorded the censoring backlash led by Anthony Comstock against this form of literature, and has noted the similarity in the crusading rhetoric against dime novels and the Essanay film of the James gang.[81] The negative criticism was obviously taken on board by Essanay and others, because the next attempt to base a film on the myth of the James gang was in 1915 with *The Near Capture of Jesse James* (Luna Productions), followed six years later by two productions that featured Jesse James Jr. In 1927 Fred Thompson played the role of the outlaw in *Jesse James* (Paramount), and the Studio Relations Committee was hit by a slew of letters, particularly from viewers in the South, censoring the company for giving succour to outlaws and cautioning against making a criminal into a hero. This was obviously something that was still a consideration in 1939, when the reviewer for the *Motion Picture Herald* concluded his wholly positive review by noting this version's wholesomeness: 'The moral equation, important these days to showmen and public, is solved with complete candor. Both cause and result of the James' decade of outlawry are shown impartially. The picture is therefore suitable for exhibition to Americans of all ages, times and places. It may well turn out to be an American classic.'[82]

To get the picture to the point where they could still exploit the infamy of Jesse James, yet remain relatively uncontroversial, Fox undertook lengthy negotiations with the PCA. Their first completed script was rejected as unsuitable 'for the reason it is hardly more than the glorification of a man who is a bandit and a killer'.[83] This problem had been encountered before by the PCA and successfully overcome in *Robin Hood of Eldorado* where the representative of the law was played up, 'making him the voice for morality', and Breen suggested a similar strategy for *Jesse James*.[84] When the film's preproduction publicity began to circulate, Hays and Breen received letters complaining about the 'glorification of a killer', the negative influence this would have on the nation's youth, and the poor image it presented of America abroad. Even this negative view could be turned around, however, as it was in *Motion Picture* magazine's feature 'Hollywood Declares War on Dictators': 'Whatever Jesse James may have been in real life, 20th Century-Fox recently pictured him as a good American who simply went berserk. Getting across the point that injustice makes American blood boil—and stay hot.'[85] This reading was governed by a need to make the film conform to the wider requirement that Hollywood appear an essential voice in the defence of American democracy and free speech rather than by any explicit message in the film itself.

On the release of *Jesse James*, Warner Bros. wrote to Hays asking for leave to register the title 'John Dillinger, Outlaw', a title that had previously been rejected. Warners felt there should be no differentiation between their title and 'Jesse James'. Hays did not agree and wrote back citing previous industry-wide decisions not to make any film about, or which drew upon, the exploits of John Dillinger. At the end of a lengthy letter justifying his decision, Hays wrote:

> Perhaps this distinction [between Dillinger and Jesse James] is vague and difficult to state in words, but I believe it is genuine. The same distinction is hinted at in the language of the Production Code 'revenge in modern times shall not be justified'. When a legendary or historical figure is the central figure it may be properly distinguished from a similar story presenting an actual criminal figure from current life. One reason is that the mythical or legendary character does not so readily induce imitation because present day audiences are not so likely to identify themselves with him. This reasoning does not apply to Jesse James as certainly as it does to Robin Hood, but it applies to Jesse James much more than it does to John Dillinger and there has been some worry as you know about Jesse James. The technique of Robin Hood's operations are certainly passé; the technique of Jesse James' crimes is at least outmoded; the technique of John Dillinger is that used today, except only as it is prevented by current techniques of the officers of the law.[86]

This debate had earlier been rehearsed in *Scarface* (1932), in which a newspaperman who attempts to get the chief of police's comments on the 'colourful character' of Tony Camonte is instead given a lecture in civic ethics:

Colourful! What colour is a crawling louse? Say listen. That's the attitude of too many morons in this country. They think these hoodlums are some kind of demagogues. What do they do about a guy like Camonte? They sentimentalise, romance, make jokes about him. They had some excuse for glorifying our old Western badmen. They met in the middle of the street, at high noon and waited for each other to draw. But these fiends sneak up and shoot a guy in the back and then run away.

The contrast between the romantic outlaw of the Old West and the modern urban gangster became almost a commonplace in the early 1930s. In his cultural study of the gangster, David E. Ruth quotes from a 1931 *Cosmopolitan* article: 'few have the bravado of the outlaws of the western plains—healthy, red-corpuscled men, quick on the draw and usually comparatively "square shooters." . . . the 1931-model gunman is more often than not a chicken breasted Broadway gigolo type—tubercular or otherwise diseased . . . at heart a miserable coward and a "snitch" '.[87] In the same year, writing about a clutch of gangster films for the *National Board of Review*, James Shelly Hamilton noted how the 'vitality' of the genre was matched only by pictures of the 'Wild West' and the war, but then set the latter firmly in the past and out of harm's way:

> These two fields where active adventure and physical clash predominate, have become something like story-book lands, and the things that happen in them, no matter how interesting or exciting, touch us no more nearly than any other vivid fiction; but the gang wars belong to here and now, with the vital reality of something that might be happening at the present moment in the next street. No wonder the pictures about them fascinate us, sometimes to the verge of terror and anger.[88]

The 'story-book land' of the Wild West outlaw was most obviously occupied by the legend of Robin Hood.

The making of Jesse James into an American Robin Hood was a process begun even before Robert Ford played out his cowardly act.[89] Major John N. Edwards, a contemporary chronicler of the James gang's exploits (and the figure upon whom Major Rufus Cobb, the newspaper editor in the film, is clearly based), headed up the list of mythologisers who sought to make capital out of the comparison.[90] According to historian Michael Fellman, the myth of Jesse James was rooted in a widespread attempt by those involved in guerrilla activities in Missouri to justify their actions by drawing upon the long tradition of mythical noble bandits which helped turn their acts of terrorism into the ennobling defence of the Lost Cause:

> In this symbolic context, he was both a gritty social bandit and an anarchic superhuman figure—striking out against the very social forces which had ground down the southern cause during the war and had continued to wear down American farmers and small-town residents after the war.[91]

Neither the placement of the Western outlaw in a dim and distant past nor the parallels with Robin Hood could entirely assuage public outcries about the glorification of the criminal. In response to a movie trailer for *Belle Starr—The Bandit Queen* (1941), starring Gene Tierney (Fox's second attempt to emulate the success of *Jesse James*, following on the heels of *The Return of Frank James* in which Tierney had played the female lead), the Tulsa *Tribune* ran a satirical and critical editorial on Hollywood's glamorisation of outlaw figures. It concluded:

> knowing Hollywood's current taste in such scenarios and also the price paid for the same we are beginning work on a little playlet based on the life of Jack the Ripper. In this work we see Jack as a earnest and manly young London sneak thief who becomes so persecuted by the tyrannical forces of the law that he takes to eviscerating women in dark alleys. More or less in self defence until he is brought down by a cowardly blow from a Bobbie's truncheon. We have no doubt that Hollywood would stamp this up and make a great movie of it, probably with Henry Fonda in the lead role, in which case we aren't going to see that one either.[92]

The box-office success of *Jesse James* meant that Hollywood persisted in looking to outlaw figures, both fictional and historical, on whom to build an American legend and who could also address contemporary concerns in the form of allegory.

When MGM first began work on the script for *Billy the Kid* at the beginning of 1939, they used the basic story they had produced in 1930. The screenwriters edited out some of the less plausible bits of plot, like Garrett helping Billy to give himself up by frying bacon outside of his hideout, and dropped the ending which has Billy ride off with his girl by his side. But they kept the names (or variations of them) of the principal historical characters who were involved in the

22. *Billy the Kid*
Despite this publicity still, the 1941 version of the Billy the Kid story once
again failed to supply a convincing love story

Lincoln County War alongside key events, like the burning of the
McSween home. By mid-1940, however, when the script had gone
through five writers, the story was completely different from the 1930
version, all the historical character names, except of course Billy the
Kid, had been changed, and none of the historically documented
incidents of the 'War' were included. Gone, too, were the over-stressed
references to Robin Hood that had figured prominently in earlier
versions, such as Harvey Fergusson's March 1939 draft of a scene in
which Pat Garrett meets with Governor Lew Wallace to discuss Billy
the Kid's situation:

> 'He must be a remarkable man' the Governor said. 'He seems to
> take cattle from wherever and whenever he pleases. You can
> hardly call it stealing because no one tries to stop him. He has so
> many friends amongst the native people. They all hide him and
> feed him, and none of them will tell you where he is. Why the
> man is a regular Robin Hood'. 'Robin Hood' Pat said 'Why that's

one gun slinger I've never heard of'. 'Robin Hood used a bow and arrow.; 'Part Apache I suppose', Pat remarked. 'No he was an Englishman', the Governor said. 'And he made the law look ridiculous'. 'Then he is just what Billy the Kid is doing, don't you see? You got to bring him in before we can establish respect for the law in this country'.[93]

By ridding itself of the historical context that anchors the myth of Billy the Kid, the film was able to concentrate on creating an overt allegory of the need to defend law and free speech against men of violence with ambition to rule. By playing Billy off against one side then the other, allowing him to exact bloody justice before reining him in at the close, the film was able to contain potential Code violations.

Billy first goes to work for Dan Hickey (Gene Lockhart), who has plans to take over the cattle business. Opposed to him is the Englishman Eric Keating (Ian Hunter, who played King Richard in *The Adventures of Robin Hood*). Billy's initial job is to orchestrate a stampede of Keating's cattle. During the stampede and the ensuing gun battle, Billy meets an old boyhood friend from Silver City, Jim Sherwood (another veiled reference to Robin Hood—a reference is also found in a trailer for the film which calls Billy the Kid the 'Robin Hood of the Rio Grande'). Sherwood (Brian Donlevy) introduces Billy to his boss, Keating, who refuses to carry a gun and puts his trust in the essential goodness of man and in the need to steadfastly uphold the law by legal means. He explains to Billy as they ride together through Monument Valley:

> You know, things are gonna happen in this county. Guns and shooting are going out. Law and order's on the march. You better look out or they'll run you over. The good people want to live together as good peaceful citizens. And when they get together there isn't a man fast enough on the draw, or tough enough to stand against them. Not even Hannibal, Napoleon or Billy the Kid.

This coded allusion to a Europe of dictators needs little elucidation, except to note that it was not present in the draft versions of the script. It first appears in a retake script in April 1941, suggesting the screen-writers and producers' desire to give the story a contemporary currency. The other voice for free speech, the town's would-be newspaperman, also makes a very late entry into the script's development. Midway through the film the newspaperman prints an anti-Hickey letter,

Hickey's men suggest they throw him into jail again where he was when first introduced. Hickey responds: 'It won't learn him anything to be locked up. Trouble is you can't lock up his mind.' His answer is to have one of his henchmen make the newspaper man literally eat his words (they push a rolled up newspaper down his throat), whereupon Billy saves him and switches to Keating's side.

The development of these pointed allusions to the war in Europe was given greater resonance when a character declares that the country is on the 'edge of a full-scale war', a line that was eventually cut from the film. No doubt it was eliminated because it assumed rather too forcefully and prematurely that America's neutrality was evaporating or, more circumspectly, that America's internal social and political divisions were leading towards violent confrontation. The producers also eliminated some of Hickey's dialogue where he is aligned with the isolationist America First movement:

> Hickey; turning to Cass 'Billy's one of us.' He looks at Billy—
> 'a real patriot'. He smiles—'I didn't tell you Keating is an
> Englishman—and this part of the country is for Americans'. He
> looks back at Cass—'We're doing our country a real service, aren't
> we, Cass?' (Cass smiles because he feels he has to. Hickey starts to
> the door, then stops and turns to Billy) 'By the way, Kid, I don't
> think the boys will get along with that Mexican'. Billy—'Then
> they won't get along with me'.

The scene remained, but the business about 'America for Americans' is only alluded to through Hickey's use of red, white and blue gambling chips to explain to Billy how the situation in this part of the country is split between his camp and Keating's—an allusion that is so innocuous that it only makes sense when what it replaced is known. Nevertheless, it is part of a consistent programme that establishes this film as pro-intervention. Because the film is set in the past, however, the producers can always disclaim this position. Ambiguity and suggestion allow for what Ruth Vasey has called the 'transparent principle of "deniability" '.[94]

Keating soon assumes the role of father figure in Billy's life (Billy's real father had been shot in the back in Silver City and a corrupt judicial system let the perpetrator go free; it was this event that caused Billy to take to a life of crime). He appears to be winning Billy over to his way of thinking, a point laid on rather thickly when Billy's sidekick, the Mexican, Pedro, is killed by Hickey's men, and Billy resists taking immediate revenge. The Governor makes Keating a Marshal. Keating rides into town to serve warrants on the Hickey gang, but he is ambushed and killed. Despite Sherwood's best attempts to hold Billy in check and let the law take its course, Billy hits out, coldly gunning down Hickey's accomplices before shooting Hickey in the back, a sign that Billy has now become what he most hates. In an act of suicide, left-handed Billy straps his gun on his right hip and lets Sherwood beat him to the draw.

By cutting out any attempt to offer a historical account of the Lincoln County War, the film is able to focus on Billy as mythic hero, a man born of his times, who serves a purpose—the meeting of violence with violence—and then vanishes to make way for a more peaceful and civilised society. Released in the autumn of 1941, *Billy the Kid* is perhaps the most overt allegory on the international conflicts facing America in the months before its entry into the war. Westerns produced earlier in the cycle offer a much less transparent political position.

In the 1939/40 cycle of Westerns, Hollywood successfully managed to integrate romantic dramas of courtship with the spectacular adventures of Westerns, creating what Dana Polan (1986) has called a 'unifying effect'. In his study of postwar narrative, Polan argues that there was a marked shift during the war years from a prewar classical narrativity where films are marked by a 'unifying effect—the forming of personal and political destiny into one logic' to a wartime and postwar American cinema where the unifying effect undergoes a 'derouting' or 'detouring'. Prewar cinema's concern with establishing a stable space to allow for the formation of the couple was no longer a given:

> Indeed, in the moment of victory and after, where even the forcing of narrative resolution to the commitment to the war effort will be lacking, narrative can seem to turn fundamentally unstable, fundamentally unable to move forward. Narrative here becomes a virtual antinarrative: nonstories dominated by an endless cyclicity or a predictable and inevitable descent into the stasis of death or unchanging passivity.[95]

Polan's claims about the changes in Hollywood narratives are based on the arguments of French critics Raymond Bellour and Daniel Dayan that the late 1930s Western is a 'symptomatic' Hollywood narrative which is 'classically American in the way it forges a coincidence of personal story and national destiny through the elaboration of a systematic style of filming and narrating'.[96] For Polan, the 'buckling' of this model can be best seen in a *film noir* like *Detour* (PRC, 1945), which is 'nothing so much as a vast bad-joke version of the classic narrative'. The hero's westward journey in search of his lover becomes a 'nightmare parody of the American romance'.[97] The romantic denouement that Bellour and Dayan find, respectively, in *The Westerner* and *Stagecoach*, and Westerns in general, as being characteristic of 'classical' Hollywood cinema was, however, the effect of a number of converging and intersecting cultural, social, political, industrial and historically located determinants. These films are better viewed as anomalies within Hollywood's production, rather than symptomatic models of a classical paradigm.

Discussing contemporary critics' fascination with *film noir*, Marc Vernet argues that these critics are guilty of mythologising prewar Hollywood: 'Paradoxically, *film noir* is loved for representing a past that it in fact occults, a past that the enthusiast hardly knows, if at all, a bit of the pre-war in the post-war period'.[98] Dayan, Bellour, and Polan by extension, fall into this paradigm. By making claims about prewar Hollywood based on a few selected films produced at the end of the decade, they hide from view the fact that 1930s Hollywood narratives could be as equally 'buckled', 'derouted' and 'detoured'. Few films produced in the 1940s can match the nihilism of *Last Flight* (Warner Bros., 1931), the narrative absurdities of *Dynamite* (MGM, 1929), or the celebration of, and attack on, female sexuality in *Female* (Warner Bros., 1933).

Westerns produced towards the end of the decade do manifest the symptoms of 'classical Hollywood narrative' but this was due to unique events both inside and outside Hollywood. It is unlikely Hollywood would have invested so heavily in Westerns without the threat to break up the system of block and blind booking. Equally, the need to produce politically engaged films (which were also uncontroversial) to assuage both domestic and international parties gave impetus to the production of Westerns. Moreover, only Westerns made towards the end of the decade can be described as establishing a 'stable place' for the formation of the couple. One need only remember the endings of *Cimarron*, *Three Godfathers*, *Ramona*, *The Plainsman*, or the un-convincing denouement of *Billy the Kid* (1930), to recognise how precarious is the couple in 1930s Westerns.

Westerns served an immediate political purpose by helping Hollywood negotiate between, on the one hand, the demands of the antitrust lobby led by the independent exhibitors, and on the other, the need to continue to make prestige pictures that would capture a first-run metropolitan audience. Through the casting of the leading male matinee idols, the focus on the woman's role, the successful integration of romance plots, and the incorporation of adult themes and settings, Westerns were transformed.

Further questions of how 'America' was represented in the A-feature Western remain to be answered, however. Whose voices are heard, and whose are suppressed? Who is given space to live and prosper within the Republic, and who is denied entry? How are conflicts represented and resolved? Because of the specificity of their geographical and historical setting, A-feature Westerns are preoccupied with the idea of nation-building. With its ingrained celebration of American exceptionalism, the frontier myth provided the most readily available narrative paradigm. I would argue, however, that the myth operates as little more than a frame upon which more significant themes can be engaged.

6

Dixie Cowboys
Representing the Nation

The 1939/40 Westerns were recognised by both the industry and its critics as having an ideological accent that enabled Hollywood to practise a limited and cautious form of propaganda for the defence of American 'values'. In turn, this was offered as proof that the industry's self-regulating body was not imposing monopolistic practices that censored the dissemination of films which addressed contemporary issues. All of the major studios participated in the 1939/40 cycle of Westerns, and for most of the studios these Westerns constituted their principal prestige pictures for that season.

Domestically and internationally beleaguered, Hollywood turned to the theme of 'Americanism', an ambiguous concept that allowed the studios to suggest that they were dealing with contentious political issues on the domestic front, while denying any stake in either an 'America First' or an interventionist platform. Writing in 1933, Leon Samson considered Americanism to be neither a tradition or a territory:

> but a doctrine—what socialism is to a socialist . . . a solemn assent
> to a handful of final notions—democracy, liberty, opportunity, to
> all of which the American adheres rationalistically much as the
> socialist adheres to his socialism—because it does him good,
> because it gives him work, because, so he thinks, it guarantees him
> happiness.[1]

In a rather feeble bid to keep markets open for their products, the theme of 'Americanism' enabled the studios to maintain that their products were internally focused and therefore politically neutral on international affairs.

Specifically, 'Americanism' meant the production of films based on American history. Westerns were promoted as American history alongside films on historical figures like Alexander Graham Bell, Abraham Lincoln, Stephen Foster, and events as disparate as the building of the Panama Canal, the Civil War, and horse breeding in Kentucky. This focus on American history, however, invoked concomitant concerns for the constitution of an American national identity: in a republic founded upon contradictory principles (of individual rights and democratic consensus), fear of the dissolution of the Union through sectional conflict continued to reverberate. In this respect, Western narratives can be read as 'double-coded' in articulating contemporary disunity through historical representation. It is my contention that in the 1930s representations of the South and its problematic status within the Union came to define the Western's ideological provenance.

As Westerns are allegorical forms especially open to reinvention, producers of Westerns understood that their films were presenting sets of presupposed meanings, which their audience recognised as allegories on the state of the nation. Such a process of 'reading' has much in common with Michael Denning's theorisation of the dime novel as allegory. He suggests that this particular fictional world is 'less a representation of the real world than a microcosm . . . individual characters are less individuals than figures for social groups.'[2]

> This allegorical mode of reading depends upon the existence of a master plot by which to read the disguises; and that master plot was in working class cultures of the nineteenth-century the story of the Republic itself. The stories of individuals and of individual families become types of the citizens of the Republic, both in utopian images of its fulfilment as the cooperative commonwealth and in the stories of its betrayal, as it becomes a land of tramps and millionaires.[3]

The case Denning makes for popular culture and late-nineteenth-century workers still has validity well into the twentieth century. Narratives of a betrayed but finally saved republic run throughout the series Westerns of the 1930s, a narrative conceit that owed much to the magnification of social divisions engendered by the Great Depression. Moreover, series Westerns display a marked use of nineteenth-century performance traditions drawn from theatrical melodramas, song forms, variety skits and blackface minstrelsy. These anachronisms help form a shared imagined heritage for the series Western's audience which resembles Benedict Anderson's (1991) concept of narrative works (novels and newspapers) that help create the 'remarkable confidence of community in anonymity which is the hallmark of modern nations'.[4]

The function of the South in series Westerns is to offer their audience a dramatisation of the fears and conflicts that appear to divide them from the rest of the Union, using the West as a site where these tensions can be resolved. For A-feature Westerns, the South functions more obliquely to raise issues of *national* tension and conflict in a historically located, yet mythological context. Here, sectional conflict derived from the tensions of the Civil War are restaged in an ideologically unmarked West where otherwise irreconcilable schisms can be resolved. Approaching 1930s A-feature Westerns in these terms illustrates that it is *fear of secession* that Westerns register and not, as has been frequently argued, the structuralist opposition between savagery and civilisation. In that model, 'civilisation' is symbolised by Europe and eastern culture, which come to stand in for the Old World. It is significant that in 1930s Westerns the Old World is more generally positioned as *Southern*. Sectional conflict is formulated through representations of the South, which Westerns are then able to resolve through their displacement into a dramatic arena—the West—where American identities are not yet fixed, and where the contradiction between individual determination and communal responsibility is contained. The accommodation of contradiction and conflict is achieved through the means of *disguise*: Westerns operate not only as a mask for the South—revealing its virtues while repressing its evils—but for the Union as a whole.

The idea of disguise as a vehicle for telling a particular story of the South (in effect addressing the state of the Union) is not unique to Westerns. A similar function is fundamental to America's first indigenous mass art-form, blackface minstrelsy. In nineteenth-century minstrelsy the disguise of burnt cork permitted European immigrant cultures to find a common language in their shared whiteness, formed out of the negative construction of blackness. This is the view offered by Alexander Saxton in *The Rise and Fall of the White Republic* (1990). Focusing on both Westerns and blackface minstrelsy, Saxton adopts from Gramsci an ideological analysis of the emerging mass media and popular culture of nineteenth-century America for an understanding of American racism. Saxton argues that both the Western hero and the blackface minstrel are products of an American construction of white egalitarianism formulated around the vernacular hero who was definitively 'American'. His work reveals how race comes to displace class in the formation of an American identity that is distinct from a European one. As a justification for imperialist expansion (initially at the expense of the Indian population), Saxton specifies how white supremacy met the needs of class coalitions at the point of America's industrialisation.[5]

Minstrelsy's performance of an American racism, as David R. Roediger (1991) has also argued, has its roots in the foundation of the Republic that declared its independence from Europe through the call of 'deference to no one'.[6] This statement of equality was profoundly qualified by the presence of slavery within the Republic. Roediger shows how 'Blacks, free and slave, could be stigmatised precisely because slavery thrived in republican America, indeed that they could be stigmatised as the *antithesis* of republican citizens'.[7] Roediger argues that this lived contradiction acted as the means by which white American working classes were able to reconcile their economic dependency on an employer where dependency ideologically militated against the rhetoric of living in a republic. This is a significant reconciliation, because as Alan Trachtenberg (1982) has argued, in this period and well into the twentieth century, labour thought of itself as upholding 'nothing so much as the fundamental American traditions of republicanism and equality'. Indeed, labour considered itself as having 'the most authentic voice of America'.[8] Blackface provided the white worker with the 'psychological wage' of being 'not black' and 'not slave'. It is in this space that blackface minstrelsy derives its meaning.

The black mask performed the inclusion/exclusion around which white American identity could be constructed. Blackface also enabled, as Michael Rogin (1996) has argued, for a similar positioning of the Southern States inside and outside the Union:

> If a Puritan mission or a liberal tradition engendered the United States . . . then the slave-holding South is an exception outside the national consensus. Placing blackface, slavery, and race at the center, by contrast, makes the South organic to American national identity.[9]

Westerns side-step this problematic inclusion of the South in the Union by disguising the Southerner as a cowboy. Westerns came to offer an alternative to blackface minstrelsy for rehearsing fissures in the Republic, simultaneously shoring up white male American identity and confirming the Union. The rise of the Western as a recognisable genre occurred as the popularity of blackface minstrelsy was on the wane. Supported by a predominantly Northern audience, blackface evoked images of a static, racially interdependent antebellum South where issues of *class* division are magnified. In contrast, Westerns construct a dynamic republic where non-white races are either suppressed or excluded, and class conflict and national disunity are resolved.

Outside their shared vernacular heritage and ideological projects, blackface minstrelsy and Westerns appear in Saxton's thesis to be wholly autonomous from one another. From my analysis of the function of disguise in 1930s Westerns, it is possible to argue that the blackface minstrel and the cowboy are actually more closely linked than has hitherto been suggested. This is particularly evident in Southern vernacular music and in the films of Gene Autry, where the performance traditions of blackface are restaged. Further, by recognising how the South is re-presented through blackface, it becomes possible to identify why A-feature Westerns, when they evoke the Civil War, take a pro-Southern stance.

With Hollywood's promotion of the theme of 'Americanism' came a set of concerns around the representation of the nation. In order to assemble an audience under a consensually agreed definition of the American body politic, Hollywood drew upon historical narratives of the building of the nation. The destabilisations produced by the Depression and America's uncertain international situation provoked a particular 'return' to foundation myths. Historical Westerns offered a privileged site for re-reading stories of the emergence of the American nation. These Western settings provided an ostensibly 'neutral' arena in which these stories could be played out as tales of individual struggles against the wilderness, the settlement of the West, the conquest of savagery by civilisation, the lionising of the pioneer. This is the familiar terrain upon which the Western canon has been constructed. The return to the seeming neutrality of the frontier myth at this time belies a far more complex set of negotiations at work in Hollywood's construction of American identity, however. Rather than replay epic stories of the winning of the West (as exemplified in films such as *The Covered Wagon* and *The Big Trail*), A-feature Westerns of 1939–41 invoke frontier mythology with a view to recasting it in terms of the fissures represented by the Civil War. This shift away from the narrative of confrontation between savagery (represented by the Indian) and civilisation (represented by the pioneer) to a confrontation between North and South on America's Western frontier (hence the repeated use of the 'border' states of Missouri and Kansas as the settings for many of these films) redraws the ground upon which a conceptualisation of the Western at the close of the 1930s must be understood. In the restaging of these former fissures, Hollywood A-feature Westerns aim to address contemporary anxieties around political fragmentation, American identity and nationhood. The Civil War operated as a means of establishing an instantly recognisable set of national conflicts and divisions: it becomes the trope through which conflict in the 1939–41 Western is rehearsed and contained and it would continue to be a major theme in Westerns through the 1940s and 1950s.

Southern Identities: Passage West

The Civil War picture had fallen out of favour with film producers after the controversial success of *The Birth of a Nation*, and although there was the occasional attempt to resurrect the genre during the 1930s, most notably with *So Red the Rose* (Paramount, 1935), these films had not produced any significant action at the box office.[10] With the major exception of *Jezebel* (Warner Bros., 1938), the hullabaloo following the publication of Margaret Mitchell's *Gone With the Wind* (1936) produced surprisingly few films about the antebellum South until the adaptation in 1939 conclusively proved that the representation of Southern history had box-office potential. Contemporary representations of the South, such as *Trail of the Lonesome Pine* (Paramount, 1936), *Banjo On My Knee* (20th Century-Fox, 1936) and *They Won't Forget* (Warner Bros., 1937), tended to show a grotesque vision of the South cast adrift from the rest of the Union, still struggling with defeat. Films such as *Fury* (MGM, 1936), *I Am a Fugitive from a Chain Gang* (Warner Bros., 1932) and *Boy Slaves* (RKO, 1938), which respectively depict lynching, the inhuman treatment of prisoners and child labour, are self-evidently set in the South, although the films themselves deny any specific location.[11]

In an attempt to boost the figures for Westerns produced during the mid-1930s, a number of encyclopaedias and histories of the genre include *Trail of the Lonesome Pine*, which was both a box-office success (making over $1 million in profit on its domestic release alone) and the first film to use the three-strip Technicolor process on location. However, only by a critical sleight of hand is it a Western. The film is an adaptation of John Fox Jr's 'famous novel' (as it is puffed in the credits) published in 1908, dramatised by Eugene Walter in 1912 and then made into a photoplay in 1912, 1914 and again in 1923. The story concerns a feud between two mountain families which has lasted generations and is brought to a head with the arrival of the railroad. The time of the drama is not specified in the film, but it is either in the present or the very recent past:

> Among the American mountains there are forgotten valleys where peoples dwell shut in. Old worlds, old ways, old codes have lived on unchanged.
>
> Each family is at war with the other over deadly feuds whose beginnings they cannot remember. But their hatred is their patriotism, their quaint customs are their religion. Such a feud has been carried on for generations by the Tollivers and Falins.

This opening text crawl gives way to the prologue, where we are introduced to the two families, both young and old, shooting at each other. In a pause in the shooting the cry of a new-born baby is heard and her mother prays for peace. There are no Indians in this film, no cowboys, no covered wagons, no moving frontier, just two savage families of hillbillies isolated from the rest of America.[12] Why, then, is this film so often cited as a Western? The answer lies both in a particular understanding and cultural construction of the South, and in the way Hollywood marketed its films.

In the case of the Tollivers and Falins, all they have ever known is the savage side of the divide. Both families are dirt poor; the Tolliver women go barefoot (there are no Falin women), and the men own little more than their guns. Apart from the sporadic outbursts of violence, however, life is fairly tolerable. Jud Tolliver, the father of the family, spends his time playing with the kids, refusing to grow up himself. His daughter, June (Sylvia Sydney), scampers aimlessly around the hills trying to put off marriage to her cousin Dave (Henry Fonda), who has recently been shot by one of the Falins and is suffering from an infected wound. Mammy (Beulah Bondi) is a dried-up husk of a woman whose burden is to suffer for those too thick-headed to realise that they live in a hostile world.

Into this world comes Jack Hale (Fred MacMurray), a railroad engineer who is bringing the line through the Falin's property but who needs the coal on the Tolliver's land. If the line is to go ahead with the minimum of fuss he has to bring the feud to a conclusion, or at least broker some kind of compromise. He wins the Tollivers over by offering them $5,000 in thirty days and a percentage of company earnings, but more importantly he saves Dave's arm from gangrene.

23. *Trail of the Lonesome Pine*
The illiterate Tolliver family ponder over the 'squirrel tracks and
chicken scratches' on a cheque

The family had hoped to heal the wound with herbal remedies, which,
like their illiteracy, is a sign of their backwardness. Dave tells Jack
'those squirrel tracks and chicken scratches don't mean nothing to me'.
When the first cheque arrives, the Tollivers are at a loss to figure out
what it is.

June soon becomes infatuated with Jack, but she remains a 'little
savage' in his eyes until she leaves the mountains and goes to town to
get an education. By then Dave's jealousy has got the better of him,
and he and Jack fight it out on the dirt streets of Gaptown. The Falins
join in the fray, which then sees Jack fighting alongside Dave. Held off
by the sheriff, the Falins vow to break their agreement with the
railroad. Small acts of sabotage lead to the final conflagration, when
they dynamite the bridge upon which sits a steam shovel. Unknown to
them the youngest Tolliver is playing engineer in the cabin of the
shovel; the ugly kid, the shovel and the bridge are blown up. June, who
has become something of a modern woman, returns to the mountain
seeking revenge. Instead of continuing the feud, Dave goes to the

Falins offering his hand in peace—it is Mammy's birthday and he finally gives her her greatest wish, an end to the fighting. Buck Falin accepts Dave's hand, but his son refuses and shoots Dave in the back. Buck then fills his son full of holes and carries Dave home.

Progress is the saviour of the Tollivers, but Dave embraces it only at the film's end because it changes the certainty of his world and also because it has come between him and June. Progress is beneficent, the railroad is not the rapacious monster it is in *Jesse James*, nor is it an anonymous force that pays little heed to the needs of those that stand in its way, as in Autry's films. Both the Falins and the Tollivers are treated fairly and there is not even a hint of underhandedness in Jack's dealings. They are gently but firmly persuaded to enter into the modern world, since all that holds them back is their hatred of the other family.

It is the women and children who most assertively lead their family into the future. The Tolliver's theme song, sung by Tater (Fuzzy Knight) in a crooning style reminiscent of Bing Crosby, is woven around the refrain 'love is everywhere', an image in harmony with the beautiful lake that their house looks out upon and with the autumnal colours of the trees that they live amongst. The Falins, who are without women, demand that Tater sings 'Stack-O-Lee' to accompany their fight with Dave. 'Stack-O-Lee' or 'Staggerlee' was a song much recorded by both black and white musicians. It tells the story of badman Staggerlee who shoots Billy Lyon over an argument about his hat, an image of banal depravity that is in keeping with the barren rocky hollow where the Falins live. Progress is only possible because the land, as in series Westerns, has provided hitherto hidden wealth.

For W.J. Cash, the South's reliance on cotton and tobacco, which held the region in a spiral of economic depression, vitiated progress. In *Trail of the Lonesome Pine*, progress is brought to the South through the agency of the railroad, which transforms the South, saving it from itself. This idea has parallels with Roosevelt's New Deal in the South, which was greeted, according to Cash, with great enthusiasm even though the 'basic Rooseveltian ideas, with their emphasis on the social values as against the individual, and on the necessity of revising all values in the light of the conditions created by the machine and the disappearance of the frontier, ran directly contrary to the basic Southern attitudes'.[13]

In his introduction to W.J. Cash's seminal work *The Mind of the South* (1941), Bertram Wyatt-Brown notes how 'Frederick Jackson Turner's hypothesis of a moving frontier as the defining key to

American society dominated historical thinking in the 1930s' and, in particular, how much it informed Cash's understanding of the South. For Cash, the South was not formed out of the aristocratic pretensions of a few Virginians, but out of physical contact with the wilderness where the cherished but fallacious ideal of the chivalrous gentleman met the 'frontier swagger' of the backwoodsman. To illuminate his point he quotes another writer on the subject of the Southerner:

> Sent to jail for fighting in the courthouse, he made the walls of the prison resound with unaccustomed shouts of merriment and revelry. Starting to fight a duel, he laid down his hand at poker, to resume it with a smile when he returned, and went on the field laughing with his friends, as to a picnic. Yet no one knew better the proprieties of life than himself—when to put off levity and treat grave subjects and persons with proper respect.

Cash recognises this is an 'overdrawn and idealised measure' of the Southerner, but he remains sympathetic to this image even as he recognises these characteristics as symptoms of a wider economic malaise that kept the South isolated from the rest of the nation.[14] Cash argues that the South as frontier continues into the twentieth century: the Civil War wrecked what little civilisation the South had established, and the thirty years of Yankee-imposed reconstruction made the 'frontier absolute and continual'. The South's reaction to reconstruction condemned it to a regressive agricultural, social, economic and political system.[15]

Cash is principally concerned with the culture of the Old South, but in the Southeast and in the four-state region of the Southwest—Oklahoma, Arkansas, Texas and Missouri—the frontier mentality had an even stronger hold on the popular imagination. In his study of the Dust Bowl migration and Okie culture in California, James N. Gregory notes that the Southwest 'did not develop the caste-like social structure of the Old South'. Cotton had come late to the region so that the plantation system and the large black population did not hold the same influence. Instead the population was marked by an 'attachment to their Western heritage':

> With 'no leisure class to romanticise cotton farming', observed anthropologist Oscar Lewis in his study of a central Texas county, cotton, despite its preeminence, 'could at no time compete with ranching in capturing the imagination of the people as an ideal way of life'. The other was oil, the zone's footloose second

industry. Complementing in many ways the folklore of the cattle West, the boom and bust oil economy kept the pioneer mythology of the second chance and the quick strike alive long after the agricultural system had lost its resilience.[16]

However, during the first half of the twentieth century, the romantic myth of the 'second chance' did not forestall massive migration out of the South either to industrialised Northern cities like Chicago and Detroit, or to California. This was accompanied by major shifts in employment and living arrangements as well as agricultural modernisation and environmental changes. 'By 1950', writes Gregory, 'Oklahoma had lost 55 percent of its agricultural labor force, Arkansas 52 percent, Texas 51 percent, and Missouri 47 percent. At mid-century, rural farm areas in the Western South supported two million fewer people than just twenty years earlier.'[17]

In a manner similar to Cash's writing of the South into Turner's frontier, film critics have been able to write *Trail of the Lonesome Pine* into the Western, which is principally figured through the movement of the Tollivers from isolated savagery into communal civilisation. This movement is not possible in the South described by Cash: it does not embrace progress and therefore does not join the modern Union. Instead, it remains isolated and backward.

The production of *Trail of the Lonesome Pine* was motivated in part by the continued exploitability of the property it was based upon and in part by the popularity of Erskine Caldwell's novel *Tobacco Road* (1932), a best-selling title and a huge success as a theatrical adaptation on Broadway in 1933, when it set a new record for the longest continuous run of any American play. While the utter depravity of Caldwell's poor whites made the book and play all but unfilmable (if it was to be faithful to its source), its notoriety and the public profile of Southern writers such as William Faulkner and Thomas Wolfe meant that Hollywood was certain to film properties that in some way emulated its milieu and character types. The box-office success of *Trail of the Lonesome Pine* in 1936 guaranteed that it would be imitated. Fox found a vehicle in *Banjo on My Knee*, which Faulkner worked on uncredited. Released in December 1936, *Banjo on My Knee* starred Barbara Stanwyck, Joel McCrea and Walter Brennan, and told, in producer Darryl Zanuck's words, 'a beautiful love story laid among a certain type of river people that exist on the Mississippi today'.

Newly wed Pearl's (Stanwyck) patience is sorely tested by her husband Ernie (Joel McCrea), who consistently absents himself from the narrative and their bed whenever it looks as if they are finally going to consummate the marriage. This is a problem for Pearl, but in the film's scheme of things it is an even bigger headache for her father-in-law Newt (Walter Brennan), who has waited many a year to play 'St Louis Blues' outside his son and daughter-in-law's bedroom on their first night of matrimony. Newt's neighbours had serenaded him and his bride with the song and now it is his turn to pass on this totem of good luck and blessing for his future grandchild. The setting is a cluster of rafts tied to an island in the middle of the Mississippi; like the Tollivers and the Falins, Newt's family lives an isolated existence. But the emphasis on consummating the marriage, the excessive drinking and drunkenness and no sight of a beneficent world of progress or some hidden or unrealised wealth to relieve Newt and kin of their poverty shifts the story away from the Arcadia in which the Tollivers and Falins fought their feud.

The film caused initial difficulties between the production company and the PCA. A reader of the first complete script complained about the 'excessive drinking' and the 'suggestive running gag showing Newt's efforts to have Pearl and Ernie sleep together so that the marriage may be consummated'. Darryl Zanuck, in a fit of outrage, responded with a three-page tightly typed letter which made the counter-complaint that 'Your reader has injected smut and sex where none was ever intended . . . It is a real human romantic drama, about real human beings . . . They are not drunks, they are not whores.'[18] Somewhat disingenuously, Zanuck felt that his film had been slighted. The PCA reader's view is not without foundation, for even after a number of changes had been made in the script to bring it in line with the Code, the film can still be read as sexually suggestive. But if the characters were to have any credence as a 'certain type of river people' they needed to be given traits which are by necessity vulgar—given Hollywood's world-view how else to characterise an underclass? For Zanuck the vulgar is ameliorated by playing on stereotyped ideas of an American vernacular, and by the construction of the characters as childlike. As such, for Zanuck at least, sexual innuendo simply does not exist.

Following a series of implausible incidents, Pearl and Newt end up performing in the New Orleans bar Cafe Creole, where she wows a slumming sophisticated audience with sentimental ditties and he gets them dancing by playing his bones and banjo and banging out a medley of minstrel tunes on his weird musical contraption that harnesses all sorts of homemade instruments. This is a *declassé* version of the kind of novelty act contemporaneously performed by the

Hoosier Hot Shots, a comedy hillbilly group who found fame playing on the same bill as Gene Autry on WLS's *National Barn Dance* in the 1930s. Smiley Burnette also made this kind of performance central to his act and is often seen playing novelty instruments. In the 1940s Spike Jones and His City Slickers would popularise yet another variant.[19] Despite their success and acclaim, Newt and Pearl drift back to their river home where he finally plays 'St Louis Blues' as Pearl and Ernie consummate their marriage in the film's closing moments.

The film's opening scenes create a view of a primitive yet vital community which draws upon the combined stereotypes of poor Southern whites and blackface minstrels. One of the marginal characters, Buddy (Buddy Ebson), performs accompanying dances to Newt's music-making both on the rafts and at the Cafe Creole, and belongs firmly within the minstrel tradition. The film is a grand farce, a celebration of vernacular Americana and was well received by the American press, who responded positively to the 'novel characters and situation'.[20] Though the film delves into the same pool of stories, character types and general Southern location as *Trail of the Lonesome Pine*, it could never be mistaken for a Western. Like the characters in *Tobacco Road*, Newt and his family absolutely shun modernity, choosing instead to remain like isolated children in an adult America. Unlike the Virginian, who in the early stages of the book moves from being a young man who takes pleasure in childish pranks to being an absolute believer in the sanctity of property and the owner's right to protect it (an even greater acceptance of responsibility than his marriage), or the Tollivers and the Falins who eventually embrace the outside world, Newt is happy to continue to exist in blissful ignorance of greater America. For Newt, the Southern frontier is the only world he cares for.

The smaller production companies were acutely aware of the wider shifts and changes in Hollywood's cycles and trends, despite the fact that most of the critical writing on series Westerns holds the genre in isolation from the rest of Hollywood. The box-office success of *Trail of the Lonesome Pine* was exploited by the Autry vehicle *Yodelin' Kid From Pine Ridge* (Republic, 1937). The story's context is given in the opening credit crawl: 'Contrary to general belief large cattle ranches are to be found among the turpentine forests of Florida and Georgia'. Rather than the South moving West, here, the West moves South. The film begins with a barefoot Milly Baynum (Betty Bronson) emulating Sylvia Sydney's character. She is shown running in and out of the trees before coming to attention when she hears Gene Autry's yodelling. Instead of feuding families, the conflict is between cattle ranchers and turpentiners—between cowboys and hillbillies.

The film replays the same plot as *Tumbling Tumbleweeds*. Autry sides with the turpentiners against his father, who is unknowingly in cahoots with a band of crooked cattlemen, who want not only to burn off the forest to create a prairie but also intend to steal Autry's father's land and stock. Disowned by his father but loved by Milly, Autry leaves Georgia and becomes a champion rodeo rider. Some years later he returns in the company of the Millhouse Wild West Show. In the parade to herald their arrival, Autry (accompanied by the comic string band The Tennessee Ramblers) sings about the Southwest, confirming and reinforcing the idea of the West in the South introduced in the opening text crawl. By the end of the movie the real villains are brought to book, and the cowboys symbolically link hands with the hillbillies. Milly has learnt to read and wear store-bought clothes and shoes, becoming a fitting partner for Autry.

In Westerns, the Southern frontier is erased and the South is eventually included in the Union. Secession or isolation thereby becomes a moot point. Southern savagery evaporates, the 'semi-barbarous' public burning and lynching of Negroes becomes the semi-legitimate private (i.e. corporate) hanging of horse-thieves, the poor disenfranchised white becomes the democratic cowboy. Conflicts are, then, determined by a symbolic North/South divide where the West provides the space in which the Union can be reunited. Marcus Klein records Theodore Roosevelt's observation, in *Ranch Life and the Hunting Trail*, that although cowboys might come from anywhere, they were prevailingly Southerners, 'as might be considered to be appropriate beyond the mere fact of the matter, because Southerners were better candidates than other Americans for a role of proud and sure defeat'.[21]

The process of assimilating the South, or at least the Southerner, into the West began in earnest with the publication and success of Owen Wister's *The Virginian* (1902). By making the hero a Southerner, Wister uses the West to appropriate the perceived values of the antebellum South, while suppressing the heritage of slavery. In a passage following the lynching of cattle rustlers, the hero's boss Judge Henry persuades the heroine of the righteousness of this act:

> For in all sincerity I see no likeness in principle whatever between burning Southern Negroes in public and hanging Wyoming

horse-thieves in private. I consider the burning a proof that the South is semi-barbarous, and the hanging a proof that Wyoming is determined to be civilised. We do not torture our criminals when we lynch them. We do not invite spectators to enjoy their death agony. We put no such hideous disgrace upon the United States.

Despite the gaping holes in Judge Henry's argument, the heroine surrenders to his polemic, as she will also surrender her heart to the hero. Confronted by a man formed in the mould of a chivalrous romantic hero, her Eastern rationalism is doomed. Thomas McGuane has noted how Wister's book could not have been called 'The Michigander' because the narrative demands a hero birthed in romanticism and not realism. This romanticism comes from the South, not the East or the North and not yet the West, for that, at least in fiction, is still an empty stage. The West will allow the Southerner to cleanse and renew himself, to make himself over again as an American. Without the blank space of the West which allows the South actively to reinvent itself, the Southerner is forced either to remain in a state of suspended savagery or to be the passive recipient of the benefits of Northern benevolence.

That other great formative Western narrative, Zane Grey's *Riders of the Purple Sage* (1912), similarly has a Southern hero gone West. Born in Missouri, Lassiter moves with his sister Milly and his parents to Texas. After Milly's abduction, he trails her to Utah where the story is set. Milly has died before he finds her, but he is temporarily reunited towards the end of the story with his niece, Bess, the Masked Rider, who believes her father to be the infamous rustler Oldring. As the forces of evil close in, Lassiter reveals Bess's true parents with the aid of a faded miniature portrait:

> You are Milly Erne's child. Your name is Elizabeth Erne. You're not Oldring's daughter. You're the daughter of Frank Erne, a man once my best friend. Look! Here's his picture beside Milly's. He was handsome, an' as fine an' gallant a Southern gentleman as I ever seen. Frank come of an old family. You come of the best blood, lass, an' blood tells.[22]

This linking of the Westerner to the South, through the idea of bloodlines, gives him or her an undisputed, transparent Anglo-Saxon heritage and a distinct American identity. That is, it simultaneously racialises and democratises the cowboy/girl. The image of a class-bound South is evacuated and a classless but racialised West is substituted.

In Andy Adams' *Log of a Cowboy* (1903) the South again acts as a means of establishing an unimpeachable American identity—white, Anglo-Saxon Protestant. The book opens: 'Just why my father moved, at the close of the civil war, from Georgia to Texas, is to this good hour a mystery to me. While we did not exactly belong to the poor whites, we classed with them in poverty, being renters; but I am inclined to think my parents were intellectually superior to that common type of the South.' Adams' hero may have been poor—but not trash—and becoming a cowboy is his proving ground. The theme is continued in the autobiography of the African-American Nat Love: *The Life and Adventures of Nat Love. Better Known in the Cattle Country as 'Deadwood Dick'. A True History of Slavery Days, Life on the Great Cattle Ranges and on the 'Wild and Woolly' West, Based on Facts, and Personal Experiences of the Author*. First published in 1907, the book attempted to find its market in the wake of the success of *The Virginian* by offering the 'real' Deadwood Dick as opposed to the dime novel hero who bore the same name. Nat Love's story shifts from recalling a childhood spent in slavery, and his family's struggle to survive the immediate postwar years, to becoming a cowboy. Through a shared enthusiasm for working with cattle, horseplay, 'tall story' telling and an absolute contempt and hatred of Mexicans and Indians, Love finds comradeship with other cowboys. After his move to the West he never again mentions his family and his life as a slave. In the West, he is able to take control over his own life, to function as an equal to other men. In this narrative, slavery is interchangeable with class, its racial under-pinnings repressed and displaced onto Indians and Mexicans. As with the Anglo-Saxon, in the classless West his race becomes invisible, but manifested through his representation of the Indian and Mexican as Other.

Like the Virginian, Nat Love's Southern past is left behind. Also like his white counterpart, his life as a cowboy comes to an end with the rude arrival of modernity. The Virginian becomes a businessman and Nat Love finds work as a Pullman porter. Love's story is an archetypical American drama of aspiration and assimilation com-pounded through his use of the formal narrative strategies of the Great White Western to achieve his goals. Paradoxically, his autobiography speaks both to the genre's agenda of racial exclusion in his hatred of Indians and Mexicans *and* to its ability to absorb difference. The Western frontier helps form the American out of the Southerner, which in turn gives way to the modern world in which both the Virginian and Nat Love are able to find a space. This process of assimilation and progress was a key theme in both the novel and adaptation of *Cimarron*.

Both book and film conform to the thesis that Alexander Saxton develops in *The Rise and Fall of the White Republic*, that the West operated as an assimilationist space in which white egalitarianism was established through a contradictory racist programme of exclusion. By focusing on a woman's passage from domestic innocent to professional politician, *Cimarron* suggests a radical vision of American democratic principles, but one which is contradicted by a reactionary project of exclusion based on white supremacy.

The Venables are an old Southern family who moved to Kansas after the war. Led by the mother, they are at odds both with Yancey's dreams of adventure and the town's Midwestern notions of bourgeois temperance. The opening chapter sets up the themes of family blood-lines, regional identity and racial hierarchy that will have such an important effect on Sabra's experience of frontier life. Sabra's Southern ancestry gives her fortitude, bearing and a sense of distinction. But without her husband Yancey Cravat she would become like the rest of her family, an isolated and decadent member of an irrelevant aristocracy. This idea is played to lesser effect in the character of Ruth Cameron (Marguerite Churchill) in Fox's epic *The Big Trail* (1930). She is an orphaned Southern belle, dressed like her namesakes the Cameron girls in the early stages of *The Birth of a Nation*. She is charged with escorting her younger brother and sister on a westward-heading wagon train out of Missouri. Without the Westerner played by John Wayne to aid her transformation from innocent to pioneering woman, she would have barely survived the first mile of the journey.

The Venables have transplanted Southern culture wholesale into Kansas where Ferber sets them off against the puritan Midwesterners. Their garden walls off the outside world, forbidding 'that course vulgarian, the Kansas sunflower'. Felice Venable bemoans the impossibility of growing Spanish moss in a Northern climate: 'A neighboring mid-west matron, miffed, resents this. "But that's a parasite! And real creepy, almost. I was in South Carolina and saw it. Kind of floating, like ghosts. And no earthly good" '. The foods at their table are also Southern: 'The frying pan and the deep-fat kettle (both, perhaps, as much as anything responsible for the tragedy of '64) still spattered their deadly fusillade in this household'. Despite their lack of great wealth they retain black servants, a 'remnant of Mississippi feudalism'. Above the family dining table a black boy, Isaiah, who 'looked a simian version of one of Raphael's ceilinged angels', fans the diners as they listen both captivated and horrified by Yancey's monologue on the adventures awaiting him and Sabra in the Oklahoma territory.[23]

This first scene of the novel is repeated in the film, though the extent to which the Venables' Southern identity is outlined is much reduced and is transferred away from the garden and food and onto Felice Venable's belief that Yancey has Indian blood in him: 'Some half-breeds are no darker', a line that echoes *Showboat*'s 'one drop of Negro blood'. Whatever Yancey's racial pedigree, Sabra has married beneath herself. Despite her unstinting loyalty and love for her husband, this class tension provides much of the initial dramatic intrigue. To make matters worse, Yancey uses his newspaper to petition for Indian rights. He finds this petition unproblematic, despite his endless enthusiasm for exploiting the opportunities for self-advancement and adventure offered by the government's confiscation of Indian lands.

Because the town of Osage must obey the law of government, Yancey's first task after he sets up his newspaper office is to prove that Lon Yountis killed the city's previous newspaper proprietor. Yancey is the agent of both government and God. The latter is confirmed when he is asked to lead the city's first prayer meeting, held in one of the many wood and canvas saloons. All the city turns up, good and bad, even the Jew, Sol Levy, whom Yancey had earlier saved from a 'crucifixion' at the hands of Yountis.[24] The only representative missing is Isaiah. This character is the familiar black child-fool who wishes to be like his 'Massa', but clearly never can. On Sunday the Cravats walk to church along the muddy and anarchic streets. Stopped in their tracks by howls of laughter they turn to see Isaiah following behind dressed in an unselfconscious comic attempt to mimic Yancey. The minstrel legacy of the black man/boy attempting to be white lies beneath this scene. Yancey turns him back to their house with the promise to buy him a proper suit to assuage his disappointment about not going with the family to church. This exclusion is crucial to the film's ideological project of offering what appears to be an 'open door' policy to the American democratic promise but which is, in actuality, exclusive. By first excluding Isaiah from the community and then later having him killed trying to protect Yancey's child, the film represses the presence of blacks within America.

The novel is much more vicious in its racial portrayal of Isaiah.

Constantly referred to as monkey-like, he sleeps in a 'kennel' and is expelled from the narrative when he makes an Osage serving girl pregnant. The Osages, unlike other Indian tribes (according to Ferber's version), absolutely forbid miscegenation between themselves and blacks. Their race is pure, having only ever mixed with white blood. No doubt this saves them from becoming a vanishing tribe, for Yancey believes Indians to be 'a naturally sterile race'.[25] Isaiah and the Indian girl are kidnapped by the Osages. She and her baby are sewn into a fresh cow hide that is left to shrink in the heat of the sun. Isaiah is bound to a stake and is tortured by a rattlesnake tied on a leather leash: as the dew forms on the ground, the leather stretches, allowing the snake to reach Isaiah, and he dies a horrible death.

When it is discovered their son wishes to marry an Indian, Yancey explains to Sabra that 'Cim's like your father, Lewis Venable. Weak stuff, but good stock. Ruby's pure Indian blood and a magnificent animal. It's hard on you now my darling. But their children and their grandchildren are going to be such stuff as Americans are made of.'[26] But when black, white and red cultures mix, it produces a grotesque comic vision: 'Arita Red Feather's dialect became a bewildering thing in which her native Osage, Sabra's refined diction, and Isaiah's Southern Negro accent were rolled into an almost unintelligible jargon. "I'm gwine wash um clothes big rain water extremely nice um make um clothes white fo' true" '.[27] The corrupting element is black and it must be expunged.

The significance of Isaiah's exclusion lies in the fact that he acts as a representative of the Old South. His symbolic value can be understood through Saxton's reading of the Old South. The setting in which minstrelsy is performed functions as a place existing outside of time, a nostalgic symbol for what has been lost to the new urban dweller and the westering migrant:

> What has been left behind collectively may be a rural past, but individually it is childhood. New cities and new frontiers, attractive to conspiring and perspiring adults, have little room for children; and the South, in the legend of blackface minstrelsy, became the antithesis to both.[28]

By shifting the story out of the Old South (represented by the Venables and Isaiah) and into the New West (represented by Yancey) the characters are shown to be encountering adulthood, as is America. The theme of maturation is present not only in the story's historically epic scope—Oklahoma's shift from territory to State—but also in the discourses on racial and ethnic assimilation and on the role of women within the public sphere. With the exclusion of Isaiah, racial and ethnic assimilation is carried by the less problematic figure of the Indian and achieved through Sabra's eventual conversion into a racially tolerant matriarch. As an act of miscegenation, the marriage of her son to the daughter of the Osage chief is mitigated through the bride's status as a princess and because her tribe are oil-rich.

The displacement of the issue of miscegenation between white and black onto the Indian allows the story to maintain the myth of America as a nation able to assimilate all races and ethnicities. The long-standing image of the vanishing Indian, either through genocide or assimilation, means that the race does not pose a threat to the dominance of the white bloodline, nor does the Indian present a challenge to the presumption of an egalitarian America. The self-evident hierarchy between white and black, on the other hand, contradicts this egalitarianism; hence the need to exclude black men and women from narratives of nation-building. Further, because Sabra's son has married the daughter of a chief there is a tacit re-establishment of class hierarchies that were left behind in the Old South. These shibboleths of assimilation facilitate Sabra's conversion from Southern belle to American woman: positing an image of assimilation and national unity without having to face the very real negation of this promise posed by the exclusion and segregation of African-Americans.

Corporate Carpetbaggers

In his report to Jack Warner on the script of *Virginia City* (1940), Joseph Breen suggested he 'change the word "Southerner's" to "your" in order not to deliberately offend your Southern patrons who might not think the war is over yet'.[29] Breen was paying heed to the Southern box office, but he really had no need to worry. Westerns produced during 1939–41 were fundamentally supportive of Southern romanticism. Aided in part by the casting of stars with female marquee appeal such as Robert Taylor and Tyrone Power, the Southerner's transformation into a Westerner helped to romanticise the Westerner.

By the end of 1940, sympathetic Southern characters in Westerns had become commonplace: Wallace Beery's Reb in *Wyoming* (aka *Badman of Wyoming*, MGM, 1940)—in the same year he played a Union soldier in *The Man From Dakota* (MGM); Robert Taylor's

24. *The Westerner*
Judge Roy Bean (Walter Brennan) meets his death dressed in his old
Confederate uniform

Southern aristocrat in *Stand Up and Fight*; Cagney's populist figure in
The Oklahoma Kid; William Holden's Missourian in *Arizona*. Southern
figures who fail fully to fuse their identities with the new nation
emerging in the West are still allowed to die nobly: Marlene Dietrich's
Frenchy, who brings her black maid with her from New Orleans in
Destry Rides Again; John Carradine's Southern gambler, who redeems
himself during the Indian attack in *Stagecoach*; Walter Brennan's Judge
Roy Bean, who dies in his old Confederate uniform in *The Westerner*.
The Southerner in Westerns simultaneously evoked political fissures in
the Union and, paradoxically, a nostalgia for a 'lost' America *and* a
progressive desire to build a 'new' America.

The 1939/40 Western whole-heartedly adopted the series Western's
theme of the threat to home and family. In a bar room scene from *The
Oklahoma Kid*, which concludes with the Kid outwitting two deputies
and then mounting his horse in best series Western fashion, the Judge
challenges the Kid's patriotism. The Kid retorts:

> In the first place the white people steal the land from the Indians.
> Right. They get paid for it, yeah, a measly dollar and forty cents
> an acre; price agreed at the point of a gun. Then the immigrants
> sweat and strain and break their hearts carving out a civilisation.
> Fine. Great. Then when they all get pretty and prosperous along
> come the grafters, land grabbers and politicians, and with one
> hand skim off the cream and with the other scoop up the gravy.

This explicit criticism of 'grafters, land grabbers and politicians' is a
common rhetorical device in this cycle of Westerns, though perhaps
more forcefully made here.

Although A-feature Westerns used the major theme of series
Westerns—the threat to home and land through repossession—the
availability of large budgets meant that the major studios were able to
create a more monstrous visualisation of the forces imperilling the
common man who seeks only to fulfil Jefferson's promise of a nation of
self-sufficient farmers. The threat posed to communities in this cycle
of Westerns takes the form of organised crime syndicates in *The
Oklahoma Kid*, *Dodge City* and *Destry Rides Again*; cattle barons
in *The Westerner*; monopolists in *Arizona*; stock market speculators in
Union Pacific; demagogues in *Santa Fé Trail* and *Dark Command*;
Mexican bandits in *Virginia City*; Indians under foreign influence
in *Drums Along the Mohawk* and *Northwest Passage*; arms traders in
Allegheny Uprising; religious persecution in *Brigham Young*. But it is the
railroad—'Hell on wheels that claims a man's life for every day of
the year' (*Union Pacific*)—that offers the primary threat.

In *Dodge City*, the race at the beginning of the film between the
train and the stagecoach is a celebration of the transforming power of
technology and industrialisation, but in its wake it brings lawlessness. In *Jesse James* and *The Return of Frank James* the railroad is
unequivocally the villain: 'The St Louis-Midland's got this whole State
hog-tied. They got the police, they got the courts, they got everything
. . . The railroad's got too much at stake to let two little farmer's-
boys . . . bollox things up.' In *Stand Up and Fight*, set in the antebellum
South, the conflict initially centres on the competition between a
mule-powered haulage company (which is being surreptitiously used
in the illegal trading of slaves) and the recent arrival in Cumberland of
the Ohio and Baltimore railroad. In *Let Freedom Ring*, Nelson Eddy's
character returns home after getting an Eastern education to discover
the railroad is running roughshod over his neighbours and friends. It
is not the railroad *per se* that is the problem, since the people are

not against the benefits it can bring. Rather, it is the undemocratic means that the railroad owners use to squash any obstacle or voice of resistance.

The appeal is to the might of the railroad industry—and by extension all industrial and business corporations—to treat fairly those with whom it deals. A similar position was held by Roosevelt in a campaign speech he made in Chicago in October 1936: 'The people of America have no quarrel with business. They insist only that the power of concentrated wealth shall not be abused.'[30] Nothing can stop progress, nor is it deemed undesirable, but it must also be accountable to the people and recognise their rights. This was a story that had been consistently played out in Gene Autry's Westerns.

Like *Jesse James*, *The Return of Frank James* and *Destry Rides Again*, *The Westerner* (United Artists, 1940) is not particularly concerned with the 'Frontier', but with the establishment and defence of a Jeffersonian pastoral idyll. Greg Toland's photography manages powerfully to evoke the destruction of homes, families, crops and the ever-present threat to repossess the land. The film closes with the return of the exiled families and an image of lush fertile land waiting to be harvested. In *Stagecoach*, the Ringo Kid's drive for vengeance is motivated by the destruction of his family. The resolution of the film, which sees him successfully exact an eye for an eye, is completed by his ride on a buckboard across the border with the prostitute Dallas (Claire Trevor) to build a new life and family, a proposition given plausibility by the central dramatic device around the birth of Lucy Mallory's child and the mothering role assumed by Dallas. *Arizona* concerns one woman's dream to own a ranch; to achieve this, and against sound advice, she borrows money. When her dream ranch is almost complete the villain calls in the debt. The film is brought to its climax by the threat of repossession, not the confrontation between civilisation and savagery.

More than any other previous holder of the office, President Roosevelt aligned himself with Jeffersonian ideals. In 'Is There a Jefferson on the Horizon?' (a review of a book on Jefferson and Hamilton) Roosevelt argued that 'Jefferson, a veritable Westerner of his day' was needed again to counter the rise of the new Hamiltonians who echo their forebear in his 'fondness for his Chamber of Commerce and his contempt for the opinion of the masses'.[31] In Westerns of this period, a long-standing conception of the American body politic as pulled between the contending forces of government controlled by commerce and government controlled by the people is also expressed in localised divisions drawn from representations of the Civil War.

In the Jesse James 'trilogy' produced by 20th Century-Fox—*Jesse James* (1939), *The Return of Frank James* (1940) and *Belle Starr—The Bandit Queen* (1941)—the South is used to invoke a pastoral vision of America *against* which progress must be measured. In the Warner Bros. 'trilogy' starring Errol Flynn, directed by Michael Curtiz and scripted by Robert Buckler—*Dodge City* (1939), *Virginia City* (1940) and, *Santa Fé Trail* (1940)—the South is used to invoke fissures in the Union which are resolved through its displacement and incorporation into the West, out of which a new Union evolves.

Jesse James makes use of both Southern and Western iconography, enabling the film to speak to concerns raised by the Depression while simultaneously addressing itself to a mythological past. In this manner it plays out a similar function to *Gone With the Wind*. In a comparative analysis of *Gone With the Wind* and *The Grapes of Wrath*, Thomas H. Pauly has written:

> Though it was less daring and less accomplished than Ford's work as an artistic creation, *Gone With the Wind* was similarly preoccupied with the problem of survival in the face of financial deprivation and social upheaval. Both movies also demonstrate a nostalgic longing for the agrarian way of life which is ruthlessly being replaced by the fearful new economic forces of capitalism and industrialisation. By way of extension, both reflect an intense concern for the devastating consequences of these conditions upon self-reliant individualism and family unity, two of America's most cherished beliefs. In each case, however, serious concern for these implications is dissipated into indulgent sentimentalism so that the audience's anxieties are alleviated rather than aggravated.[32]

While images of the West are deeply inscribed in the myth of Jesse James and indicated in the film's opening text crawl (which celebrates the role played by the railroads in opening up the West while condemning the manner in which this was achieved), they are confounded by the opening scenes of a sleazy railroad employee (Brian Donlevy) conning farmers out of their land. These scenes share little in common with the kind of Western iconography found in, for example, *Dodge City* or *Stagecoach*. Instead of adobe ranch houses or the isolated prairie cabin, the film presents neat wooden homes occupied by 'salt of the earth' types cast to approximate Hollywood's idea of Dorothea Lange's or Walker Evans' Dust Bowl migrants: an old couple with young children, a mother and adolescent, the Jameses. In each case there is a marked absence of a strong patriarchal figure. It is images like these (rather than the often remarked-on presence of actors Henry Fonda, John Carradine and Jane Darwell who also starred in *The Grapes of Wrath*) that conclusively link the film to the Depression.

As in *The Grapes of Wrath* and *Gone With the Wind*, the underlying theme in *Jesse James* is that of loss: of land, home, family, community, and a way of life. The characters must struggle against almost insurmountable odds to reassert their values and needs, and in so doing they emerge more resilient than ever. According to Pauly, during this period the Civil War functioned as a way of addressing the problems of the Depression without having to allude to it directly. By looking back to a time when America was divided against itself, and by suggesting how the country had dealt with these divisions, Hollywood could offer up a palliative for contemporary tensions. All the A-feature Westerns dealt with from the period discussed here (with the exception of *Drums Along the Mohawk* and the other 'Revolution' Westerns) use the lead-up to and/or the repercussions of the Civil War as a key factor in their representation of conflict.

These films present the promise of a prosperous future through an idealisation of the past. This helps to explain the otherwise gratuitous presence in *Jesse James* of the character Pinky: the James' 'Faithful Darkie', an Uncle Tom and Mammy rolled into one. As a pliant symbol of slavery and the antebellum South without its heinous connotations, Pinky is crucial to this nostalgic construction of American history because he suggests an unproblematic past. The problems faced by the Jameses and their community are external (large corporations in the guise of the railroad) not internal (race). Like Scarlett O'Hara and the Joads, the Jameses are faced by overwhelming and impersonal odds. With the Jameses forced into a life of crime, the film switches from rural melodrama to Western. As such, the multifaceted conflicts of post Civil War America are reduced to a set of uncontroversial and simplistic oppositions, in which it becomes possible for the community to galvanise itself into action and to overcome the common enemy.

The ambivalence displayed towards Jesse as hero/villain, and the generic hybridity of the film as a rural melodrama and Western, are absent from *The Return of Frank James*. The film opens where its precursor closed, with the death of Jesse, and then cuts to find Frank back on the land steering a plough through rocky Ozark soil. As in *Jesse James*, this Arcadian dream is again vanquished when the Governor pardons the Ford brothers. For the greater part of its second act, the film is set in the Rocky Mountains, where Frank takes his pant legs out of his boot tops and stops looking like a farmer and more like a gunfighter. Colorado is the West and Missouri is now the Old South, although at times an audience could be forgiven for confusing the two since there are more blacks working in subservient positions in Denver, Colorado than in Liberty, Missouri.

The connection with the Old South is more fully developed in *Frank James* and is particularly apparent in the court room scene where the Civil War is metaphorically refought. Frank has given himself up to the law (which is still in the employ of the railroad) in order to save an innocent Pinky from hanging. Here Frank's innate goodness is fully established (he gives up his freedom to save a 'Negro'), and the representation of the railroad owners as Yankee carpetbaggers is confirmed. Unlike Jesse, Frank never gives up his commitment to community and the idea of the family. As a result, he finally makes it back into society after the Governor makes an unexplained *volte face* and pardons him. Wrongs have been made right, and with Gene Tierney's character as an inducement he may move West permanently.

Capitalising on Gene Tierney's success in *The Return of Frank James*, 20th-Century Fox gave her the title role in *Belle Starr—The Bandit Queen*. The film opens with an image of the war-torn South being turned back into productive farm land. With the prompting of an old rag doll turned up by a plough, one of Belle Starr's ex-slaves tells her story to his son: 'She was what the white folks calls a legend'. Tierney plays the part as if she was Scarlett O'Hara, at times pushing her performance into a virtual parody of Vivian Leigh's. The crucial distinction between the two, however, is that Belle Starr takes to a life of crime rather than hoping for a better tomorrow. She and her husband continue to fight for the lost cause after Lee's surrender, motivated by the occupying Union forces' wanton destruction of her home and property as a punishment for harbouring a wounded guerrilla, her husband-to-be (Randolph Scott). Like Jesse James before him, Scott's character starts with apparent justification by pursuing his own war against the North, but, also like Jesse, he soon crosses over into criminal activity and pays the price (Paramount's 1938 film *The Texans* uses a similar narrative structure). Belle is killed trying to get him to pull back from his criminal activities. By the end he has recognised the error of his ways and submits to the due process of the law, but only after he and his persecuting Union officer have covered up the fact of Belle's death so that an American legend can be born: one that attests to the nation's abhorrence of tyranny and injustice. The film ends by returning to where it began on an image of peaceful work and pastoral fertility—American Arcadia.

The Jesse James 'trilogy' used the South and the repercussions of the Civil War as a way to explore the impact of external forces on individuals. The Warner Bros. 'trilogy' used the Civil War as a historical backdrop for its epic visualisation of nation-building. *Dodge City* opens with the prologue, 'The Civil War has ended, armies disbanded—the nation turns to building the West. Kansas 1866.' The railroad is reaching West and Colonel Dodge stops long enough to give a new town his name. He hopes that it will one day blossom to become the 'flower of the prairie'. Wade Hatton (Errol Flynn) turns down his offer to become the town's policeman and heads south to Texas to get into the cattle business. Nine years lapse and Dodge City has turned into a den of sin and vice where honest ranchers are duped and families are, at best, forced to move on to Wichita or, worse, are all but destroyed. The Union and Confederate armies may have been disbanded but the old allegiances still hold sway; the conflicting forces in the town are neatly divided into North and South, where the singing of their respective anthems motivates the battle in the saloon. Wade Hatton, who had fought on the side of the South, again refuses the badge of sheriff—his business is cattle—but eventually he finds a sense of social obligation when the town's 'sheriff', played by a little boy, is killed. Time and again the message is reinforced that the West needs men like Flynn—strong men for desperate times—to accept responsibility if the Union is to be held. Because Hatton has fought for the South, yet has accepted responsibility, he is well placed to see this vision accomplished. The villains, aligned with the North, represent unrestrained capitalism, the enemy of the commonwealth.

Regardless of whether he is playing a Southerner or a Northerner, Flynn's characters in the 'trilogy' are based on the figure of the Southern cavalier. Noting the influence of Sir Walter Scott's romances on the Southern imagination, where the antimodern martial ideal fused republican and romantic tradition, moral and aesthetic appeal, T.J. Jackson Lears writes:

> The fusion seemed most compelling to slave-holding Southerners, whose chivalric posturing and enthusiasm for Scott have become proverbial. Though the political importance of Southern medievalism has been exaggerated, there is no doubt that proslavery critics of Northern commercialism held aloft the image of the aristocratic country gentleman, who fought hard and rode

25. *Virginia City*
Confederate spy Miss Haynes (Miriam Hopkins) masquerades
as a saloon girl

hard and cared not a fig for money matters. The image was more than a piece of ideological mystification; it was grounded in Southern customs and traditions which were reinforced by the Civil War. The widespread obeisance to notions of personal honor, the persistence of dueling, and the proliferation of military schools designed to produce 'officers and gentlemen'—all underscored the importance of premodern martial ideals among upper-class Southerners well into the twentieth century.[33]

Flynn's character assumes many of the Southern aristocrat's virtues and abilities but, significantly, these are democratised by being fused with the figure of the cowboy.

As with the two films that exploited the success of *Jesse James*, *Virginia City* and *Sante Fé Trail* similarly extended the scope of their Southern references beyond that of their predecessor. *Virginia City* opens in the closing year of the war. Flynn is a Union officer who must stop Randolph Scott's Southern officer from shipping bullion out of Virginia City. The two figures are brought together when they join

26. *Santa Fé Trail*
'So perish all such enemies of the Union'—Robert E. Lee. John Brown
(Raymond Massey) prepares to go to his grave

forces to defeat the common enemy in the guise of Mexican bandits.
This theme of reconciliation and unity is echoed in the love story
between Flynn's character and the Southern belle (and spy) Miss
Hayne (Miriam Hopkins), who masquerades as a saloon singer and
dancer. Having refused to give up the location of the Confederates'

buried booty to the Union authorities, believing it should be used to help rebuild the South, Flynn's character is condemned to death. In a desperate bid to save his life, Miss Hayne appeals to President Lincoln for clemency. It is on the eve of Lee's surrender to Grant. 'We have lost, then', she says. 'Not lost. Found', responds Lincoln. 'You're coming back into the Union, Miss Hayne. You came over two thousand miles to save the life of a man who was once your enemy. I think very likely you're in love with him. To me you two are symbols of what I hope we can do for our country.' Lincoln is a beneficent and strong patriarch, an absent figure in so many of Hollywood's Depression narratives: from series Westerns to the gangster film; from Deanna Durbin to W.C. Fields' films. During the Depression Lincoln acted as a key mythological figure invoked by 'mainstream New Deal Populism' to suggest the possibility of resolution for troubled times. The radical Popular Front, as Michael Denning argues, 'was more likely to invoke John Brown'.[34]

Santa Fé Trail's setting is 'Bloody Kansas'. Like *Virginia City*, it attempts to strike a sympathetic balance and a unity between the North and South. Again, this is attempted via a friendship between officers and through the love story. The threat to peace and stability is provided by the figure of John Brown. By substituting Brown for the Mexican bandits, the film shifts its concerns away from an external peril and onto a domestic threat. Brown's objective is to 'break up the American Union as it now exists . . . with the entire nation in a state of chaos we can dictate our terms.' The newly graduated West Point officers—all of whom will go on to illustrious careers during the Civil War—are sent to break up the armed gangs who are terrorising Kansas. The film's sympathies are almost wholly on the side of the South, with Flynn playing the hero J.E.B. Stuart and the moral centre provided by the figure of Jeff Davis (who tells the graduates their duty is to the 'defence of the rights of man'). Brown, on the other hand, is played by Raymond Massey as a demagogic madman. Northern rationalism provided by George Custer (Ronald Reagan) —playing second fiddle to Stuart in both love and war—strikes a poor balance: 'There's a purpose to that madness, one that can't easily be dismissed'. But it is dismissed: the scenes of desolation wrought by Brown and his 'army' and the sight of the enfeebled slaves he has 'freed', who wish only to go back to the security of the plantation, all but annihilates the possibility of seeing the 'purpose' in the 'madness'. The film is little better than an apologia for the South's Peculiar Institution. But a defence of slavery is not the film's objective. The question of slavery, if not the Rights of Man, was answered by the Civil War. Brown is a symbol of tyranny, used as a potent figure to warn against the tolerance or support of radicalism. After Brown is hanged, Robert E. Lee portentously remarks: 'So perish all such enemies of the Union, all such foes of the human race'. The film received solid praise from the trade press, which picked up on its 'accent on Americana' and 'romance'. *Motion Picture Daily* noted that the film is 'made more significant and stronger through the inclusion of high returns of foreboding'. None of the reviews criticised the film for its Southern sympathies but instead emphasised the cliché of 'brother . . . against brother and friend against friend'. *Variety* noted, however, that the

> Picture shrewdly does not take sides on the slave issue . . . the audience always is more wrapped up in the carryings-on of the cavalrymen, the pursuit of Miss de Havilland by JEB and Custer or the rugged comedy of "Big Boy" Williams and Alan Baxter.

There is also no record in the PCA files of either censor concerns or public outcry about the film's representations.[35]

Republic Pictures' biggest production up to this point, *The Dark Command* (1940), exploited a similar setting to *Sante Fé Trail*. Yet, by making all of its leading characters' allegiances ambiguous, it kept its distance from any implied support for the Old South. This feat was achieved by making the hero Bob Seton (John Wayne) a Texas cowboy who refuses to get embroiled in partisan arguments, and by making the villain Will Cantrell (Walter Pidgeon) a guerrilla who exploits the war for his own ends rather than for any ideological purpose. The heroine, played by Claire Trevor (her second pairing with Wayne after the success of *Stagecoach*) is the daughter of the town's banker, the Scotsman Angus McCloud. Apart from the shooting incident between McCloud's son Fletcher (Roy Rogers) and a Free Soiler, the family avoids declaring any particular sympathies. McCloud is basically an honest but arrogant and rich banker. It is his arrogance rather than any pro-Southern sentiments which fuels the townspeople's distrust of him, causing a run on the bank. The monstrous fanaticism of John Brown, creating a compelling and credible tyrannical figure, is absent in the character of Cantrell. Where Brown fights for a cause, Cantrell is motivated by self-interest: he believes life has been unfair to him and he has bad blood from his father's side. Nevertheless, Cantrell wages a war of terror against the good citizens of Lawrence, Kansas. In the final scene he and his men set fire to the town, Republic's own version of *Gone With the Wind*'s burning of Atlanta. Bob Seton kills Cantrell and, in an echo of the sentiments expressed at the end of *The Westerner*, he declares: 'We got a saying down in Texas. It takes a good fire to burn down the weeds—it lets the flowers grow.' Out of the turmoil of war comes peace and prosperity.

As allegories of the domestic or international scene, Westerns were hardly opaque. They were, however, uniformly ambiguous about the pressures that informed Hollywood's production of A-feature Westerns in this period: the issues of intervention or isolation; of whether the threat to the Republic was internal or external; of whether monopoly capitalism or rogue individuals were to blame for the fractured commonwealth; of whether appeals should be made to greater self-sufficiency or to federal aid to heal these fractures. The Civil War provides a historical moment when the Union faced its most fearsome test and survived. The bias towards the South, then, is not an indication of the sympathies of individual or collective filmmakers nor a means of exploiting the Southern box office, but a symbolic act of *rapprochement*.

Conclusion

At the conclusion of this study, readers with a bias towards the canon of 'great' Westerns will have found few, if any, new titles to add to their lists of Hollywood's crowning achievements. By examining how Hollywood and its subsidiary forms of discourse 'positioned' and understood the Western, I have, however, radically revised the ground for further study of the genre. By shifting debate away from the overarching paradigm of the frontier myth, and by analysing Westerns from the perspective of their production and consumption contexts, I have offered a more historically grounded and culturally responsive understanding of the genre than has hitherto been undertaken.

I have based the study on an empirical investigation to understand why Hollywood produced Westerns and to frame a new method for approaching textual readings of the films. These readings have repositioned critical orthodoxies as a result of respecting the parameters established and sanctioned by both the industry and its initial consumers, the press, fan magazines, censorship boards and industry correspondence.

Most critical writings on Westerns and society assume that there are grounds for reading of the films allegorically. I have retrieved this general approach but have allowed the material studied to determine what these readings might have been for a contemporary audience. While an audience is hypothetically free to read whatever it cares to within a particular film or group of films, this study has argued that Hollywood and its media satellites offered historical and cultural boundaries by which those readings were most likely to be set. Thus, late 1930s Westerns were deliberately 'double-coded': received both as 'harmless entertainment' and as engaged on a political, social and cultural front. This engagement might be with the escalating conflict

27. *Union Pacific*
Publicity still, connecting the Old West with new America

in Europe and Asia, with a nation divided by the Depression, with the role of women within films and by extension society, with the representation of adult sexual and leisure activities, or with ethnic assimilation. This was not primarily because Hollywood had found a social conscience, but because it found it politically and therefore financially expedient. The genre's 'fall' and 'renaissance', then, was less to do with any notion of *Zeitgeist* than with Hollywood's particular needs in maintaining a stable context within which it could best control and exploit its markets. The cyclical production of Westerns during the 1930s is neither the 'cultural watershed' that Robert Sklar has argued of its 'disappearance' in the early 1930s, nor is its ascendency in 1939 explained by Michael Coyne's view that the time was 'evidently ripe for the Western'.

Since the dime novel stories of the late nineteenth century, Westerns have been conceived as narratives of the Republic. The forms and accents of that story have changed across time and across audiences: series Westerns, for example, tell a different story from the Western epic and revise the story as told in dime novels, but all address themselves to a commonwealth. Apart from marking the broad differences in address to this 'imagined community', I have also argued that Westerns appealed to a female audience, rather than maintaining the orthodox conception of the genre as having an exclusively male appeal. While I have shown this to be the case with series Westerns (and the singing cowboy in particular), I have also shown how Hollywood sought to attract women to A-feature Westerns. Nonetheless there is much work to be done in this area: from dime novels through turn-of-the-century magazine fiction and Western novels, specifically those by B.M. Bower (which equalled if not exceeded the sales of *The Virginian*), to early cowboy and Indian motion pictures into the 1910s and on through the appeal of silent stars such as Tom Mix and W.S. Hart.

Within my own time frame, there is still much room for further exploration. For instance, both female reception of the South of the Border cycle and the function of racial and sexual masquerade upon which the cycle was based offer rich avenues for further research. Through the analysis of the singing cowboy and the performance traditions he drew upon, I have suggested how this might be done. This entails a consideration of those Hollywood films and practices lying outside orthodox critical positions around gender, myth and the canon, and apart from film theories that exclude consideration of a wider cultural context. The benefits of this approach can be seen in recent studies of film which contextualise analyses of gender and sexuality in this way, and suggest methodologies for extending similar research into class and race.[1] Particularly in the chapters concerned with series Westerns, this study contributes to the process of opening up film studies to the influence of cultural history that takes seriously cultural forms addressed to apparently marginal audiences.

Notes

Introduction

1. Cormac McCarthy, *The Crossing* (London: Picador, 1994), p. 155.
2. On the difficulties in ascribing a film's quality see Lea Jacobs, 'The B Film and the Problem of Cultural Distinction', *Screen*, 33: 1 (Spring 1992), pp. 1–13.
3. Michael Denning, *Mechanic Accents: Dime Novels and Working-Class Culture in America* (London: Verso, 1987), p. 163.
4. André Bazin, *What is Cinema?*, Volume II (Berkeley: University of California Press, 1971).
5. Editor's English introduction to Jean-Louis Leutrat, 'L'Histoire comme diffraction d'une identité', *IRIS*, 2: 2 (1984), pp. 57–67.
6. Tag Gallagher, 'Shoot-Out at the Genre Corral: Problems in the Evolution of the Western' in Barry Keith Grant (ed.), *Film Genre Reader* (Austin: University of Texas Press, 1986), pp. 203–4.
7. Steve Neale, 'Questions of Genre', *Screen*, 31: 1 (Spring 1990), pp. 45–66.
8. Ibid., pp. 45–66.
9. Frederick Jackson Turner, 'The Significance of the Frontier in American History' in American Historical Association, *Annual Report*, 1893 (Washington, DC), 1893), pp. 199–227.
10. Charles S. Peterson, 'Speaking for the Past' in Clyde A. Milner II, Carol A. O'Connor and Martha A. Sandweiss (eds), *The Oxford History of the American West* (New York and Oxford: Oxford University Press, 1994), p. 744.
11. Ibid., p. 748.
12. Ibid., p. 749.
13. Ibid., p. 751.
14. Gerald D. Nash, *Creating the West: Historical Interpretations 1890–1990* (Albuquerque: University of New Mexico Press, 1991).

15. Henry Nash Smith, *Virgin Land: The American West as Symbol and Myth* (New York: Vintage Books, 1950).
16. John H. Lenihan, *Showdown: Confronting Modern America in the Western Film* (Urbana and Chicago: University of Illinois Press, 1985), pp. 24–5.
17. Richard Slotkin, 'Part IV: Democracy and Force: the Western and the Cold War, 1946–1960' in *Gunfighter Nation: The Myth of the Frontier in Twentieth Century America* (New York: Harper Perennial, 1993), pp. 347–488.
18. John G. Cawelti, *The Six Gun Mystique* (Bowling Green, OH: Bowling Green University Popular Press, 1971); Jim Kitses, *Horizons West* (London: Thames and Hudson, 1969); Will Wright, *Six Guns and Society: A Structural Study of the Western* (Berkeley: University of California Press, 1975).
19. *Regeneration Through Violence: The Mythology of the American Frontier, 1600–1860* (Middletown, CT: Wesleyan University Press, 1978); *The Fatal Environment: The Myth of the Frontier in the Age of Industrialisation, 1800–1890* (New York: Atheneum, 1985); *Gunfighter Nation: The Myth of the Frontier in Twentieth Century America* (New York: Harper Perennial, 1993).
20. Cited in Peterson, 'Speaking for the Past', p. 767.
21. Richard White, '*It's Your Misfortune and None of My Own': A New History of the American West* (Norman and London: University of Oklahoma Press, 1991).
22. Denning, *Mechanic Accents*, p. 163.
23. For a mapping out of the distinctions between Roosevelt's, Wister's and Remington's Western heroes and the heroes of the early Western film see Peter Stanfield, *Horse Opera: The Strange History of the 1930s Singing Cowboy* (forthcoming). This study looks in detail at the antecedents, history, production and audience for the singing cowboy.
24. Zeese Papanikolas, *Trickster in the Land of Dreams* (Lincoln: University of Nebraska Press, 1995), pp. 73–4.
25. Marcus Klein, *Easterns, Westerns and Private Eyes: American Matters, 1870–1900* (London: University of Wisconsin Press, 1994), pp. 67–130.
26. Ibid., pp. 94, 98.
27. Denning, *Mechanic Accents*, p. 161.
28. Lee Clark Mitchell, *Westerns: Making the Man in Fiction and Film* (Chicago: University of Chicago Press, 1997); Robert Murray Davis, *Playing Cowboys: Low Culture and High Art in the Western* (Norman: University of Oklahoma Press, 1992).
29. Davis, *Playing Cowboys*, p. xi.

Chapter One

1. *Picture Play*, 34: 2, April 1931, p. 60.
2. *New York Times*, 13 December 1931.
3. Tino Balio (ed.), *Grand Design: Hollywood as a Modern Business Enterprise, 1930–1939* (Berkeley: University of California Press, 1993), p. 310.
4. Ibid., p. 179.
5. *Exhibitors Herald-World*, 17 August 1929, pp. 40−5. The second major response to the survey was published 21 September 1929, pp. 21−5.
6. *Exhibitors Herald-World*, 12 April 1930, pp. 36−52.
7. *Exhibitors Herald-World*, 12 April 1930, pp. 36−52.
8. *Exhibitors Herald-World*, 12 April 1930, p. 37.
9. *Exhibitors Herald-World*, 12 April 1930, pp. 36−52.
10. *Exhibitors Herald-World*, 12 April 1930, pp. 36−52.
11. *Exhibitors Herald-World*, 12 April 1930, pp. 36−52.
12. *New York Times*, 6 January 1929.
13. *New York Times*, 26 December 1929.
14. *Picture Play*, 34: 2, April 1931, p. 60.
15. See advertisement in *Exhibitors Herald-World*, 16 November 1929.
16. See news item on the film's exploitation, *Exhibitors Herald-World*, 30 November 1929, p. 44.
17. These posters are reproduced in Bruce Hershenson, *Cowboy Movie Posters* (West Plains, MO: Bruce Hershenson, n.d.), n.p.
18. Donald Crafton, *The Talkies: American Cinema's Transition to Sound 1926–1931* (New York: Charles Scribners Sons, Simon and Schuster, 1998), p. 282.
19. Paul Seale, '"A Host of Others": Towards a Nonlinear History of Poverty Row and the Coming of Sound', *Wide Angle*, 13: 1 (January 1991), p. 78.
20. For more on antitrust litigation see Ernest Borneman, 'United States versus Hollywood: The Case Study of an Antitrust Suit' in Tino Balio (ed.), *The American Film Industry* (Madison: University of Wisconsin Press, 1985), pp. 449−62.
21. *Picture Play*, 33: 4, December 1930, p. 99.
22. *Motion Picture*, 39: 6, July 1930, p. 3.
23. Gaylyn Studlar, *This Mad Masquerade: Stardom and Masculinity in the Jazz Age* (New York: Columbia University Press), p. 194.
24. Richard Maltby made this point in a note to the author, Donald Crafton (*The Talkies*, p. 504) notes the difficulties audiences encountered at some screenings of early talkies when the actor's voice failed to live up to the imagination of the listener/viewer, a shortcoming that was compounded by the 'screenwriter's awkward intrusion of public lovemaking in the audience's private realm'. Laughter, Crafton notes, was a fairly frequent response to love scenes in early sound cinema. Presumably, the Latin lover, by speaking in the 'language of love' overcomes the audience's embarrassment.

25. Ruth Vasey, *The World According to Hollywood 1918–1939* (Exeter: University of Exeter Press, 1997), p. 121.
26. Miriam Hansen, 'Pleasure, Ambivalence, Identification: Valentino and Female Spectatorship' in Christine Gledhill (ed.). *'Stardom: Industry of Desire* (London: Routledge, 1991), p. 275.
27. *Motion Picture*, 40: 3, October 1930, p. 9.
28. *Motion Picture*, 39: 5, June 1930, p. 4.
29. *Exhibitors Herald-World*, 17 May 1930, pp. 8–9.
30. Edna Ferber, *Cimarron* (New York: Buccaneer Books, n.d.), p. 16.
31. Ibid., p. 219.
32. Hansen, 'Pleasure, Ambivalence, Identification', pp. 259–60.
33. Ed Buscombe (ed.), *The BFI Companion to the Western* (London: British Film Institute and Andre Deutsch, 1988), p. 255.
34. *Picture Play*, 24: 3, May 1931, p. 68.
35. Ferber, *Cimarron*, p. 210.
36. Laura Mulvey, 'Visual Pleasure and Narrative Cinema' in Gerald Mast and Marshall Cohen (eds), *Film Theory and Criticism: I Introductory Readings*, 3rd edn (Oxford: Oxford University Press, 1985), pp. 803–16. See also, for example, Janet Bergstrom, 'Alienation, Segmentation, Hypnosis: Interview with Raymond Bellour', *Camera Obscura* 3/4, p. 87, which contains the much-quoted and little-developed statement about women as the *princee producteur* of Western narratives.
37. *Variety*, 28 January 1931.
38. *New York Times*, Film Reviews, 4 February 1931.
39. *Picture Play*, 24: 3, May 1931, p. 68.
40. *Variety*, 28 January 1931.
41. *Picturegoer*, 1: 15, 5 September 1931, p. 18.
42. *Variety*, 28 January 1931.
43. *Photoplay*, February 1931.
44. *Picture Play*, 24: 3, May 1931, p. 68.
45. *Variety*, 28 January 1931.
46. Joel Finler, *The Hollywood Story* (London: Pyramid Books, 1989), pp. 175–6 for one account of RKO's misfortunes. Also Richard B. Jewell with V. Harbin, *The RKO Story* (London: Octopus Books, 1982), p. 32. This source gives the cost of the production as $565,000. Balio, *Grand Design*, records that the film earned $1.38 million, but still made a loss. He further notes 'Declining admissions during the Depression put a damper on the production of silent-style epics, musical extravaganzas, prestige costume pictures, and other expensive productions' (p. 182).
47. *Picture Play*, 24: 3, May 1931, p. 68.
48. For the context to Joy's motives for supporting the film see Balio, *Grand Design*, pp. 41–8.
49. Richard Maltby, *Reforming the Movies* (New York: Oxford University Press, forthcoming).

50. King Vidor, interview, *New York Times*, 6 July 1930.

51. King Vidor, interview, *New York Times*, 6 July 1930.

52. Christine Bold, *Selling The Wild West: Popular Fiction, 1860–1960* (Bloomington and Indianapolis: Indiana University Press, 1987), pp. 117–18.

53. *Motion Picture*, 40: 4, November 1930, p. 61.

54. *Variety*, 29 October 1930.

55. Quoted in *Variety*, 29 October 1930.

56. Quoted in *Variety*, 29 October 1930.

57. *Variety*, 29 October 1930.

58. *Motion Picture*, 40: 6, January 1931, p. 59.

59. *New York Times*, 25 October 1930.

60. *New York Times*, 19 October 1930. For further discussion of the marketing of these widescreen films see John Belton, *Widescreen Cinema* (London Harvard University Press, 1992), pp. 34–51.

61. *New York Times*, 19 October 1930.

62. *Exhibitors Herald-World*, 7 June 1930, p. 23.

63. *Picture Play*, 34: 2, April 1931, p. 60.

64. For coverage of Hollywood's recruitment and use of vaudeville performers and their effect on movie content see Henry Jenkins, *What Made Pistachio Nuts* (New York: Columbia University Press, 1992), pp. 153–84. For coverage of the recruitment of Broadway talent see Robert Sklar, *City Boys* (Princeton, NJ: Princeton University Press, 1992), p. 23.

65. On Fox Film Corporation's talent-buying spree see 'Fox in Talkies Only: Signs 200 Show Folk' *New York Times*, 25 March 1929.

66. *Exhibitors Herald-World*, 31 May 1930, p. 141.

67. *Picture Play*, 32: 1, March 1930, p. 43.

68. *Exhibitors Herald-World*, 31 May 1930, p. 141.

69. *Picture Play*, 34: 2, April 1931, p. 37.

70. *Motion Picture*, 41: 6, July 1931, pp. 67–7, 116.

71. Seale, ' "A Host of Others" ', p. 81.

72. Crafton, *The Talkies*, p. 181. He also notes, 'The studios could not afford a shotgun approach to distribution (for example sending comedies and Westerns to small towns, opera and "class" theatrical adaptations to the cities). Hollywood wanted to make only one kind of film—the profitable kind' (p. 126). He also offers an illuminating break-down of the difficulties the major studios and independents encountered in the early years of the Depression (pp. 193–216).

73. Giuliana Muscio, *Hollywood's New Deal* (Philadelphia: Temple University Press, 1997), p. 121.

Chapter Two

1. Paul Searle, ' "A Host of Others": Towards a Nonlinear History of Poverty Row and the Coming of Sound' *Wide Angle*, 13: 1 (January 1991), p. 80.
2. Ibid., p. 93.
3. W.H. Brenner, Cozy Theater, Winchester. Ind. Gen Pat., *Motion Picture Herald*, 30 November 1935, p. 84.
4. *Motion Picture Herald*, 19 January 1935, p. 83.
5. Brian Taves, 'The B Film: Hollywood's Other Half' in Tino Balio (ed.), *The Grand Design: Hollywood as a Modern Business Enterprise, 1930–1939* (Berkeley: University of California Press, 1993), p. 322.
6. *Motion Picture Herald*, 20 May 1935, p. 26, and 15 July 1935, p. 59.
7. *Motion Picture Herald*, 28 September 1935, p. 344.
8. *Motion Picture Herald*, 1 June 1935, p. 55.
9. C.L. Niles, Niles Theatre, Anamosa, Iowa. Gen Pat., *Motion Picture Herald*, 30 November 1935, p. 84.
10. Douglas Gomery, *The Hollywood Studio System* (London: Macmillan/ British Film Institute, 1986), pp. 183–4.
11. Owen Wister, *The Virginian: A Horseman of the Plains*, reprint of 1929 illustrated edition (Lincoln: University of Nebraska Press, 1992), p. 184.
12. David R. Roediger, *The Wages of Whiteness: Race and the Making of the American Working Class* (London: Verso, 1991), pp. 117–18.
13. Lawrence Cohen (ed.), *Nothing But the Blues: The Music and the Musicians* (New York: Abbeville Press, 1993), p. 252.
14. Emmett Miller, *The Minstrel Man from Georgia* (Columbia Legacy, 483584 2, 1996). His 1928 recording, 'Lovesick Blues' is also on *Okeh Western Swing* (Epic, EPC 22124, 1982), along with tracks by The Light Crust Dough Boys, The Sweet Violet Boys, Bob Wills and His Texas Playboys, and a host of others. See Nick Tosches, *Country: Living Legends and Dying Metaphors in America's Biggest Music*, rev. edn (London: Secker and Warburg, 1985).
15. On the diversity of styles displayed by Southern rural musicians (black and white) prior to attempts to standardise country music, listen to *Roots N'Blues: The Retrospective (1925–1950)* (Columbia Legacy, C4k 47911, 1992). Also, *Before the Blues: The Early American Black Music Scene*, Volumes 1–3 (Yazoo, 2015/6/7), which despite its title contains both black and white recordings from the 1920s and 1930s—hardly 'before the blues'. A variety of non-cowboy yodelling styles, including many of those referred to in my text, can be found on *White Country Blues (1926–1938)* (Columbia Legacy, Col 472886 2, 1994).
16. Quoted in Wayne W. Daniel, *Pickin' on Peachtree: A History of Country Music in Atlanta, Georgia* (Chicago: University of Illinois Press, 1990), p. 30.

17. Sleevenotes to Cliff Carlisle, *Blue Yodeler and Steel Guitar Wizard*, Arhoole (CD 7039, 1996).
18. Colin Escott, *Hank Williams: The Biography* (New York: Little Brown and Co., 1994), p. 15.
19. W.J. Cash, *The Mind of the South* (1941) (New York: Vintage Books, 1991), p. 283.
20. Nolan Porterfield, *Jimmie Rodgers: The Life and Times of America's Blue Yodeler* (Chicago: University of Illinois Press 1992).
21. Quoted in P. Kingswood and S. Costello (eds), *Country: The Music and Musicians*, 2nd edn (New York: Abbeville, 1994), p. 335.
22. Richard White, *'It's Your Misfortune and None of My Own': A New History of the American West* (Norman: University of Oklahoma Press, 1991), pp. 482–3.
23. James N. Gregory, *American Exodus: The Dust Bowl Migration and Okie Culture in California* (Oxford: Oxford University Press, 1989), pp. 102–3.
24. Peter Guralnick, *Lost Highways: Journeys and Arrivals of American Musicians* (New York: Harper and Row, 1989), p. 19.
25. Ronnie Pugh has suggested that Autry was given pre-release recordings of Rodgers by the latter's publisher, who hoped to gain exposure and royalties from Autry's performances on the *National Barn Dance* and via his budget label releases. This might explain, to some extent, Autry's mimicry. See Richard A. Peterson, *Creating Country Music: Fabricating Authenticity* (Chicago: University of Chicago Press, 1997), p. 86.
26. Escott, *Hank Williams*, p. 45.
27. *Variety* (New York), 116: 13, 11 December 1934, pp. 1, 52.
28. Cash, *Mind of the South*, p. 262.
29. G. Fowler and B. Crawford, *Border Radio* (New York: Limelight Edition, 1990).
30. *Motion Picture Herald*, 22 February 1936, p. 99.
31. For more on the relationship between the major Hollywood studios and radio promotion see Michele Hilmes, 'The Ban That Never Was: Hollywood and the Broadcasting Industry in 1932', *The Velvet Light Trap*, 23 (Spring 1989), pp. 39–49. Also, Michelle Hilmes, *Hollywood and Broadcasting: From Radio to Cable* (Urbana: University of Chicago Press, 1992).
32. Escott, *Hank Williams*, p. 105.
33. Alton Delmore, *Truth is Stranger Than Publicity*, ed. Charles K. Wolfe (Nashville: Country Music Foundation, 1995), p. 99.
34. In a surviving transcription disc of a Light Crust Dough Boys radio programme (reissued on Jambalaya, CW 207, France 1990), the master of ceremonies announces that the Dough Boys are heading to Hollywood to appear in a Gene Autry film. The title is not mentioned, but their performance can be seen in *Oh, Susanna!* (Republic, 1936).

35. Charles K. Wolfe, *Tennessee Strings: The Story of Country Music in Tennessee* (Knoxville: University of Tennessee Press, 1977), p. 56.

36. Daniel, *Pickin' on Peachtree*, pp. 15–44.

37. Bill C. Malone, *Singing Cowboys and Musical Mountaineers: Southern Culture and the Roots of Country Music* (Georgia: University of Georgia Press 1993), p. 91.

38. N.H. Thorpe, *Songs of the Cowboy* (1908) (Lincoln: University of Nebraska Press, 1984), with a forward by Guy Logsdon.

39. Guy Logsdon, Mary Rogers and William Jacobson, *Saddle Seranaders* (Salt Lake City: Gibbs and Smith, 1995), p. 9.

40. *Harper's Monthly*, (September 1895), pp. 602–17.

41. *The Log of A Cowboy: A Narrative of the Old Trail Days* (1903) (New York: Airmont Publishing Company 1969), p. 141:

   Two little niggers upstairs in bed,
   One turned ober to de oder an' said
   'How 'bout dat shortnin' bread,
   How 'bout dat shortnin' bread?'

42. Malone, *Singing Cowboys*, p. 83.

43. Bill C. Malone, *Country Music, USA* (Wellingborough, Northamptonshire: Equation, 1985), p. 130.

44. A major survey of Gene Autry recordings are on *Sing, Cowboy, Sing: The Gene Autry Collection* (Rhino, 1997). The best collection of recordings produced before he went to Hollywood is *Blues Singer 1929–31, Booger Rooger Saturday Nite* Roots and Blues (Columbia, CK 64987, 1997). This has many of Autry's more risqué performances and clearly shows the debt he owes to Rodgers. Tex Ritter's 1930s recordings are collected on *Blood on the Saddle* (Bear Family Records, BCD 16260, 1999). See Guy Logsden, *The Whorehouse Bells Were Ringing* (Urbana: University of Illinois, 1989) for the real low-down on low-down dirty cowboy songs. Collections of pre-1940 recordings of cowboy songs on CD can be found on *Back in the Saddle Again* (New World Records NW314/315-2) and *Western Cowboy Ballads and Songs 1925–1939* (Frémeaux and Assoccies FA 034). These double CD sets contain such classics of the genre as Harry McClintock's 'The Old Chisholm Trail', Carl T. Sprague's 'When the Work's All Done This Fall', Patsy Montana's 'I want to be a Cowboy's Sweetheart', Tex Owens' 'Cattle Call', alongside early recordings by Autry, Sons of the Pioneers, Tex Ritter, Bob Wills, Jimmie Rodgers, and Ken Maynard giving his all on 'The Lone Star Trail' and 'Home on the Range'. However, neither of these sets can compete with *When I Was a Cowboy: Early American Songs of the West, Classic Recordings from the 1920s and 30s*, Volumes 1 and 2 (Yazoo, 2022 and 2023, 1996), which offer forty-six performances and include Dick Devall's transcendent unaccompanied rendition of 'Tom Sherman's Barroom'.

45. Gene Autry with M. Herskowitz, *Back in the Saddle Again* (New York: Doubleday, 1978), p. 1.

46. See, for example, the biographical sketch in Autry's first published song collection *Cowboy Songs and Mountain Ballads* (Chicago: M.M. Cole Pub. Co., 1932).

47. Peter C. Rollins, *Will Rogers: A Bio-Bibliography* (Westport CT: Greenwood Press, 1984), p. 18.

48. Ibid., p. 48.

49. T.J. Jackson Lears, *No Place of Grace: Antimodernism and the Transformation of American Culture 1880–1920* (New York: Pantheon Books, 1981), p. 141.

50. Ibid., p. 301.

51. Ibid., p. 166.

52. Owen Wister, 'The Evolution of the Cow Puncher', *Harper's Monthly*, 91 (September 1895), pp. 602–17.

53. Bryan B. Sterling and Frances N. Sterling (eds), *A Will Rogers Treasury: Reflections and Observations* (New York: Crown Publishers, 1982), pp. 3–4.

54. James Agee, *On Film: Reviews and Comments* (Boston: Beacon Press, 1964), p. 407.

Chapter Three

1. Robert Sklar, *City Boys: Cagney, Bogart, Garfield* Princeton NJ: Princeton University Press, 1992), p. 9.

2. Robert Warshow, 'The Movie Chronicle: The Westerner' (1954) in *The Immediate Experience* (New York: Atheneum Books, 1962), p. 94.

3. George N. Fenin and William K. Everson, *The Western: From Silents to the Seventies* (London: Penguin, 1977), p. 214.

4. Jon Tuska, *The Vanishing Legion: A History of Mascot Pictures 1927–35* (London: McFarland and Co., 1982), p. 162.

5. Jane Tompkins, *West of Everything: The Inner Life of Westerns* (Oxford: Oxford University Press, 1992).

6. Packy Smith and Ed Hulse (eds), *Don Miller's Hollywood Corral: A Comprehensive B-Western Roundup* (Burbank: Riverwood Press, 1993), p. xii.

7. Tuska, *Vanishing Legion*, p. 165.

8. Ed Buscombe (ed.), *The BFI Companion to the Western* (London: British Film Institute and Andre Deutsch, 1988), p. 194.

9. David Rothel, *The Gene Autry Book* (Madison: North Carolina, 1988), p. 13.

10. Kim Newman, *Wild West Movies* (London: Bloomsbury, 1990), p. 42.

11. Ian Cameron and Douglas Pye (eds), *The Movie Book of the Western* (London: Studio Vista, 1996), p. 10.

12. *Motion Picture Herald*, 5 January 1935, p. 60.
13. P.A. McConnell, Emerson Theatre, Hartford, Ark. Small Town and General Pat., *Motion Picture Herald*, 13 April 1935.
14. M.S. Porter, Orpheum Theatre, Nelsonville, Ohio. Small Town and Rural Pat., *Motion Picture Herald*, 16 February 1935, p. 72.
15. G. Carey, Strand Theatre, Paris, Ark. Family Pat., *Motion Picture Herald*, 23 February 1935, p. 80.
16. A.N. Miles, Eminence Theatre, Eminence, Ky. Small Town Pat., *Motion Picture Herald*, 21 September 1935, p. 53.
17. E.J. McClurg, Grand Theatre, Preston, Idaho. Rural and Small Town Pat., *Motion Picture Herald*, 6 June 1935.
18. Charles T. Nelson, Fay Theatre, Jasper, Fla. Small Town and Rural Pat., *Motion Picture Herald*, 7 September 1935, p. 59.
19. Walter Holifield, Elite Theatre, Greenleaf, Kan. Small Town Pat., *Motion Picture Herald*, 7 September 1935, p. 59.
20. *Motion Picture Herald*, 1 February 1936, p. 55.
21. Mary Hayes Davis, Dixie Crewiston, Fla. Small Town Pat., *Motion Picture Herald*, 27 April 1935, p. 58.
22. *Motion Picture Herald*, 15 June 1935, p. 59.
23. J.W. Noah, New Liberty and Ideal Theatres, Ft. Worth, Texas. General Pat., 27 April 1935, p. 58.
24. Gene Autry with M. Herskowitz, *Back in the Saddle Again* (New York: Doubleday, 1978), p. 40.
25. *Motion Picture Herald*, 9 November 1935, p. 2.
26. *Motion Picture Herald*, 19 October 1935, pp. 47–51.
27. *Motion Picture Herald*, 7 December 1935, p. 67.
28. *Motion Picture Herald*, 5 October 1935, pp. 26–7.
29. Twenty-five of Bing Crosby's renditions of cowboy songs can be heard on *I'm An Old Cowhand, 1933–44* (Living Era CD AJA 5160, 1996).
30. For complete listings of box-office attractions see Smith and Hulse (eds), *Don Miller's Hollywood Corral* pp. 505–16.
31. A Salty Holmes recording, 'I Want My Mama', can be heard on *Harmonica Masters* (Yazoo 2019, 1996).
32. *Hollywood Reporter*, 21 April 1938, p. 3.
33. Noted in David Rothel, *The Gene Autry Book* (Madison: North Carolina, 1988), p. 144. Donald Crafton, 'The Jazz Singer's Reception in the Media and at the Box Office' in David Bordwell and Noel Carroll (eds), *Post-Theory: Reconstructing Film Studies* (Madison: University of Wisconsin Press, 1996), pp. 460–80.
34. There had been two earlier adaptations of William Colt McDonald's Three Mesquiteers novels: *Law of the 45s* (Beacon, 1935) and *Powdersmoke Range* (RKO, 1935).
35. Autry, *Back in the Saddle Again*, p. 53.

36. John Opie, *The Law of the Land: Two Hundred Years of American Farmland Policy* (Lincoln: University of Nebraska Press, 1994), p. 152.
37. James N. Gregory, *American Exodus: The Dust Bowl Migration and Okie Culture in California* (New York: Oxford University Press, 1989), p. 75.
38. Michael Denning, *Mechanic Accents: Dime Novels and Working-Class Culture in America* (London: Verso, 1987), p. 200.
39. Dale Cockrell, *Demons of Disorder: Early Blackface Minstrels and Their World* (Cambridge: Cambridge University Press, 1997), p. 169.
40. Ibid., p. 141.
41. *Hollywood Reporter*, 4 August 1938, p. 3.
42. Richard White, 'It's Your Misfortune and None of My Own': A New History of the American West (London: University of Oklahoma Press, 1991), p. 230.
43. Ibid., pp. 436–8.
44. Richard Maltby, *Reforming the Movies* (New York: Oxford University Press, forthcoming).
45. Michael Denning, *The Cultural Front: The Laboring of American Culture in the Twentieth Century* (London and New York: Verso, 1996), p. 30.
46. Autry, *Back in the Saddle Again*, p. 66.
47. Lizzie Franck, *Script Girls: Women Screenwriters in Hollywood* (London: British Film Institute, 1994), pp. 74–5.
48. Pamela Grundy, ' "We Always Tried to Be Good People". Respectability, Crazy Water Crystals and Hillbilly Music on the Air, 1933–1935', *Journal of American History*, 81: 4 (March 1995), p. 1613. For a short but informed overview of women in country music see Ruth A. Banes, 'Dixie's Daughters: The Country Music Female' in Melton A. McLarin and Richard A. Peterson (eds), *You Wrote My Life: Lyrical Themes in Country Music* (Philadelphia: Gordon and Breach, 1992), pp. 81–112.
49. Teresa Jordan, *Cowgirls: Women of the American West* (Lincoln and London: University of Nebraska Pressl Bison edition, 1992), p. 291. Also, Christine Bold, 'Malaeska's Revenge; or, The Dime Novel Tradition in Popular Fiction' in Richard Aquila (ed.), *Wanted Dead or Alive: The American West in Popular Fiction* (Urbana and Chicago: University of Illinois Press, 1996), pp. 32–3.
50. Marcus Klein, *Easterns, Westerns and Private Eyes: American Matters, 1870–1900* (Madison: University of Wisconsin Press, 1994), p. 101.
51. Denning, *Mechanic Accents*, pp. 193–4.
52. Zane Grey, *Riders of the Purple Sage* (Oxford: Oxford University Press, 1995), p. xxxiv.
53. Ibid., p. 245.
54. Ibid., p. 264.
55. Denning, *Mechanic Accents*, p. 77.
56. Ibid., p. 153.
57. Ibid., pp. 146–7.

58. Ibid., p. 147.
59. Quoted in Ibid., p. 177.
60. Mary Beth Hamilton, *The Queen of Camp: Mae West, Sex and Popular Culture* (London: Pandora, 1996), p. 133.
61. J.W. Williamson, *Hillbillyland: What the Movies Did to the Mountains and What the Mountains Did to the Movies* (Chapel Hill and London: University of North Carolina, 1995), p. 24. Williamson uses the court jester to make sense of the hillbilly clown, a figure that apparently did not appear in American popular culture until the end of the first quarter of the twentieth century, see pp. 38–9.
62. See, for example, *The Haunted Churchyard: or Old King Brady the Detective and the Mystery of the Iron Vault* (1890), reprinted in *The Dime Novel Detective*, (ed.) Gary Hoppenstand (Bowling Green, OH: Bowling Green University Popular Press, 1982).
63. See correspondence in PCA file on *Showboat*, Margaret Herrick Library, American Motion Picture and Science (AMPAS), Letter dated 17 October 1935.
64. The Cabin Kids wre a troupe of African-American youths who specialised in this kind of comic performance. They also appear in the W.C. Fields/Bing Crosby film *Mississippi* (A. Edward Sutherland, 1935).
65. There is a comparable joke in the Wheeler and Woolsey comedy *So This is Africa* (1932).
66. Smith and Hulse (eds), *Don Miller's Hollywood Corral* p. 177.
67. James H. Dormon, 'Shaping the Popular Image of Post-Reconstruction American Blacks: The "Coon Song" Phenomenon of the Gilded Age', *American Quarterly*, 40: 4 (1988), pp. 440–77.
68. Cultural responses to these strikes are discussed in Michael Denning, *The Cultural Front: The Laboring of American Culture in the Twentieth Century* (London: Verso, 1996), pp. 259–82.
69. Smith and Hulse (eds), *Don Miller's Hollywood Corral* p. 178.
70. Steve Neale, 'Melo Talk: On the Meaning and the Use of the Term "Melodrama" in the American Trade Press', *The Velvet Light Trap*, 32 (Fall 1993), p. 81.
71. *Hollywood Reporter*, 15 October 1938.

Chapter Four

1. Rick Altman, 'Reusable Packaging: Generic Products and the Recycling Process' in Nick Browne (ed.), *Refiguring American Film Genres: Theory and History* (Berkeley: University of California Press, 1998), pp. 1–41.
2. Ibid., p. 4.
3. Ibid., p. 11.
4. Ibid., pp. 11–12.
5. Ibid., p. 16.

6. Tino Balio (ed.), *Grand Design: Hollywood as a Modern Business Enterprise, 1930–1939* (New York: Charles Schribner's Sons, 1993), p. 311.

7. Anne O'Hare McCormick, *New York Times*, 20 December 1931.

8. Robert Sklar, *City Boys: Cagney, Bogart, Garfield* (Princeton, NJ: Princeton University Press, 1992), p. 8.

9. Tino Balio (ed.), *The American Film Industry*, rev. edn (Madison: University of Wisconsin Press, 1985), p. 255.

10. Ibid., pp. 255–6.

11. Anne O'Hare McCormick, *New York Times*, 6 December 1931.

12. Ed Buscombe (ed.), *The BFI Companion to the Western* (London: British Film Institute and Deutsch, 1988), p. 426.

13. Balio (ed.), *Grand Design*, p. 193.

14. *Motion Picture Herald*, 22 February 1936, p. 59/62.

15. *Screen Romances Album*, 1: 1, February 1931, p. 13.

16. *Three Godfathers*, PCA file, Margaret Herrick Library, AMPAS.

17. *Hollywood Reporter*, 12 February 1936.

18. *Variety*, 11 March 1936.

19. *Film Daily*, 7 March 1936.

20. *Variety*, 12 February 1936.

21. *Motion Picture Daily*, 13 February 1936.

22. Babies would be used again in *The Cisco Kid and the Lady* (20th Century-Fox, Herbert Leeds, 1940), in *Wells Fargo, Stagecoach, Drums Along the Mohawk*, and in *Jesse James*; the scene where Zee has just given birth and wishes she and the baby had died is the most emotionally intense moment in any of the 1939/40 Westerns.

23. *Motion Picture Herald*, 22 June 1935, p. 31.

24. *Motion Picture Herald*, 8 June 1935, p. 76.

25. *New Statesman*, 13 February 1937.

26. *Paramount Service*, 19: 26, 26 December 1936, p. 1.

27. *The Spectator*, 19 February 1937. Reprinted in *The Pleasure Dome: The Collected Film Criticism 1935–40*, ed. John Russell Taylor (Oxford: Oxford University Press, 1980), p. 131.

28. See Robert Anderson, 'The Role of the Western Film Genre in Industry Competition 1907–11', *Journal of the University Film Association*, 31: 2 (Spring 1979), pp. 19–26.

29. *Hollywood Reporter*, 15 October 1938, p. 5.

30. Greene, *Pleasure Dome*, pp. 116–17.

31. *Monthly Film Bulletin*, 4: 38, 28 February 1937, p. 37.

32. *Monthly Film Bulletin*, 3: 34, 31 October 1936, p. 175.

33. *Monthly Film Bulletin*, 3: 28, 30 April 1936, p. 68.

34. *Monthly Film Bulletin*, 3: 27, 31 March 1936, p. 51.

35. *Monthly Film Bulletin*, 3: 34, 31 October 1936, p. 177.

36. *Paramount Service*, 20: 1, 9 January 1937, p. 12.

37. *Paramount Service*, 20: 1, 9 January 1937, p. 14.

38. *Paramount Service*, 20: 1, 9 January 1937, p. 12.
39. *Screen Romances Album*, 1: 1, February 1931, p. 41.
40. *Hollywood Reporter*, 14 January 1939, p. 3.
41. André Bazin, *What is Cinema?*, Volume II (Berkeley: University of California Press, 1971).
42. Michael Coyne, *The Crowded Prairie: American National Identity in the Hollywood Western* (London: I.B. Tauris, 1997), p. 16.
43. Buscombe, *BFI Companion*, pp. 38-9.
44. Ibid., p. 39.
45. Ibid., pp. 42-3.
46. Giuliana Muscio, *Hollywood's New Deal* (Philadelphia: Temple University Press, 1997), p. 131.
47. Richard Maltby, 'The Production Code and the Hays Office' in Balio (ed.), *Grand Design*, p. 69.
48. See also Muscio, *Hollywood's New Deal*, pp. 114-15.
49. Lea Jacobs, *The Wages of Sin: Censorship and the Fallen Woman Film 1928-1942* (Berkeley: University of California Press, 1997), p. x.
50. Ibid., p. 35.
51. Ibid., p. 35.
52. Maltby, 'The Production Code', p. 40.

Chapter Five

1. Roscoe Williams, *Moving Picture Daily*, 7 February 1939.
2. March 1939, reprinted in Stanley Hochman (ed.), *From Quasimodo to Scarlett O'Hara: A National Board of Review Anthology, 1920-1940* (New York: Ungar Publishing, 1982), pp. 293-4.
3. *Film Daily*, 15 February 1939.
4. *New York Times*, 3 March 1939.
5. *New York Herald-Tribune*, 3 March 1939.
6. *Hollywood Reporter*, 3 February 1939.
7. 'The Making of a Scenario' reprinted in Hochman (ed.), *From Quasimodo to Scarlett O'Hara*, p. 408.
8. *New York Daily News*, 3 March 1939.
9. National Board of Review, March 1939.
10. *Motion Picture Herald*, 25 January 1939, p. 13.
11. *Hollywood Reporter*, 28 April 1938, pp. 1, 6.
12. *Hollywood Reporter*, 11 May 1938, p. 1.
13. *Motion Picture Herald*, 14 January 1939, p. 13.
14. *Motion Picture Herald*, 7 January 1939, p. 9.
15. *New York Times*, 15 January 1939 A.
16. *New York Times*, 15 January 1939 A.
17. Richard Maltby, *Reforming the Movies* (New York: Oxford University Press, forthcoming).

18. See Matthew Bernstein, *Walter Wanger: Hollywood Independent* (Berkeley: University of California Press, 1994).
19. *Motion Picture Herald*, 18 February 1939, p. 7.
20. *Motion Picture Herald*, 25 February 1939, p. 12.
21. Maltby, *Reforming the Movies*.
22. Cited in the *New York Times*, 28 March 1939. In April, Joe Breen wrote to producing companies asking for footage from their recent films 'depicting high spots in American history' for a movie 'being made for showing in Federal buildings and New York and Frisco fairs'. This was part of the PCA's propaganda drive to show Hollywood was alive to the needs of American democracy. Telegram, 12 April 1939, in AMPAS *Man of Conquest* File.
23. Maltby, *Reforming the Movies*.
24. Ibid.
25. *New York Times*, 28 March 1939.
26. *New York Times*, 28 March 1939.
27. *Motion Picture Herald*, 4 February 1939, p. 68.
28. Ruthy Vasey, *The World According to Hollywood 1918–1939* (Exeter: University of Exeter Press, 1997), p. 156.
29. *New York Times*, 23 April 1939.
30. *Time*, clipping in *Let Freedom Ring* AMPAS file, n.d.
31. Outside of Westerns, Hollywood's tentative approach to the question of labour can be seen in films such as *Boy Slaves* (RKO, 1938). Though it is essentially about the exploitation of child labour—an uncontroversial topic other than in the recognition that it exists—the film is better read as a veiled commentary on the exploitation of migrant workers. This theme would be more fully exploited in *The Grapes of Wrath* (1940). In either case, these films are less a testimony to Hollywood's politicisation than a recognition that it needed to counter claims that, through the agency of the PCA, it censored and blocked films with a social conscience. For more on Hollywood's history of representing labour and the working-classes, see Stephen J. Ross, *Working Class Hollywood: Silent Film and the Shaping of Class in America* (Princeton, NJ: Princeton University Press, 1998).
32. *Motion Picture*, 42: 3, April 1939, p. 18.
33. *Motion Picture*, 42: 4, May 1939, pp. 28–9, 80–1.
34. *Motion Picture*, 42: 4, May 1939, p. 28.
35. *Motion Picture*, 42: 4, May 1939, p. 80.
36. *Motion Picture*, 42: 4, May 1939, pp. 80–1.
37. *Motion Picture Herald*, 18 March 1939, p. 67.
38. *Motion Picture Daily*, 20 February 1939.
39. *Picture Play*, February 1940, p. 71.
40. *Motion Picture Herald*, 14 January 1939, p. 46.
41. *New York Times*, 12 March 1939.

42. *New York Times*, 25 December 1938.
43. *Motion Picture Herald*, 27 January 1939.
44. *Motion Picture*, 42: 7, February 1939, p. 4.
45. *Motion Picture*, 42: 9, April, 1939, p. 81.
46. *Motion Picture*, 42: 11, June 1939, p. 26.
47. *Motion Picture*, 43: 1, August, 1939, p. 13.
48. *New York Times*, 4 August 1935 B.
49. Robert Sklar, *City Boys: Cagney, Bogart, Garfield* (Princeton, NJ: Princeton University Press, 1992), p. 228.
50. *Motion Picture*, 42: 10, May 1939, p. 74.
51. *Film Daily*, 15 March 1939.
52. *Motion Picture*, 42: 8, p. 18.
53. *Motion Picture*, 42: 8, March 1939, p. 18.
54. *Motion Picture*, 42: 9, April 1939, p. 18.
55. *Variety*, 20 November 1940.
56. *New York Times*, 3 December 1939.
57. Thanks to Richard Maltby for pointing out this connection.
58. Synopsis in *Destry Rides Again* AMPAS File.
59. *Variety*, 29 November 1939.
60. *New York Times*, 30 November 1939.
61. *New York Herald*, 30 November 1939.
62. *Motion Picture Herald*, 2 December 1939.
63. For further contemporary discussion of her persona see Helen Hover, 'Stepping Off Her High Horse', in *Picture Play* February 1940, pp. 60–1, 71–2.
64. Synopsis in *Destry Rides Again* AMPAS File.
65. *Motion Picture*, 42: 4, May 1939, p. 90.
66. *New York Times*, August 1940.
67. *New York Times*, 4 August 1935 B.
68. O'Brien's novelty was the size of his chest, which is invariably displayed at some point in his films, here as he takes a bath in a barrel, sans hat, with Chris Pin Martin in attendance.
69. Robert C. Allen, *Horrible Prettiness: Burlesque and American Culture* (Chapel Hill and London: University of North Carolina Press, 1991), pp. 73–8.
70. To M.J. Siegel from Breen, 9 November 1938, *Man of Conquest* AMPAS file.
71. *Time*, clipping (n.d.), *Stagecoach* AMPAS file.
72. *Time* clipping (n.d.) and memos, *Stagecoach* AMPAS file.
73. *Honky Tonk* AMPAS file.
74. *New York Times*, 7 May 1939.
75. *New York Times*, 25 December 1938.
76. *Hollywood Reporter* 21 July 1938, p. 5.
77. *Time* review (n.d.) AMPAS file.

78. *New York Times*, 4 September 1938 A.

79. *New York Times*, 8 January 1939 A.

80. Cited in Matthew Solomon, 'Dime Novels and Early Cinema as the Nickelodeon Period Begins: Outlaw and Detective Stories', paper given at Bradford conference on early cinema, May 1995.

81. Ibid.

82. *Motion Picture Herald*, 14 January 1939, p. 43.

83. *Jesse James* AMPAS file, Memo., 12 April 1938.

84. Ibid.

85. *Motion Picture*, 42: 4, May 1939, pp. 28–9, 80–1.

86. *Jesse James* AMPAS file, letter from Wm. Hays, 2 March 1939.

87. David E. Ruth, *Inventing the Public Enemy: The Gangster in American Culture, 1918–1934* (Chicago: University of Chicago, 1996), p. 91.

88. 'Some Gangster Films' May 1931, reprinted in Hochman (ed.), *From Quasimodo to Scarlett O'Hara*, pp. 143–9.

89. American interest in Robin Hood was part of the late-nineteenth-century/early-twentieth-century preoccupation with mediaevalism as a source of inspiration and rejuvenation to counter the negative affects of modernisation. See T.J. Jackson Lears, *No Place of Grace: Antimodernism and the Transformation of American Culture, 1880–1920* (New York: Pantheon Books, 1981), pp. 93–182.

90. See Michael Fellman, *Inside War: The Guerrilla Conflict in Missouri During the American Civil War* (New York: Oxford University Press, 1989), pp. 247–66.

91. Ibid., p. 263.

92. Tulsa *Tribune*, 24 September 1941, Tulsa, Oklahoma, clipping in *Belle Starr* AMPAS file.

93. Extract from early treatment (3 March 1939) #333–f.1573.

94. Vasey, *World According to Hollywood*, p. 107.

95. Dana Polan, *Power and Paranoia: History, Narrative and the American Cinema, 1940–1950* (New York: Columbia University Press, 1986), p. 31.

96. Ibid., p. 26.

97. Ibid., p. 31.

98. Marc Vernet, '*Film Noir* on the Edge of Doom' in Joan Copjec (ed.), *Shades of Noir* (London: Verso, 1996), pp. 1–32.

Chapter Six

1. Cited in Michael Denning, *The Cultural Front: The Labouring of American Culture in the Twentieth Century* (London and New York: Verso, 1996), p. 431.

2. Michael Denning, *Mechanic Accents: Dime Novels and Working-Class Culture in America* (London: Verso, 1987), p. 72.

3. Ibid., p. 153.

4. Benedict Anderson, *Imagined Communities*, (rev. edn London: Verso, 1991), p. 36.

5. Alexander Saxton, *The Rise and Fall of the White Republic: Class Politics and Mass Culture in 19th Century America* (London: Verso, 1990).

6. David R. Roediger, *The Wages of Whiteness: Race and the Making of the American Working Class* (London: Verso, 1991).

7. Ibid., p. 36.

8. Alan Trachtenberg, *The Incorporation of America: Culture and Society in the Gilded Age* (New York: Hill and Wang, 1982), p. 96.

9. Michael Rogin, *Blackface, White Noise: Jewish Immigrants in the Hollywood Melting Pot* (Berkeley: University of California Press, 1996), p. 42.

10. For general accounts of Hollywood's representation see Jack Temple Kirby, *Media-Made Dixie* (Baton Rouge: Louisiana State University Press, 1978) and Edward D.C. Campbell, Jr., *The Celluloid South: Hollywood and the Southern Myth* (Knoxville: University of Tennessee Press, 1981).

11. See Richard Maltby, ' "Usable Bonds": *I Am a Fugitive from a Chain Gang*' and the Politics of 1932', paper delivered at the Irish Film Centre, Dublin, February 1997.

12. For more on the representation of hillbillies, although without mention of the *Trail of the Lonesome Pine*, see J.W. Williamson, *Hillbillyland: What the Movies Did to the Mountains and What the Mountains Did to the Movies* (Chapel Hill and London University of North Carolina, 1995).

13. W.J. Cash, *The Mind of the South* (1941) (New York: Vintage Books, 1991), p. 364.

14. Ibid., pp. 71–2.

15. Ibid., p. 105.

16. James N. Gregory, *American Exodus: The Dust Bowl Migration and Okie Culture in California* (New York and Oxford: Oxford University Press, 1989), p. 4.

17. Ibid., pp. 6–7.

18. Letter dated 24 August 1936, *Banjo On My Knee* PCA file, Margaret Herrick Library, AMPAS.

19. Spike Jones can be seen to good effect in the Eddie Cantor variety film *Thank Your Lucky Stars* (David Butler, Warner Bros., 1943).

20. See press clippings in the *Banjo On My Knee* PCA file, Margaret Herrick Library, AMPAS.

21. Marcus Klein, *Easterns, Westerns and Private Eyes: American Matters, 1870–1900* (Madison: University of Wisconsin Press, 1994), p. 83.

22. Zane Grey, *Riders of the Purple Sage* (Oxford: Oxford University Press, 1995), p. 241.

23. Edna Ferber, *Cimarron* (1930) (New York: Buccaneer Books, n.d.), pp. 2–4.

24. The crucifixion is more overt in the novel, p. 144. However, unlike the

film, it keeps the character of Sol Levy very much isolated within the growing community. The Australian censor demanded the scene cut from release prints. See file in AMPAS, Margaret Herrick Library.

25. Ferber, *Cimarron*, p. 103. For a historical account of this construction of Indian potency see Brian Dippie, *The Vanishing American: White Attitudes and US Policy* (Middletown, CN: Wesleyan University Press, 1982).
26. Ferber, *Cimarron*, p. 274.
27. Ibid., p. 163.
28. Saxon, *Rise and Fall*, p. 174.
29. AMPAS *Virginia City* file, 1 November 1939.
30. Franklin D. Roosevelt, *Selected Speeches, Messages, Press Conferences, and Letters*, ed. Basil Rauch, (New York: Rinehart and Co., 1957), p. 159.
31. Ibid., pp. 43–7.
32. Thomas H. Pauly, '*Gone With the Wind* and *The Grapes of Wrath* as Hollywood Histories of the Depression' in Richard Harwell (ed.), *Gone With the Wind as Book and Film* (Columbia, SC: University of South Carolina Press, 1992).
33. T.J. Jackson Lears, *No Place of Grace: Antimodernism and the Transformation of American Culture 1880–1920* (New York: Pantheon Books, 1981), p. 99.
34. Denning, *Cultural Front* pp. 130–1 and p. 499, n. 32.
35. Clippings held in *Santa Fé Trail* PCA file, Margaret Herrick Library, AMPAS. *Motion Picture Daily*, 16 December 1940.

Conclusion

1. For example, Richard Maltby, *Reforming the Movies: Politics, Censorship, and the Institutions of the American Cinema, 1908–1939* (New York: Oxford University Press, forthcoming), Lea Jacobs, *The Wages of Sin: Censorship and the Fallen Woman Film 1928–1942* (Berkeley: University of California Press, 1997), Henry Jenkins, *What Made Pistachio Nuts* (New York: Columbia University Press, 1992), Ruth Vasey, *The World According to Hollywood 1918–1939* (Exeter: University of Exeter Press, 1997), Gaylyn Studlar, *This Mad Masquerade: Stardom and Masculinity in the Jazz Age* (New York: Columbia University Press, 1997), Steve Neale, *Genre and Hollywood* (London: Routledge, 2000), Frank Krutnik, *Inventing Jerry Lewis* (Washington: Smithsonian Institution, 2000), Lee Grieveson, *Policing Cinema: Regulating Early American Cinema* (Berkeley: University of California Press, forthcoming), Janet Staiger, *Bad Women: Regulating Sexuality in Early American Cinema* (Minneapolis and London: Minnesota University Press, 1995). On race and class, two fine recent examples are Daniel Bernardi (ed.), *The Birth of Whiteness: Race and the Emergence of US Cinema* (New Jersey: Rutgers University Press, 1996) and Stephen J. Ross, *Working-Class Hollywood: Silent Film and the Shaping of*

Class in America (Princeton, NJ: Princeton University Press, 1998). On the Western's role in the 'Americanisation' of American cinema see Richard Abel's superb *The Red Rooster Scare: Making Cinema American, 1900–1910* (Berkeley: University of California Press, 1999).

Bibliography

Abel, Richard. *The Red Rooster Scare: Making Cinema American, 1900–1910* (Berkeley: University of California Press, 1999).

Adams, Andy. *The Log of A Cowboy: A Narrative of the Old Trail Days* (1903) (New York: Airmont Publishing Company, 1969).

Agee, James. *On Film: Reviews and Comments* (Boston: Beacon Press, 1964).

Allen, Robert C. *Horrible Prettiness: Burlesque and American Culture* (Chapel Hill and London: University of North Carolina Press, 1991).

Altman, Rick. 'Reusable Packaging: Generic Products and the Recycling Process' in Nick Browne (ed.), *Refiguring American Film Genres: Theory and History* (Berkeley: University of California Press, 1998), pp. 1–41.

Anderson, Benedict. *Imagined Communities*, rev. edn (London: Verso, 1991).

Anderson, Robert. 'The Role of the Western Film Genre in Industry Competition 1907–11, *Journal of the University Film Association* 31: 2 (Spring 1979), pp. ?

Autry, Gene with Herskowitz, M. *Back in the Saddle Again* (New York: Doubleday, 1978).

Balio, Tino (ed.). *The American Film Industry*, rev. edn (Madison: University of Wisconsin Press, 1985).

Balio, Tino (ed.). *Grand Design: Hollywood as a Modern Business Enterprise, 1930–1939* (Berkeley: University of California Press, 1993).

Banes, Ruth A. 'Dixie's Daughters: The Country Music Female' in Melton A. McLaurin and Richard A. Peterson, (eds), *You Wrote My Life: Lyrical Themes in Country Music* (Philadelphia: Gordon and Breach, 1992), pp. 81–112.

Bazin, André. *What is Cinema?*, Volume II (Berkeley: University of California Press, 1971).

Belton, John. *Widescreen Cinema* (London: Harvard University Press, 1992).

Bergstrom, Janet. 'Alienation, Segmentation, Hypnosis: Interview with Raymond Bellour', *Camera Obscura* 3/4 (?).

Bernardi, Daniel (ed.). *The Birth of Whiteness: Race and the Emergence of US Cinema* (New Jersey: Rutgers University Press, 1996).

Bernstein, Matthew. *Walter Wanger: Hollywood Independent* (Berkeley: University of California Press, 1994).

Bold, Christine. *Selling The Wild West: Popular Fiction, 1860–1960* (Bloomington and Indianapolis: Indiana University Press, 1987).

Bold, Christine. 'Malaeska's Revenge; or, The Dime Novel Tradition in Popular Fiction'. in Richard Aquila, (ed.), *Wanted Dead or Alive: The American West in Popular Fiction* (Urbana and Chicago: University of Illinois Press, 1996), pp. 32–3.

Borneman, Ernest. 'United States versus Hollywood: The Case Study of an Antitrust Suit' in Tino Balio (ed.), *The American Film Industry*, rev. edn (Madison: University of Wisconsin Press, 1985), pp. 449–62.

Buscombe, Edward (ed.). *The BFI Companion to the Western* (London: British Film Institute and Andre Deutsch, 1988).

Buscombe, Edward. *Stagecoach* (London: British Film Institute, 1992).

Buscombe, Edward and Pearson, Roberta (eds). *Back in the Saddle Again: New Essays on the Western* (London: British Film Institute, 1998).

Cameron, Ian and Pye, Douglas (eds). *The Movie Book of the Western* (London: Studio Vista, 1996)

Campbell, Edward D.C. *The Celluloid South: Hollywood and the Southern Myth* (Knoxville: University of Tennessee Press, 1981).

Cash, W.J. *The Mind of the South* (New York: Vintage Books, 1991).

Cawelti, John G. *The Six Gun Mystique* (Bowling Green, OH: Bowling Green University Popular Press, 1971).

Cockrell, Dale. *Demons of Disorder: Early Blackface Minstrels and Their World* (Cambridge: Cambridge University Press, 1997).

Cohen, Lawrence (ed.). *Nothing But the Blues: The Music and the Musicians* (New York: Abbeville Press, 1993).

Coyne, Michael. *The Crowded Prairie: American National Identity in the Hollywood Western* (London: I.B. Tauris, 1997).

Crafton, Donald. *The Talkies: American Cinema's Transition to Sound 1926–1931* (New York: Charles Scribners Sons, Simon & Schuster, 1998).

Daniel, Wayne W. *Pickin' on Peachtree: A History of Country Music in Atlanta, Georgia* (Chicago: University of Illinois Press, 1990).

Davis, Robert Murray. *Playing Cowboys: Low Culture and High Art in the Western* (Norman and London: University of Oklahoma Press, 1992).

Delmore, Alton. *Truth is Stranger Than Publicity*, ed. Charles K. Wolfe (Nashville: Country Music Foundation, 1995).

Denning, Michael. *Mechanic Accents: Dime Novels and Working-Class Culture in America* (London: Verso, 1987).

Denning, Michael. *The Cultural Front: The Laboring of American Culture in the Twentieth Century* (London and New York: Verso, 1996).

Dippie, Brian. *The Vanishing American: White Attitudes and US Policy* (Middletown, CN: Wesleyan University Press, 1982).

Dormon, James H. 'Shaping the Popular Image of Post-Reconstruction American Blacks: The "Coon Song" Phenomenon of the Gilded Age', *American Quarterly*, 40: 4 (1988), pp. 440–77.

Escott, Colin. *Hank Williams: The Biography* (New York: Little Brown & Co., 1994).

Fellman, Michael. *Inside War: The Guerrilla Conflict in Missouri During the American Civil War* (New York and Oxford: Oxford University Press, 1989).

Fenin, George N. and Everson, William K. *The Western: From Silents to the Seventies* (Harmondsworth: Penguin, 1977).

Ferber, Edna. *Cimarron* (New York: Buccaneer Books, n. d.).

Finler, Joel. *The Hollywood Story* (London: Pyramid Books, 1989).

Fowler, G. and Crawford, B. *Border Radio* (New York: Limelight Edition, 1990).

Francke, Lizzie. *Script Girls: Women Screenwriters in Hollywood* (London: British Film Institute, 1994).

Gallagher, Tag. 'Shoot-Out at the Genre Corral: Problems in the Evolution of the Western' in Barry Keith Grant (ed.), *Film Genre Reader* (Austin: University of Texas Press, 1986), pp. 203–4.

Gomery, Douglas. *The Hollywood Studio System* (London: Macmillan/British Film Institute, 1986).

Greene, Graham. *The Pleasure Dome: The Collected Film Criticism 1935–40*, ed. John Russell Taylor (Oxford: Oxford University Press, 1980).

Gregory, James N. *American Exodus: The Dust Bowl Migration and Okie Culture in California* (Oxford: Oxford University Press, 1989).

Grey, Zane. *Riders of the Purple Sage* (Oxford: Oxford University Press, 1995).

Grundy, Pamela. ' "We Always Tried to Be Good People": Respectability, Crazy Water Crystals, and Hillbilly Music on the Air, 1933–1935', *Journal of American History*, 81: 4 (March 1995), pp. 1591–1620.

Guralnick, Peter. *Lost Highways: Journeys and Arrivals of American Musicians* (New York: Harper & Row, 1989).

Hamilton, Mary Beth. *The Queen of Camp: Mae West, Sex and Popular Culture* (London: Pandora, 1996).

Hansen, Miriam. 'Pleasure, Ambivalence, Identification: Valentino and Female Spectatorship' in Christine Gledhill, (ed.), *Stardom: Industry of Desire* (London: Routledge, 1991).

Hershenson, Bruce. *Cowboy Movie Posters* (West Plains, MO: Bruce Hershenson, n.d.).

Hilmes, Michele. 'The Ban That Never Was: Hollywood and the Broadcasting Industry in 1932', *The Velvet Light Trap*, 23, (Spring 1989), pp. 39–49.

Hilmes, Michelle. *Hollywood and Broadcasting: From Radio to Cable* (Urbana: University of Chicago Press, 1992).

Hochman, Stanley (ed.). *From Quasimodo to Scarlett O'Hara: A National Board of Review Anthology, 1920–1940* (New York: Ungar Publishing, 1982).

Jacobs, Lea. 'The B Film and the Problem of Cultural Distinction', *Screen*, 33: 1 (Spring 1992), pp. 1–13.

Jacobs, Lea. *The Wages of Sin: Censorship and the Fallen Woman Film 1928–1942* (Berkeley: University of California Press, 1997).

Jenkins, Henry. *What Made Pistachio Nuts* (New York: Columbia University Press, 1992).

Jewell, Richard B., with Harbin, V. *The RKO Story* (London: Octopus Books, 1982).

Jordan, Teresa. *Cowgirls: Women of the American West* (Lincoln and London: University of Nebraska Press, Bison edition, 1992).

Kingswood, P. and Costello, S. (eds). *Country: The Music and Musicians*, 2nd edn (New York: Abbeville, 1994).

Kirby, Jack Temple. *Media-Made Dixie* (Baton Rouge: Louisiana State University Press, 1978).

Kitses, Jim. *Horizons West* (London: Thames and Hudson, 1969).

Kitses, Jim and Rickman, Gregg (eds). *The Western Reader* (New York: Limelight Editions, 1998).

Klein, Marcus. *Easterns, Westerns and Private Eyes: American Matters, 1870–1900* (London: University of Wisconsin Press, 1994).

Lears, T.J. Jackson. *No Place of Grace: Antimodernism and the Transformation of American Culture 1880–1920* (New York: Pantheon Books, 1981).

Lenihan, John H. *Showdown: Confronting Modern America in the Western Film* (Urbana and Chicago: University of Illinois Press, 1985).

Leutrat, Jean-Louis. 'L'Histoire comme diffraction d'une identité, *IRIS*, 2: 2 (1984), pp. 57–67.

Logsdon, Guy. *The Whorehouse Bells Were Ringing* (Urbana and Chicago: University of Illinois, 1989).

Logsdon, Guy, Rogers, Mary and Jacobson, William. *Saddle Seranaders* (Salt Lake City: Gibbs and Smith, 1995).

MacNanara, Brooks. *Step Right Up: An Illustrated History of the Medicine Show* (New York: Doubleday, 1976).

Malone, Bill C. *Country Music, USA* (Wellingborough, Northamptonshire: Equation, 1985).

Malone, Bill C. *Singing Cowboys and Musical Mountaineers: Southern Culture and the Roots of Country Music* (Georgia: University of Georgia Press 1993).

Maltby, Richard. *Hollywood Cinema: An Introduction* (Oxford: Basil Blackwell, 1995).

Maltby, Richard. ' "Usable Bounds": *I Am a Fugitive from a Chain Gang* and the Politics of 1932', paper delivered at the Irish Film Centre, Dublin, February 1997.

Maltby, Richard. *Reforming the Movies: Politics, Censorship, and the Institutions of the American Cinema, 1908–1939* (New York: Oxford University Press, forthcoming).

Mitchell, Lee Clark. *Westerns: Making the Man in Fiction and Film* (Chicago: University of Chicago Press, 1997).

Mulvey, Laura. 'Visual Pleasure and Narrative Cinema' in Gerald Mast and Marshall Cohen, (eds), *Film Theory and Criticism: Introductory Readings*, 3rd edn (Oxford: Oxford University Press, 1985), pp. 803–16.

Muscio, Giuliana. *Hollywood's New Deal* (Philadelphia: Temple University Press, 1997).

Nash, Gerald D. *Creating the West: Historical Interpretations 1890–1990* (Albuquerque: University of New Mexico Press, 1991).

Neale, Steve. 'Questions of Genre', *Screen*, 31: 1 (Spring 1990), pp. 45–66.

Neale, Steve. 'Melo Talk: On the Meaning and the Use of the Term "Melodrama" in the American Trade Press', *The Velvet Light Trap*, 32 (Fall 1993), pp. 86–89.

Newman, Kim. *Wild West Movies* (London: Bloomsbury, 1990).

Ohrlin, Glen. *The Hell Bound Train: A Cowboy Songbook* (Chicago: University of Illinois Press, 1989).

Opie, John. *The Law of the Land: Two Hundred Years of American Farmland Policy* (Lincoln and London: University of Nebraska Press, 1994).

Papanikolas, Zeese. *Trickster in the Land of Dreams* (London and Lincoln: University of Nebraska Press, 1995).

Pauly, Thomas H. *'Gone With the Wind* and *The Grapes of Wrath* as Hollywood Histories of the Depression' in Richard Harwell, (ed.), *Gone With the Wind as Book and Film* (Columbia, SC: University of South Carolina Press, 1992).

Peterson, Charles S. 'Speaking for the Past' in Clyde A. Milner II, Carol A. O'Connor and Martha A. Sandweiss (eds), *The Oxford History of the American West* (New York and Oxford: Oxford University Press, 1994).

Peterson, Richard A. *Creating Country Music: Fabricating Authenticity* (Chicago: University of Chicago Press, 1997).

Polan, Dana. *Power and Paranoia: History, Narrative, and the American Cinema, 1940–1950* (New York: Columbia University Press, 1986).

Porterfield, Nolan. *Jimmie Rodgers: The Life and Times of America's Blue Yodeler*, updated edn (Chicago: University of Illinois Press 1992).

Roediger, David R. *The Wages of Whiteness: Race and the Making of the American Working Class* (London: Verso, 1991).

Rogin, Michael. *Blackface, White Noise: Jewish Immigrants in the Hollywood Melting Pot* (Berkeley: University of California Press, 1996).

Rollins, Peter C. *Will Rogers: A Bio-Bibliography* (Westport, CT: Greenwood Press, 1984).

Roosevelt, Franklin D. *Selected Speeches, Messages, Press Conferences, and Letters*, ed. Basil Rauch (New York: Rinehart and Co., 1957).

Ross, Stephen J. *Working-Class Hollywood: Silent Film and the Shaping of Class in America* (Princeton, NJ: Princeton University Press, 1998).

Rothel, David. *The Gene Autry Book* (Madison: North Carolina, 1988).

Ruth, David E. *Inventing the Public Enemy: The Gangster in American Culture, 1918–1934* (Chicago and London: University of Chicago, 1996).

Saxton, Alexander. *The Rise and Fall of the White Republic: Class Politics and Mass Culture in 19th Century America* (London: Verso, 1990).

Seale, Paul. "'A Host of Others": Towards a Nonlinear History of Poverty Row and the Coming of Sound', *Wide Angle*, Vol. 13: 1 (January 1991), pp. 72–103.

Sklar, Robert. *City Boys: Cagney, Bogart, Garfield* (Princeton, NJ: University Press, 1992).

Slotkin, Richard. *Regeneration Through Violence: The Mythology of the American Frontier, 1600–1860* (Middletown, CT: Wesleyan University Press, 1978).

Slotkin, Richard. *The Fatal Environment: The Myth of the Frontier in the Age of Industrialisation, 1800–1890* (New York: Atheneum, 1985)

Slotkin, Richard. *Gunfighter Nation: The Myth of the Frontier in Twentieth Century America* (New York: Harper Perennial, 1993).

Smith, Henry Nash. *Virgin Land: The American West as Symbol and Myth* (New York: Vintage Books, 1950).

Smith, Packy and Hulse, Ed (eds). *Don Miller's Hollywood Corral: A Comprehensive B-Western Roundup* (Burbank: Riverwood Press, 1993).

Staiger, Janet. *Bad Women: Regulating Sexuality in Early American Cinema* (Minneapolis and London: Minnesota University Press, 1995).

Stanfield, Peter. 'Cowboys' Day Off : A Story of Capital, Labour and Leisure' in William Uricchio and Nanna Verhoeff (eds), *Blurred Vistas: The Western Before 1914* (Bloomington: Indiana University Press, forthcoming).

Sterling, Bryan B. and Sterling, Frances N. (eds). *A Will Rogers Treasury: Reflections and Observations* (New York: Crown Publishers, 1982).

Studlar, Gaylyn. *This Mad Masquerade: Stardom and Masculinity in the Jazz Age* (New York: Columbia University Press, 1997).

Thorpe, N.H. *Songs of the Cowboy* (Lincoln and London: University of Nebraska Press, 1984).

Tompkins, Jane. *West of Everything: The Inner Life of Westerns* (Oxford: Oxford University Press, 1992).

Tosches, Nick. *Country: Living Legends and Dying Metaphors In America's Biggest Music*, rev. edn (London: Secker and Warburg, 1985).

Trachtenberg, Alan. *The Incorporation of America: Culture and Society in the Gilded Age* (New York: Hill and Wang, 1982).

Turner, Frederick Jackson. 'The Significance of the Frontier in American

History' in American Historical Association, *Annual Report*, 1893 (Washington DC, 1893), pp. 199–227.

Tuska, Jon. *The Vanishing Legion: A History of Mascot Pictures 1927–35* (London: McFarland & Co., 1982).

Vasey, Ruth. *The World According to Hollywood 1918–1939* (Exeter: University of Exeter Press, 1997).

Vernet, Marc. '*Film Noir* on the Edge of Doom' in Joan Copjec (ed.), *Shades of Noir* (London: Verso, 1996), pp. 1–32.

Warshow, Robert. 'The Movie Chronicle: The Westerner' (1954) in *The Immediate Experience* (New York: Atheneum Books, 1962).

White, Richard. '*It's Your Misfortune and None of My Own': A New History of the American West* (Norman and London: University of Oklahoma Press, 1991).

Williamson, J.W. *Hillbillyland: What the Movies Did to the Mountains and What the Mountains Did to the Movies* (Chapel Hill and London: University of North Carolina, 1995).

Wister, Owen. 'The Evolution of the Cow Puncher', *Harper's Monthly*, 91 (September 1895), pp. 602–17.

Wister, Owen. *The Virginian: A Horseman of the Plains*, reprint of 1929 illustrated edition (Lincoln: University of Nebraska Press, 1992).

Wolfe, Charles K. *Tennessee Strings: The Story of Country Music in Tennessee* (Knoxville: University of Tennessee Press, 1977).

Wright, Will. *Six Guns and Society: A Structural Study of the Western* (Berkeley: University of California Press, 1975).

Index

Adams, Andy 70, 208
Adventures of Robin Hood, The
  (1938) 113–4, 145, 151, 172,
  182, 188
Agee, James 77
Allen, Robert C. 175
Allegheny Uprising (1939) 214
Altman, Rick 117–21
Americanism 152–60, 193–4,
  197
Anderson, Benedict 195
Annie Oakley (1935) 124, 127, 132,
  143
Arizona (1940) 167–8, 213, 214,
  215
Arizona Legion (1939) 160
Arizonian, The (1935) 124, 127,
  133–4
Arthur, Jean 167–8
Autry, Gene 56, 59–60, 65–6,
  70–4, 75, 77, 78–90, 92–7,
  101–4, 105–7, 116, 126, 132,
  156, 174, 197, 205–6

Balio, Tino 16, 121, 123, 124
Banjo on My Knee (1936) 203
Barbary Coast (1935) 175
Barthes, Roland 61
Bazin, Andre 4–5, 144

Belle Starr—The Bandit Queen
  (1941) 169, 186, 216–19
Bellour, Raymond 190–1, 231
Big Trail, The (1930) 15, 24, 32,
  40–3, 50, 54, 119, 145, 160,
  197, 209
Billy the Kid (1930) 24, 32–3,
  44–9, 50, 52, 54, 119, 133, 160,
  186, 191
Billy the Kid (1941) 163, 179,
  186–90
blackface, *see* minstrelsy
Bold, Christine 45
Bowery, The (1934) 174–5
Boy Meets Girl (1938) 140
Brigham Young (1940) 214
Buscombe, Ed 144–5

Cagney, James 140, 160, 163–6,
  180–1
Cash, W.J. 63, 201–2, 203
casting 52–3, 143–4, 145–6,
  160–73
Cawelti, John 9
Cimarron (1931) 15, 24, 31,
  33–40, 54, 124, 145, 160, 191,
  209–12
Cockrell, Dale 92
concert saloons 173–80

Cooper, Gary 20, 21–23, 26, 28, 53, 136–7, 141–2, 143
Covered Wagon, The (1923) 18, 21, 32, 40–3, 197
Cowboy and the Lady, The (1938) 141–2, 143
Cowboy From Brooklyn, The (1938) 125
Coyne, Michael 144, 226
Crafton, Donald 54, 88

Dark Command (1940) 214, 223–4
Davis, Robert Murray 13
Denning, Michael 4, 10–12, 91, 92, 95, 99, 100, 194
Destry Rides Again (1939) 96, 141, 169–71, 175, 179, 213, 214, 215
Detour (1945) 191
Dietrich, Marlene 170–73, 175
Dodge City (1939) 155, 157, 160, 166, 175–7, 179, 214, 216, 219–20
Drums Along the Mohawk (1939) 166, 214
Dynamite (1929) 191

Eddy, Nelson 87, 125, 157, 160

Female (1933) 191
Ferber, Edna 31–2
Flynn, Errol 160, 172–3
Foran, Dick 86–7, 140
Ford, John 148–50
Francke, Lizzie 95
'Frankie and Johnny' (ballad) 129, 175
Frontier Marshall (1939) 166, 176, 179
frontier myth 7–10, 122, 137, 197

Gallagher, Tag 6
gangster films 53, 119, 120, 122, 138, 163, 184–5
Gay Desperado, The (1936) 137–8
genre theory 6–7, 9, 117–21
Gibson, Hoot 18, 19, 52, 56, 87, 125
Gone with the Wind (1939) 151, 157, 198, 216–17, 224
Grapes of Wrath, The (1940) 114, 216
Greene, Graham 137–8
Gregory, James N. 64, 91, 202–3
Grey, Zane 18, 20, 56, 83, 87, 98–9, 207–8
Grundy, Pamela 96
Gun Smoke (1931) 53, 110–11, 119–20
Guthrie, Woody 70, 74

Hamilton, Mary Beth 104
Hansen, Miriam 30, 34
Hardy, Phil 81
Hart, William S. 44, 52, 56, 71, 129
Honky Tonk (1941) 180

I Take this Woman (1931) 143
In Old Arizona (1929) 15, 17, 18, 20, 21, 24–6, 31, 49, 119
In Old Chicago (1938) 175
It Happened One Night (1934) 143

Jacobs, Lea 146–7
Jesse James (1939) 160, 162, 165–6, 176, 180, 181–6, 201, 214, 215, 216–19
Jones, Buck 18, 19, 56, 116, 120, 124, 126

Kitses, Jim 9
Klein, Marcus 11–12

Lang, Fritz 172

Lash, The (1930) 27–30
Last Flight (1931) 191
Lears, Jackson T.J. 76, 219–20
Lenihan, John H. 8
Let Freedom Ring (1939) 155, 156, 158–9, 214
Leutrat, Jean-Louis 6–7
Limerick, Patricia Nelson 9–10
Love, Nat 208

Malone, Bill 70–1
Maltby, Richard 29, 95, 146–7, 153, 154–5
Man of Conquest (1939) 144, 158–9
Maynard, Ken 18, 19, 27–8, 57, 58, 82–6, 126
McCoy, Tim 99–100
Miller, Emmett 61
minstrelsy 61, 72, 79, 92, 99, 101, 104, 106–10, 175, 194–7, 205
Mitchell, Lee Clark 13, 98
Mix, Tom 56, 71
Montana Moon (1930) 20, 52, 143
Motion Picture Producers and Distributors of America, Inc. (MPPDA) 5, 30, 33, 42–3, 154
Mulvey, Laura 38
Muscio, Giuliana 54, 145

Nash, Gerald D 8
Neale, Steve 6–7, 115
Northwest Passage (1939) 157, 214

Oklahoma Kid (1939) 155, 160, 163–6, 180–1, 213, 214
Opie, John 91
Outlaw, The (1940) 180

Painted Desert, The (1931) 20
Panama Canal (1939) 157
Papanikolas, Zeese 11–12
Peterson, Charles S. 7–8, 9

Plainsman, The (136) 116, 125, 127, 136–7, 138–9, 143, 168, 191
Polan, Dana 190–1
Powdersmoke Range (1936) 125
Power, Tyrone 160–3, 166
Presley, Elvis 64, 65, 69
Production Code Administration (PCA) 33, 106, 129, 146–7, 153–5, 170, 176–80, 183–4, 204, 212, 223
Pye, Douglas 82

Ramona (1936) 125, 127, 134–6, 139, 143, 191
Return of Frank James, The (1940) 172, 214, 215, 216–19
Ritter, Tex 70, 87, 142
Rodgers, Jimmie 60–65, 68, 69, 70, 75
Roediger, David R. 61, 196
Rogers, Roy 87
Rogers, Will 73–7, 94, 122, 134, 141
Rogin, Michael 196
Ruth, David E. 185

San Francisco (1936) 175
Sante Fe Trail (1940) 173, 214, 216, 220–3
Saxton, Alexander 195, 209
Seale, Paul 25–6, 53, 57
She Done Him Wrong (1933) 174–5
Shopworn Angel (1938) 140–1, 143
sidekicks 104–10
Sklar, Robert 78, 122, 226
Slotkin, Richard 8, 9, 34
Smith, Henry Nash 8
Spoilers, The (1942) 175
'Stack-O-Lee' (ballad) 201

Stagecoach (1939) 96, 143, 144, 145, 148–50, 155, 176, 178, 180, 191, 213, 215, 216, 223
Stand Up and Fight (1939) 155, 160, 161–3, 168, 214
Studio Relations Committee (SRC) 33, 42–3, 46–7
Studlar, Gaylyn 29

Taylor, Robert 160–3, 166, 212–13
Test Pilot (1938) 145, 151
Texans, The (1938) 145, 151
Texas Rangers (1931) 124, 127, 138, 139–40, 143
They Died With Their Boots On (1941) 173
Three Godfathers (1936) 116, 125, 126–32, 133, 135, 139, 140, 143, 191
Tobacco Road (E. Caldwell) 203, 205
Tompkins, Jane 13, 80
Trachtenberg, Alan 196
Tuska, Jon 79–81

Union Pacific (1939) 157, 158, 160, 168, 180, 214

Vasey, Ruth 30, 155, 189
Virginia City (1940) 173, 212, 214, 216, 220–3
Virginian, The (1929) 15, 17, 20, 21–25, 31, 41, 49, 110–13, 119, 137, 138, 143
Virginian, The (Wister) 206–7, 208, 227

Wanger, Walter 153, 178
Warshaw, Robert 79
Wayne, John 57, 58, 59, 97, 100–1, 105, 111–15, 120, 156, 175, 223
Wells Fargo (1937) 125
West, Mae 104, 143, 171, 174
Westerner, The 163, 176, 179, 191, 213, 214, 215, 224
White, Richard 10, 63, 92–3
widescreen 49–52
Williams, Hank 61, 62, 64
Wister, Owen 70, 71, 73, 77
Wolfe, Charles K. 67
Wright, Will 9

Yates, Herbert J. 58
yodelling 60–2